THE FUNDAMENTAL FORMS
OF SOCIAL THOUGHT

By the same author:

The Ideal Foundations of Economic Thought (London: Routledge & Kegan Paul ; New York: Oxford University Press)

The History of Economics in Its Relation to Social Development (London: Routledge & Kegan Paul; New York: Oxford University Press)

America: Ideal and Reality. The United States of 1776 in Contemporary European Philosophy (London: Routledge & Kegan Paul; New York: Humanities Press)

Jeremy Bentham's Economic Writings (3 volumes, London: George Allen & Unwin (for the Royal Economic Society); New York: Burt Franklin)

The Sociology of Knowledge (London: Routledge & Kegan Paul; New York: Free Press of Glencoe)

Social Theory and Christian Thought (London: Routledge & Kegan Paul)

Montesquieu: Pioneer of the Sociology of Knowledge (London: Routledge & Kegan Paul; Toronto: The Toronto University Press)

Dr Stark is General Editor of *Rare Masterpieces of Philosophy and Science* (London: Routledge & Kegan Paul; New Haven: The Yale University Press; 16 volumes to date)

THE FUNDAMENTAL FORMS OF SOCIAL THOUGHT

by

WERNER STARK

FORDHAM UNIVERSITY PRESS

NEW YORK · 1963

First published in the United States of America
in 1963
by Fordham University Press
New York 58

© Werner Stark 1962

Library of Congress Catalog Card Number: 63-18877

Second Printing 1965

Printed in Great Britain

CONTENTS

PREFACE

IN WRITING the present book, I have had three different, but related, aims in view. I have, first of all, tried to show what were, in point of fact, the fundamental forms of social thought which have, between them, dominated the past. This might be called, with a word perhaps too grand, my typological aim. I have secondly attempted to explain why these powerful doctrines have developed and constantly tended to reappear; that is to say, I have applied the explanatory method known as the sociology of knowledge to sociology itself. This might be called my analytical aim. And I have, thirdly and lastly, raised the question of the validity of the basic conceptions of social life which the history of ideas has thrown up. This might be called my critical aim, or, even better, my critical and constructive aim. My result can be briefly indicated by saying that I have found the appearance of all the decisive movements of thought entirely understandable. I should almost go so far as to say that the main schools had to appear. But, on a critical approach, I have been unable to attribute to all of them the same value. True, I have arrived at the conviction that none was without a sound intuition at its root, but in two cases out of three one-sidedness spoilt the picture of the social order which was built up on the basis of that intuition. Models were used which misrepresented social reality by exaggerating one or the other of its basic features, and the conclusion was forced on me that these two doctrines were right only when taken in conjunction, but decidedly wrong when taken in isolation. In other words, there seems to me now, after a close study of the development of social thought, to be above all a need for synthesis, and I have awarded the prize to the third theory because I found it to be a synthesis, a reconciliation of opposites, truer than they because it bears in itself both their fundamental truths. With this result, I hope to have made a contribution to the further development of the study of society in days to come. My book is both a key to the past, and a plea for the future, of the social sciences.

My thanks are due to Dr Alison Hanham for reading my manu-script and suggesting linguistic improvements. My obligations to Drs I. S. Grant, E. J. Popham, W. Montgomery Watt and J. R. Western as well as to Mr D. M. Leahy are recorded, at the appropriate places, in footnotes to the text.

W. STARK

To become kindred in spirit without being
kin in blood—that is what only man can do.

NIKOLAI GOGOL

Taras Bulba

I

INTRODUCTION[1]

HOWEVER WE may define society in general; whatever else
it may or may not be: one thing is certain, namely that
each and every social formation is at the same time a multiplicity and a unity. We cannot speak of a society unless there are
before us several human beings, and unless the lives of these
human beings are in some way interconnected and interrelated,
i.e. constitute a unity of some kind. This primitive fact makes it
obvious that there are—and, indeed, that there can be—only
three fundamental forms of social thought, even if these basic
approaches have produced, and incarnated themselves in, a vast
literature of amazing wealth and variation. A social philosopher
can either maintain that a social system is a unity rather than a
multiplicity, that it is one rather than many; or he can take the
view that it is a multiplicity rather than a unity, that it is many
rather than one; or, finally, he can try to develop a definition of
social life which does justice, both to the real integration of the
social order and to the real independence of the individuals comprised by it. In other words, to use a well-known cliché, he can
either see the wood rather than the trees; or he can see the trees
rather than the wood; or he can endeavour to remember that the
wood is made up of trees and that the trees between them make
up a wood. Thus blandly stated, the third possibility at once
appears superior to the other two; yet in the history of human
thinking about social reality it has played only a modest and minor

---

[1] The fundamental ideas presented in this chapter were first developed in a
lecture at Heidelberg on February 9, 1959. The text of this lecture (entitled "Die
Weltanschauungsformen und die Gesellschaftslehre") was published in the *Archiv
für Rechts- und Sozialphilosophie*, 1962.

part, even though it seems now to be at long last coming into its own.

One can best characterise the two older social philosophies —the collectivistic and holistic approach on the one hand, and the individualistic and atomistic on the other—by borrowing from the technical philosophers a pair of concepts with which they have long operated—the concepts of 'realism' and 'nominalism'. When we speak or think of beauty, we can either assume that there are indeed many beautiful objects in the world, but that beauty as such, beauty-in-itself, does not exist; that beauty is merely a word (Latin: *nomen*); or we can suppose that there exists, in fact and in truth, albeit in some supernal realm, in some higher reality, perhaps in the divine mind, an idea of beauty which gives beauty to all beautiful objects, makes them what they are, and is thus a real, if not directly observable, entity (a *res vera* or true thing). In the first case we embrace nominalism, in the second realism. Now, it is with the concept of society, as it is with the concept of beauty. Either we can say that only individuals are real, the individual human beings whom we can see and hear and touch and name, and that society is merely a word; or alternatively we can say that society is a reality of a sort, a higher kind of reality, that it is prior to the individuals, as Aristotle expressed it, and makes them all that they are and can be. In the first case, we again embrace nominalism; in the second, realism.

For modern man, the conflict between nominalism and realism, which greatly agitated the later Middle Ages, has long become a dead and decided issue. He has, by and large, plumped for nominalism and regards realism as a metaphysical, nay phantasmagoric, philosophy. There are only trees; there is no wood. Only individuals really exist; society is simply the sum of the individuals who belong to it. The argument which lies behind this common conviction can be formulated as follows: take society away, and the individuals remain; take the individuals away, and nothing is left; hence reality inheres in the individuals and society is not a real entity apart from them. Nothing could be, at first sight, more plausible than this deduction, yet a short consideration is sufficient to prove that it is far less cogent than might appear. If you take the individuals away, a great deal in fact remains: the whole physical apparatus of society will be left. The Mayas have gone: their magnificent temples still stand. On the other hand, if you take away society, very little is in fact left of the individuals. For, to be fair in this argument, you must, if you wish to carry out this thought-experiment, drain out, as it were, of the individuals all that society has deposited in them, for instance their language, and that means not only their capacity to speak, but also, since thought is clad in linguistic forms, their capacity to think. But a man who cannot think is not a real man. You might as well call the cold and dead ivory statue with which Pygmalion fell in love a real woman before the goddess Aphrodite breathed life into it. Here, again, only the physical apparatus will be left: the case is the same as that before. The truth is that individual and society are not separate or even separable realities: where the one is, the other must needs be as well, if we use the words in their full and, so to speak, empirically validated sense. And for this reason both philosophical nominalism and philosophical realism are sound, if one-sided, philosophies. The real task before us is, not to decide between them, but, on the contrary, to preserve, and, if possible, to reconcile the two.

On the heights of human thought, sociological realism and sociological nominalism, the holistic and the atomistic idea of society, have always coexisted. A fascinating proof of this is Plato's moving dialogue, 'Crito'.[1] The hour at which Socrates must die has drawn near and his old friend Crito makes a last and desperate attempt to avert the catastrophe. He urges him to flee, but the sage refuses. He will, indeed, must, obey the laws. Crito is at a loss to understand, and Socrates tries to explain his attitude to him. He imagines that The Laws, the personified essence of Athenian society, address him, their victim. 'He who disobeys us,' they say, 'is, as we maintain, thrice wrong; first, because in disobeying us, he is disobeying his parents; secondly, because we are the authors of his education; thirdly, because, having made an agreement with us that he will duly obey our commands, he neither obeys them nor convinces us that our commands are unjust.' Here, the first two points clearly imply a holistic, realistic social philosophy; the last, on the other hand, is based on an atomistic, nominalistic conception of the social bond. Let us see how and why.

You must submit to us, say The Laws, in substance, to Socrates,

[1] Cf. *The Dialogues of Plato*, translated into English by B. Jowett, ed. 1953, I, pp. 367 *seq.* Cf. especially pp. 379–383.

because children must submit to their parents and educators. Now, society is to the individual both parent and educator; the individual is to society like a child, its offspring and its ward. Society is there before the individual appears: it possesses the primacy of being. But it possesses the primacy of being not only in a temporal and causal, it possesses it also in a cultural sense. It *makes* the individual, not only as a physical entity, by procreation, but also as a cultural personality, by the educative process. This is sociological realism of the purest water. Society appears in this argument as the basic and substantive reality: the individual's being is considered to be merely secondary. His subjective existence is nothing as compared to the objective power of the social forces. Relentlessly, almost brutally, the laws, i.e. society, press their claims against Socrates, the individual, and he is constrained step by step to yield to these claims. ' "In the first place, did we not bring you into existence? Your father married your mother by our aid and begat you. Say whether you have any objection to urge against those of us who regulate marriage?" None, I should reply. "Or against those of us who after birth regulate the nurture and education of children, in which you also were trained? Were not the laws, which have the charge of education, right in commanding your father to train you in music and gymnastic?" Right, I should reply. "Well then, since you were brought into the world and nurtured and educated by us, can you deny in the first place that you are our child . . . as your fathers were before you? And if this is true, you cannot suppose that you are on equal terms with us in matters of right and wrong . . . Has a philosopher like you failed to discover that our country is more precious and higher and holier far than mother or father or any ancestor, and more to be regarded in the eyes of the gods and of men of understanding? . . ." '

These words reflect one aspect of social reality: the dependence of the part on the whole. But there is the other, complementary aspect as well: the dependence of the whole on the part. Socrates and Plato were fully aware of it. It had just been forced on their attention, and that of all Greeks, by the Sophists. In a sense, the individual, at any rate the fully grown-up individual, is sovereign, even in relation to his society. No community can survive unless its members continue to sustain it. If the laws impose their will on the citizens, the will of the citizens for its part must underpin the laws. Socrates realises that he must bow to his fate, not only because a lawfully constituted court has condemned him, but also because he himself, by his conclusive actions, has accepted, and, to that extent, one could almost say, created the laws on the basis of which this court was convened and his trial conducted and concluded. From this point of view society appears as a system of control which dominates men, not by dint of its antecedent existence and cultural superiority, but by dint of the subsequent approval of its norms by the associated individuals. Hence these individuals are here the stronger, the decisive factor. It can be said of them that they *will* the laws to have, and to continue in, validity. Socrates' death on the morrow is merely the logical consequence of his own past sovereign conduct. Insofar as he lays the emphasis here on independent individual action and not on pre-existent and unchangeable social institutions, Socrates speaks now in a very different voice and vein from before. The following sentences are assuredly not radical individualism or atomism or nominalism; yet, in their insistence on the basic freedom of the individual's will, they come very near to it. 'Having brought you into the world, and nurtured and educated you, and given you and every other citizen a share in every good which we had to give,' the philosopher makes The Laws argue, 'we further proclaim to any Athenian by the liberty, which we allow him, that if he does not like us, the laws, when he has become of age and has seen the ways of the city, and made our acquaintance, he may go where he pleases and take his goods with him. None of us laws will forbid him or interfere with anyone who does not like us and the city, and who wants to emigrate to a colony or to any other city; he may go where he likes, with his property. But he who has experience of the manner in which we order justice and administer the state, and still remains, has by so doing entered into an implied contract that he will do as we command him . . . You, Socrates, are breaking the covenants and agreements which you made with us at your leisure, not under any compulsion or deception or in enforced haste, but after you have had seventy years to think of them, during which time you were at liberty to leave the city, if we were not to your mind or if our covenants appeared to you to be unfair.'

Socrates, even under the shadow of death, acknowledges the truth-content of these words. And, in doing so, he also acknowledges, what interests us here most: that a society is not only prior to the individual in the manner his parents and educators are, but also posterior to him like his children, that, as a network of agreements, it is to a large extent a product of his will, as, from another point of view, he is a product of theirs.

The two contradictory and yet complementary theories which we have just studied in Plato's dialogue have coexisted and contended with each other all through history. The only major event has been the evolution, from their joint parentage, of the third or mediating approach which sees society, more dynamically, as a progression from multiplicity to unity rather than as either the one or the other of these two alternatives. The detail does not concern us here because we are not at the moment trying to write on the development of sociological theory, but merely endeavouring to isolate and identify fundamental or archetypal modes of social thought.[1] And yet we cannot entirely exclude the detail, the historical wealth of social theorising, from our speculations. For even while we wish to concentrate on abstract ideal types of thinking, we must remain in contact with the concrete and living manifestations of it, otherwise we are apt to lose the solid ground from under our feet.

We have won our tripartite division of the broad stream of social theorising by the method which philosophers are wont to call deductive. That is to say, we have posited a certain initial definition of social reality and then drawn (deduced) from it, by logical conclusion, an idea of the varying interpretations of which this reality seems capable. There can be no objection, in principle, to this procedure. It is bound to be sound, provided, of course, that the basic definition is in harmony with the facts, and the inferences from it in agreement with the laws of logic. And yet, deduction alone will never do. We must try to confirm our findings by inductive argument as well, or, to put the matter more simply, we must show that the abstract classification which we have thought out, can indeed be traced and recognised in the realm of observation also, in the concrete divisions into which

[1] For the (co-ordinated) coexistence of the three basic types of social theory in St. Augustine, cf. Stark, *Social Theory and Christian Thought*, 1959, pp. 1–31; for their (unco-ordinated) coexistence in Herbert Spencer, cf. Stark, "Herbert Spencer's Three Sociologies", *The American Sociological Review*, 1961, pp. 515–521. This paper was originally an address to the plenary session of the 55th Annual Meeting of the American Sociological Association in New York on August 29, 1960.

the literature of the social sciences seems to fall spontaneously, of its own accord. In this endeavour the work of Wilhelm Dilthey, the great historian of human thought, can be of considerable help to us.

Nothing could originally have been further from Dilthey's mind than a summing-up or generalising approach to the history of ideas. He was impressed, nay overwhelmed, by the tremendous scope and originality of man's spiritual effort. How could you classify and categorise the thinkers of the past, if every one of them was unique, according to the adage, more true than any other, *individuum est ineffabile*? History was to Dilthey essentially the study of the unrepeatable, in contrast to the natural sciences which investigate the repeatable and repeated. Yet, as he grew older, Dilthey came to recognise that the history of ideas is, for all its riches and richness, no random collection of individual achievements. His knowledge, gained inductively from beginning to end, garnered in a life-long study of the detail, forced him to acknowledge that ideas do not exist in splendid isolation, but, on the contrary, fall into families or traditions which link man with man and age with age. And finally he came to the conclusion that there are in the last analysis three fundamental forms of thought, which he called respectively objective idealism, naturalism, and subjective idealism. Each one of these basic attitudes has grown out of a specific intuition or experience of reality which tends to dominate the whole thought of the philosopher or scientist concerned.[1]

In the case of objective idealism, this all-decisive intuition or experience is the acquaintance with the living organism composed of material body and spiritual soul or life principle. Looking at this phenomenon, so admirable in every respect, the members of the school felt that they beheld the key to the understanding, not only of part, but of the whole of reality. Just as the meanest of creatures is a compound of matter and soul, of bone and flesh on the one hand, animation on the other, so also the great cosmos. Pantheism or panentheism is the creed of these men. Spinoza, Leibniz, Goethe, Schelling, Schleiermacher and Hegel, and among the social theorists, to some extent, Comte, represent this fundamental form of philosophic thought.

[1] The decisive text is printed, in English translation, in the appendix to H. A. Hodges' book, *Wilhelm Dilthey: An Introduction*, 1944, pp. 152 *et seq.*

B

Very different from them are the thinkers who embrace naturalism (or materialism, as it is traditionally called). Here the basic
impression which provides the golden key is, not acquaintance
with the animate, but acquaintance with the inanimate creation.
The laws of the physical universe are conceived as the regularities
which dominate all that is. Life, and even thought, are merely
epiphenomena of material reality. Democritus, Epicurus, Hobbes,
Spencer and many others have explored this possible avenue
towards the truth. In religious contexts it appears as atheism, or
at least as a tendency in that direction.

Very different again, nay, diametrically opposed to these philosophers, are the subjective idealists (or idealists of freedom, as
Dilthey prefers to call them). What moves them most and sets
the seal on all their thinking is the experience of moral conflict.
They see, in St. Paul's words, that the spirit indeed is willing,
but the flesh weak. For them, a monistic interpretation of reality,
such as the naturalists propagate it—matter is all—seems unacceptable. They are dualists. There is indeed a realm of matter
which forms the substructure of the universe, but over against it
stands a principle of life, spirit and will which is caught in conflict
with it and strives to give it form and meaning. Plato, Aquinas
and Kant are the most brilliant protagonists of this perennial
philosophy, and among the sociologists above all Vico. Needless
to say, the religious side of this system is a personalistic theism,
as that of objective idealism is the pantheistic creed, and that of
naturalism is an atheistic attitude.

This, then, was the great net in which Dilthey caught the totality of human speculation. Nothing can escape it, for at the heart
of every mental effort (the word here taken in the widest possible
sense) there sits of necessity an answer, however unformulated
and unfocused, to the ultimate question of existence. Dilthey's
division can be easily tested and confirmed. Even if it is tried on
a man who seems miles away from metaphysics, it will soon
be seen to apply. Take, for instance, a social reformer; take one
who is concerned only with detailed reforms. The way in which
he wants to see his reforms carried out will reveal what manner of
thought his is. There are some who have an altogether mechanistic
idea of purposive intervention and possible "reconstruction".
They stand as a rule on the left. Political radicalism and philosophical materialism have ever gone hand in hand. There are

others who doubt that a living whole like society can be chopped and changed about like a machine. Reform can only be the work of generations; there can indeed be growth towards better things, but no abrupt adjustment. These men stand as a rule on the right. Political conservatism and objective idealism have, throughout history, been well-assorted running mates. And then there is the third group who see the essence of improvement in moral effort. They deny that a social system is incapable of reform and rapid transformation, yet they doubt at the same time that external, quasi-mechanical intervention, say, an isolated act of rational legislation, will really change the condition of things. Those who feel like this will, on investigation, prove to have their mental roots in the tradition called by Dilthey idealism of freedom. What matters to them is not the mechanism of life nor yet the organic stream of its development, but man—the heart of man.

It appears, then, that both the deductively and the inductively reached division of the field and distinction of fundamental forms are sound. The question immediately arises whether they coincide. If they do, they powerfully confirm each other. If they do not, they must appear equally indefensible. At first sight, it is somewhat difficult to see what conceivable connection there can be between the definition of society as essentially a unity on the one hand, and the conception of the universe, in the style of pantheism, as animate rather than inanimate matter on the other. But such a connection exists; indeed, it is close; and though not immediately obvious, it is not really difficult to demonstrate.

We can see the kinship, nay coincidence, of the two typologies best if we direct our attention to three sciences which form the middle ground, as it were, between the pairs of basic thought-structure which they respectively distinguish. As objective idealism regards the all as shot through by life, mind and soul-substance, it naturally considers biology as the queen of the sciences on which the other branches of learning must model themselves. Indeed, it is permissible to say that it preaches a pan-organismic philosophy. The vast universe in all its glory is an entity of the same kind as the smallest and most contemptible animal. Some writers show this conception less, others more clearly, but the greatest of the objective idealists exhibit it with considerable clarity and purity. We may think here particularly of Leibniz and Hegel. But the realistic sociologists are also, within their narrower field, pan-organismic thinkers. Indeed, this social philosophy has not, as a rule, been formulated by saying that society is a unity rather than a multiplicity; the formula has usually been that society is an organism. This comparison between body physical on the one hand and body social on the other has constituted the connecting link of a long chain of authors from Plato and Aristotle down to Herbert Spencer and beyond. Izoulet, whose book *La Cité Moderne* (1894) achieved meteoric success in the late Victorian era, showed up its essence very well when he distinguished three entities: the *infrazoaire* or little beast—namely, the cell; the *metazoaire* or middling beast—man; and the *hyperzoaire* or big beast—society. From the point of view of objective idealism the series is, of course, not complete. It needs to be concluded by adding to the three organisms a fourth which, in Izoulet's style, could be called the *pantozoaire*, the universal organism, the organical universe. Fantastic as all this may sound, it is merely a somewhat extreme and imaginative verbalisation of a mode of thought which is widespread and always has been so, as we shall see in part I of this book.

While the connection between holistic-realistic social philosophy on the one hand and objective idealism on the other is thus fairly obvious, that between atomistic-nominalistic sociology and naturalism is a little more difficult to demonstrate. Yet the case is strictly parallel. The linking science is rational mechanics, and its less theoretical correlate, celestial mechanics, i.e. astronomy. The science of sciences is here, not physiology, but physics. Everything appears to rest on, and to result from, the interplay of mechanical, mathematically measurable and calculable forces. It is a pan-mechanistic ontology which writers like Democritus or Hobbes propagate. But atomistic-nominalistic sociology is also of this kind. It, too, regards the social cosmos as essentially an equilibrium system. If only the individual is real, then the coherence of society—or rather, the coherence of individuals in society—must be due to the balancing of individual forces. The very logic of their starting-point forces the nominalists into the pan-mechanistic fold. Social institutions are to them—nay, must be to them—objective resultants of subjective energies: the coexistence of men is like the coexistence of the sidereal bodies, each of which has its own push and pull, and all of which manage to get along with each other without mutual destruction because their attractions and repulsions fall ultimately into an abiding pattern. What Izoulet's *Cité Moderne* is to organicism, Carey's *Principles of Social Science* (1858/9) is to mechanicism: an attempt to follow the operation of the supposedly fundamental laws of physics from one level of being to another, until a consistent mechanistic world-view is built up which stretches from the molecule at the one extremity to the vastness of space on the other, including, of course, a specific sociology as well. More will be said of the sociologists who have embraced this point of view in part II.

While biology and physiology thus link objective idealism and realistic sociology, and mechanics and astronomy link naturalism and nominalistic sociology, the knot between idealism of freedom and the third sociology is tied by an entirely different science, the science of history. If the reality of realities is the struggle of the higher, form-giving, forces of existence with the lower form-resisting masses of matter, then the study which will reveal the most significant aspect of being will be historiography as the record of man's fight against fate, the Promethean Contest in which the conscious will is pitted against the mindless factors which oppose it. To the subjective idealists like Kant and Fichte it is not 'phenomenal' man that matters, man as a material entity or man as an animal—not man insofar as he is caught in the coils of the lower creation—but 'noumenal' man who rises above creatureliness and asserts his moral purpose and character and his essential freedom. The greatest historians have shared this fundamental attitude, and so have some of the most outstanding sociologists.[1] Suffice it to mention but one name, brilliant above all others, the name of Giambattista Vico. Society appears to those who see it as a straining from conflict to order, from chaos to cosmos, as a cultural formation, and not as a creation of natural laws, be they mechanical or vital, be they laws of irreducible multiplicity, or laws of pre-established unity. Of the sociologists who have taken their place in the third or 'cultural' tradition, we shall be speaking in part III of this book.

It is the conviction of the present writer that all three types of social philosophy which two thousand five hundred years of human speculation have produced, possess their own value and validity. In so far as a society is a well-knit unity, it approaches

[1] Cf. my discussion of Friedrich Meinecke, in—Stark, *Social Theory and Christian Thought*, 1959, pp. 201–245.

the kind of coherence which the body physical shows us in its purest form; in so far as a society is characterised by competition and conflict, it is reminiscent of the tensions which pervade a system of weights and counterweights in mechanical, more or less unstable, equilibrium; and in so far as a society is on the way from loose to firm integration, in so far as it reflects, and, so to speak, lives, the adage *e pluribus unum*, it appears as a sustained effort taking place in time and tending to lead from formlessness to form, and from individual near-independence to quasi-organical co-operation and communion. Yet, though all three theories reflect reality in their differing ways, they are not equally realistic: the third is far superior to the other two. Merely mechanical and fully organic coherence have never been actually observed: they are at best marginal cases, ideal types, to which observable societies may more or less approach, but which none will ever realise and reach. Moral effort, on the other hand, is characteristic of all human coexistence: the core of every political order is its system of social control, the containment of the individual and his conduct within the framework of the collective norms. There is an eternal tug of war between freedom and discipline: no society that does not, at any given moment of its existence, either rise up towards fuller union or sink down towards looser give-and-take. Society is essentially a pattern of processes, and these processes can be constructive or destructive, leading men towards each other or away from each other, as such wise writers as Georg Simmel and Leopold von Wiese have untiringly emphasised and explained. Yet there is another, different, if not unconnected, reason why the third sociology rests on firmer foundations than organistic and mechanistic theory. Physiology and physics are spurious models in the social sciences because they are concerned with a reality which man finds, not with one which he makes—a reality which man can at best describe (and utilise) in and through its outward manifestations, but which he cannot understand in its inner origination and working. History, on the other hand, is, like society, the field of man's own endeavour. Both sociology and historiography study human action—both are forms of human self-knowledge and self-realisation. And because of this, they can lead to deeper (if pragmatically—economically and technically—less helpful) insights than the natural sciences. As Vico might have expressed it: only God can know nature adequately, because He alone has made it; but to us is given adequate knowledge of the human realm, the realm of culture, because it is all our own work. This conclusion seems inevitable. A convincing distinction between the fundamental forms of social thought must needs lead to an equally compelling discrimination between error and truth.

PART ONE
Society as an Organism

II

ORGANICISM
The Normative Form

A s WE have already pointed out, the basic conviction of the theory which regards society as a unity rather than a multiplicity has classically been formulated by saying that the social order is an organism. But though this formula is well-nigh universal in the camp of the philosophical realists, it hides two rather disparate modes of thought. According to one tradition, society is really—actually and factually—an organism; what is true of the body physical is true also of the body social; the laws which control the one are identical with the laws which control the other. This doctrine can best be described as the positive or positivistic variety of sociological organicism. According to the other, contrasting, tradition, society is merely ideally, but not necessarily actually and factually, an organism. What the members of this school suggest is that the social order is organic in design. Now, the word design as here used is inherently ambiguous. When I say society is designed along organic lines, I mean that its ground plan is organic. To that extent, there is a positivistic element even in this second social theory which, for reasons which will become clear at once, we propose to call normative organicism. But a design need not be realised; the structure which rises above the organic pattern at its base, need not be in harmony with it. Here, as everywhere, the basic design may not be fulfilled. Hence there appears here a normative element which sets this doctrine off against the purely positive form of organicism. Society, fundamentally an organic system, should become so in the full sense of the word. Positive organicism is restricted to the Is; normative organicism distinguishes an Is and an Ought, yet the Ought is not really, or radically, at variance with the Is. Rather is it its true working out, its natural realisation. It is more than an idle play upon words to say, that the normative theory demands that society should become what it is—that it should become in reality what it is in design. We shall survey this form of organicism first because it is far older than the other. Its greatest representatives were Aristotle in Antiquity and St. Thomas Aquinas in the Middle Ages. But the number of its champions has always been legion.

One difficulty must be removed first. Is this order of ideas not hopelessly unscientific? Does not the spirit of science move out of the back door, as soon as the concept of design enters at the front? It must be admitted that both Aristotle and St. Thomas were teleologists in philosophy. They saw reality, not as static, but as informed and permeated, in all its breadth and depth, by a tendency towards perfection. With the great Dominican, this conviction is simply an implication of his Christian creed. Everything comes from the Creator who is Perfection; everything tends back towards Him who is Perfection. With the Stagirite, the conception is a little more naive and anthropomorphic, without, at the same time, being any the less theological. The demiurge who made the world is like the potter; the potter has first a model in his mind, and this model is the thing-to-be. When he sets to work, the thing-to-be will come into being. The clay will turn into the vessel. Design is thus before reality; reality comes into line with the design. 'If the products of art are determined to an end,' says Aristotle in his *Physics*,[1] 'obviously the products of nature are also.' The modern age, whose thinking is predominantly causalistic, not teleological, which believes that we ought to explain any and every phenomenon on the basis of the efficient causes behind it, not on the basis of an 'end' or of final 'causes' before it, finds this whole approach unsympathetic. Yet quite apart from the fact that the biological sciences have never managed to get along without some form of teleology, overt or covert, the normative type of sociological realism has a grounding in common sense which will always shield it—and shield it effectually, nay peremptorily—against the accusation of being untrustworthy and unrealistic.

[1] 199 a 17–18,

Several examples can help to demonstrate the essence and the truth-content of the theory. One is man himself, that is to say, each of us. When the baby is born, he is no more than a bundle of flesh, blood and bone. His actuality is merely physical. But combined and connected with it are potentialities which, in the fullness of time, will reveal themselves as mental and moral. When we start with the baby and trace his development to adulthood and maturity, we follow the time order, the order of generation; and this order is all modern man is normally concerned with. But when we start with the fully unfolded personality and look back and down from it towards the beginning of life, we also follow and trace an order, the order of meaning, which seemed to Aristotle far more significant than the order of generation. What it means to be a man is seen far more clearly in the grown person, in the perfect personality, than in the babe in arms—if, indeed, this meaning is discernible at all in the new-born child which has far more animal qualities than human ones properly so called. Man, as we meet him in experience, will regularly be somewhere in between the two poles—mere animality and full human stature. And he will be pushed by efficient forces behind him from the lower pole to the higher, just as he will be pulled by final (or end-originating) forces towards the higher from the lower. This is the basic pattern of explanation present in Aristotle's mind. Let extreme causalists condemn it; let them say that an end which does not as yet exist, cannot exert a pull. Experience teaches us different: we all know that growing up is both physical maturing *and* mental and moral striving, a process determined by the ideal before, as well as the real behind, us. Aristotle's teleology may be highly problematic in the sphere of nature study; it is sound and sensible in the study of man. The presence of purpose in inanimate and irrational creation is and must remain a matter of faith and not of fact; but its presence among, and its influence on, men, who are creatures of reason, cannot be doubted.

Not surprisingly, Aristotle's doctrine of society lies parallel to this his doctrine of man. Individual societies, just like individual men, are each located somewhere along a line of which one end is the state (the largely hypothetical state) in which social life (the word taken in a fuller, and not merely a physical sense) is no more than pure potentiality, while the other is a state (equally hypothetical, because never fully attained) in which this potentiality has become totally actualised. It is characteristic of Aristotle's philosophical realism and organicism that the lower end-point of this gamut—the social minimum, as it were—is not envisaged by him as a mere disconnected side-by-side existence of pre-social and a-social men, as it was to be later on by Rousseau and Kant. To him, and to St. Thomas Aquinas, man is from the very beginning a social creature, though this initial sociality has a long way to go before it reaches its acmé. It is equally characteristic of his socio-centrism that the higher end-point of the gamut receives all the value-accentuation and high-lighting. This higher end-piece, this terminal of development, which is not only the end in the sense of final point, but also in the sense of final cause, is envisaged by Aristotle as a quasi-organic state, a degree of social integration comparable to the perfect unity of the healthy body. In this sense, and to this extent, he is indeed an organicist of the purest water. Yet he did not assert that society is an organism, merely that it is designed to become and to be like one—a great, nay decisive difference from positivistic organicism.

There are several disjointed passages in Aristotle's *Politics* which show, when collected together, how great a measure of sociality he ascribed even to man at his least social. If such a thing as an isolated human being could be imagined, he would, he suggests, exhibit both objective and subjective traits of sociality. 'The individual, when isolated, is not self-sufficing',[1] Aristotle writes, and this is an objectively demonstrable, natural fact. His vital needs or survival needs alone drive man towards union with his fellows. But there is not only an objective need, there is also a subjective urge towards association and community. 'A social instinct is implanted in all men by nature.'[2] Outer influences and inner thus combine to insure the origin and the development of social life. Hence even if social history were to begin with the isolated individual, it would end in the well-established society, the social organism.

But for Aristotle, it is not the individual at all with which social history begins; it is the family. 'In the first place there must be a union of those who cannot exist without each other; namely, . . . male and female.[3]' The last and deepest root of society lies

---

[1] *Politics*, 1253 a 26. (Jowett's translation. I am grateful to Mr. D. M. Leahy for helping me to make the references to Aristotle's text more exact than I could have done on the basis of Jowett's printed version.)
[2] *Ib.*, 1253 a 29.   [3] *Ib.*, 1252 a 26.

simply in the biotic sphere. Here is an element that can be, and has been, used as a sheet-anchor for positivistic organicism. But Aristotle sees even the sexual union in normative terms. The physical conjunction of male and female is only a beginning which has in it as a potentiality, and in due course produces as an actuality, the human bond between husband and wife such as we find it among truly civilised, truly cultured partners. This precisely was Aristotle's main argument against Plato's call for sex communism among the rulers, that marriage, whatever its origins in purely physical actualities, has in it possibilities of a far nobler kind, that what begins in animal gratification, may end in spiritual love.

There are in this way two 'ends' which 'nature' holds out to the union of bed and board and which the upward-pushing and upward-pulling forces in it will strive to attain: the good family and the good society. Societies may arise both through the joining together of households and through their breaking-up. 'When several families are united, and the association aims at something more than the supply of daily needs,' Aristotle writes, 'the first society to be formed is the village. And the most natural form of the village appears to be that of a colony from the [consanguine] family, composed of the children and grand-children, who are said to be suckled with the same milk.'[1] And in another context he says: 'In the first community . . . which is the family [exchange] is obviously of no use, but it begins to be useful when the society increases. For the members of the family originally had all things in common; later, when the family divided into parts, the parts shared in many things, and different parts in different things, which they had to give in exchange for what they wanted . . .'[2] A new reality thus comes into being, the reality of social life in the narrower, quasi-technical sense of the word.

This is the 'natural' origin of the social order, its natural beginning. But it has not only a natural beginning, it also has a 'natural' end. 'The state comes into existence for the sake of a good life. And therefore, if the earlier forms of society are natural, so is the state, for it is the end of them, and the nature of a thing is its end. For what each thing is when fully developed, we call

---

[1] *Ib.*, 1252 b 15–18. "Offshoot" might be a better translation in this passage than Jowett's "colony".   [2] *Ib.*, 1257 a 19–24.

its nature.'[1] This quotation reveals to us the focal centre around which the social theory of normative organicism is built: the conception and conviction that society, when it is most developed, when it is, so to speak, most itself, is comparable to that greatest of natural phenomena, a living organism. It is a 'social body' not too different in its happy unity from the healthy body physical of animal or man.

The coincidence in type between the body social when it is in good order, and the body physical when it is in good health, is due to the fact that both, when they are what they ought to be, constitute internally harmonious wholes. 'As a body is made up of many members, and every member ought to grow in proportion, that symmetry may be preserved, . . . even so a state has many parts' and 'the same law of proportion equally holds.'[2] Perhaps we come nearest to Aristotle's decisive thought if we formulate his key-conviction as follows: body physical and body social are different in matter; a mass of material particles on the one hand, a mass of individual men on the other; but they coincide in the *form* in which this matter tends to find its final—its essential—rest and realisation.

It is probably permissible to go as far as this in ascribing 'realistic' and organismic ideas to the great philosopher from Stagira. Considering what 'form' means to him, his organicism is rather far-reaching, if our formula is at all correct. But, far-reaching as it is, it yet falls short of the extremism of the positivistic organicists. For them, the equation between body physical and body social is a scientific, literal fact; for Aristotle it is, in spite of everything, no more than a metaphor, however striking, and however happy.

We see how true this is when we consider that Aristotle, unlike his distant cousins, makes no attempt to play down or argue away the outstanding and obvious difference between body physical on the one hand and body social on the other: the fact that the former is a concrete unity with a unitary sensorium and the latter a discrete unity with general dispersal of the ability to think and feel. 'Some say', he writes, 'that the state has done a certain act,' as if it were a person. 'But a state is composite, like any other whole made up of many parts.'[3] We must hold on to this composite nature of society both in theory and in practice.

---

[1] *Ib.*, 1252 b 29–33.　　　　[2] *Ib.*, 1302 b 34–41 and 1309 b 29–30.
[3] *Ib.*, 1274 b 34, 39–40.

We should falsify the mental picture as well as the real character of social life, if we allowed it to slip from our grasp. 'There is a point at which a state may attain such a degree of unity as to be no longer a state . . . like harmony passing into unison.'[1] This last quotation is particularly significant: in the case of society, multiplicity, far from being a hindrance to, is a pre-supposition of, harmonious ordering. 'The nature of a state is to be a plurality . . . A state is not made up only of so many men, but of different kinds of men; for similars do not constitute a state. It is not like a military alliance. The usefulness of the latter depends upon its quantity'—the more soldiers, the better. But in social life, into which everyone ought to enter with his full personality, 'the elements out of which a unity is to be formed differ in kind.'[2] And as the state as such cannot act, so, too, can it not experience pleasure and pain: 'Happiness is not like the even principle in numbers, which may exist only in the whole, but in neither of the parts . . . The whole cannot be happy unless most, or all, or some of its parts enjoy happiness.'[3] In a word, a society *consists* of individuals; it is not permissible to say that it *is* an individual.

This, however, does not mean that the inner ordering of the social multiplicity may not be strikingly similar to the inner ordering of the individual units. Aristotle clearly implies that the comparison body physical/body social is valid, that it is enlightening rather than misleading. 'The state, as composed of unlikes, may be compared to the living being,'[4] he expressly states, for the living being, too, is in a sense a compound. Yet if mutual adjustedness of the parts to each other and free and frictionless co-operation are essential here and there, if there is near-identity between the two phenomena in this respect, characteristic contrast appears again as soon as we look more closely. We discover it at once if we contemplate, with Aristotle, the two bases on which the order, proportion, and harmony of the political community rest: justice and friendship. Justice can indeed be so defined that it will cover the 'right relations' between physical organs as well as those between fellow-citizens and *vice versa*. But no such definition can suppress the truth that 'justice' is a virtue, a *desideratum* and *faciendum*, in the body social, and a reality, a *datum* and *factum*, in

---

[1] *Ib.*, 1263 b 33–35.
[2] *Ib.*, 1261 a 18, 22–25, 29–30.
[3] *Ib.*, 1264 b 17–22.
[4] *Ib.*, 1277 a 5–6.

       C

the body physical. As for friendship—and friendship, says Aristotle, is the greatest good in society[1]—it has no homologue outside the social sphere: it is a link possible only between persons—indeed, only between personalities who are well on the way to perfection.

Without justice, St. Augustine was to write in a much-quoted passage, kingdoms are no more than great robber-bands.[2] Aristotle had expressed a similar conviction eight hundred years earlier, only that his formulation was scientific rather than rhetorical. Without justice, he intimated, societies are merely 'alliances of which the members live apart.'[3] Such alliances, akin in character to commercial treaties between independent cities, cannot produce the close harmonies of community life without which a state can never be likened to an organic whole. In another context he had gone even further and made it doubtful, at least by implication, whether any peaceful coexistence is at all possible among men who are not just. 'Man, when perfected, is the best of animals,' he had written, 'but, when separated from law and justice, he is the worst of all.'[4] In any case, 'justice is the bond of men in states',[5] and whether some social life be possible without it or none, one thing is certain, namely, that social integration in the sense of organic unity is unthinkable without it.

All, then, depends on justice: it is justice that raises a circle of men, the matter or raw material of society, up towards culture and community, the form of its perfection. But alas! justice is a virtue, and virtue is rarely a reality. For this reason, it will practically never be possible to say of society that it *is* truly organic in coherence—though it will ever be necessary to repeat that it *ought* to be so. Aristotle explains over and over again that men are a bad medium—too unmalleable a metal as it were—out of which to fashion a community. He refers in one place to the 'wickedness of human nature'; in another he says that 'all men, if they can, do what they will'; in a third he emphasises that 'wealth and honour . . . are objects of desire to all mankind', and this desire is in a fourth place compared to a 'wild beast'. 'The avarice of mankind is insatiable . . . men always want more and more without end; for it is of the nature of desire not to be

[1] *Nicomachean Ethic*, 1169 b 10.   [2] *De Civitate Dei*, IV, 4.
[3] *Politics*, 1280 b 8–9.   [4] *Ib.*, 1253 a 31–33.
[5] *Ib.*, 37.

24

satisfied, and most men live only for the gratification of it.' 'When absolute freedom is allowed,' Aristotle writes with a specially caustic pen, 'there is nothing to restrain the evil inherent in every man.' This evil must ever make for human disharmony. Aristotle quotes Hesiod to the effect that 'potter hates potter'— brother hates brother.[1] How far is the human race from the harmony of the truly integrated society! It may be a light in the distance that beckons us on, but however hard we push towards it, we seem unable to attain it.

Of course, we are not entirely helpless. Where the spontaneous forces driving and inviting towards organic integration fail, human art may take over and continue the effort. There is education; education generates virtue; virtue creates social unity. Yet the power of the educator is limited—as limited as any other energy in this finite world. Education can shorten the distance between the state of society as it is and the state of society as it ought to be, but it cannot eliminate it altogether. The problem remains; or, rather, the problems remain; for there are two: the practical problem of the harmony, and the theoretical problem of the definition, of society. The latter Aristotle thought to have solved by bringing in and utilising the organic simile, the body metaphor.

Aristotle is quite clear in his own mind that we are less than realistic if we call society as it is an organism. 'Government', he writes in a particularly transparent passage, 'is the subject of a single science, which has to consider what government is best and of what sort it must be, to be most in accordance with our aspirations, if there were no external impediment.'[2] In other words, the science of society deals less with the real patterns it finds, in which the essence of social life is overlaid and made well-nigh unrecognisable by the impurities which smother it; it deals with the ideal pattern which emerges if these impurities are thought away. It deals with form rather than with matter, even if in this imperfect world of ours matter often obscures form. And Aristotle thinks this is right; true knowledge to him is the knowledge of form. And the form of society is the organic whole.

The social philosophy of St. Thomas Aquinas is very similar to the one which we have just reviewed. Yet a brief glance at it

[1] *Loc. cit.*, 1263 b 23; 1312 b 3; 1311 a 30; 1287 a 30; 1267 a 41—1267 b 5; 1318 b 39; 1312 b 4.   [2] *Loc. cit.*, 1288 b 20-22.

will be instructive because the great Master of the Schools, with his meticulous method and mental discipline, makes many things explicit which are no more than implicit in his Greek mentor.

Let us first note that there is substantial agreement on the basic essentials. 'St. Thomas allowed for two extreme types of human conjunction', writes Thomas Gilby in his excellent study of Aquinas.[1] 'One corresponded to the material cause or stuff of civilised association: it was the mass into which a man was born or otherwise incorporated . . . The other corresponded to the final cause or purpose: it was a communication of minds and wills through contemplation and charity . . . Between these extremes was placed a combination, namely the political community [the sociologist would perhaps prefer to say, the empirical society] which rose from the first and aspired to the second—a mixed type and, like a mongrel, all the tougher for not being of one strain.' The thought-pattern summed up in these sentences coincides to all intents and purposes with that basic to Aristotle's *Politics*. There is the natural, i.e. nature-given, raw material of the as yet culturally and ethically unformed society at the beginning of development; there is the natural, in the sense of essence-revealing, image of the perfected community at its end; and there is, in between, the half-ordered social system of observable reality in which men actually live—men who are always and in every respect on a pilgrimage between their first physical birth and their last spiritual destination.

While these conceptions are no more than a christianised version of Aristotelean convictions, St. Thomas offers a clear-cut characterisation of empirical society which goes far beyond anything the Greeks had to offer on this head. What helps him to this mental clarity, is his scholastic habit of making relevant definitions and distinctions. A society is obviously a whole; the question is—what kind of a whole? Now wholes fall, first of all, into two broad categories: logical wholes and real wholes. Logical wholes are intra-mental wholes; the mind sees several entities together and treats them, on the basis of a more or less conscious fiction, for convenience sake as a totality. If I say 'all

[1] English edition under the title *Principality and Polity*, 1958, American edition under the title *The Political Thought of Thomas Aquinas*, 1958, p. 261. Both this work and Father Gilby's *Between Community and Society*, 1953, are to be warmly recommended. Their terminology may, however, cause some difficulty to those of us who have become accustomed to Ferdinand Tönnies' definitions.

the gold in the world', I am talking as if it were one thing; I use the verb which refers to 'it' in the singular: 'all the gold in the world *is* this or that'. Yet in point of fact there is no unitary substance here: some gold is in Fort Knox, and some is, in the form of a ring, on my finger. The unity of the whole exists here only in thought, but not in life. In life there is distance and diversity. The extreme individualists and mechanists were to subsume society under this definition. In reality there are, according to them, only individual men, no more. Society is merely a shorthand term which we use because it is linguistically helpful, but which must not be thought to stand for a tangible, integrated reality. Real wholes, on the other hand, are totalities in extramental life, and not merely in speech and thought. The unity of the whole is factual, tangible, independent of the enregistering and observing mind. There really *is* a composite whole, in addition to the individual items which constitute it and which it comprises. 'All the grains of gold in the gold bar before me' is a phrase which designates a real whole. We need not sum the grains up in our mind to make them into a quasi-thing. The ingot *is* a thing, with nothing 'quasi' about it, as we notice at once when we drop the bar to the ground or toss it into the air. It is characteristic of St. Thomas' organicism that he allots the social system to this second type of totality. A society is to him more than the sum of its members.

For the extreme collectivists and organicists, the matter ended there. But not for St. Thomas. He makes further enlightening distinctions. A real whole may be a substantial whole, or it may be an 'accidental' whole. (This latter term is somewhat misleading.) A substantial whole is, as the name implies, a composite, yet coherent substance. Such is the bar of gold. Such is the body composed of cells. An accidental whole is not a substance, but a system of relations: it is a relational whole. (As relation is, in philosophical terminology, an *accidens*—or contingent characteristic—of substances, the term used here becomes understandable.) Now, a society is to St. Thomas not a substantial whole: it is not, in other words, like the body physical, a unitary thing. Its coherence is constituted by the relationships between substances (i.e. men). Certainly, it is a matter of fact, of life, not only of fiction, of speech. But St. Thomas does not hypostatise its reality into a material or tangible substantiality. 'This is the difference between the natural body of man and the mystical body of the church,' he writes,[1] 'that the members of the body natural are all together [i.e. in corporeal contact], and the members of the body mystical are not.' A society to him is many, though many tied together by nature, and not merely by concept or contract. Men do co-operate; indeed, they must co-operate; their very physical nature, with its inherent and imperative needs, forces them into a pattern that is distantly comparable and conceptually kindred with the pattern of divided and integrated labour in the living organism. But to say that for this reason society *is* an organism in the ontological sense of the word seemed to St. Thomas a vast exaggeration that he would not let pass. Wherever the body-metaphor crops up, he carefully dissociates himself from it.[2] The members of a group *reputantur quasi* unum corpus; the church *dicitur* unum corpus mysticum *per similitudinem* ad corpus naturale; omnes homines *possunt considerari* ut unus homo, *reputatur* communitas quasi unus homo:[3] a group is being considered (reputatur) *as if it were* one body; the church *is being called* a mystical body because of its *similarity* to the body natural; all men together *may* be looked upon (understand: for some purposes) as one individual: however 'real' society as a system of given relations may be, 'body social' is merely a metaphor.

A very good insight into the sociological conceptions of the Saint is also afforded by the article in which he discusses the question whether the devil is the head of the wicked.[4] In so far as men possess free will and commit sins of their own account, they must needs appear as independent personalities and irreducible selves. In other words, they appear as a multiplicity rather than a unity. There can thus be no close comparison between the 'body' of the fallen and the body physical in which the members always do the behest of the head and have no determination of their own. Yet there *is* a sense in which the devil can reasonably be described as the head of the wicked: he is their leader as it were, and they follow him as soldiers follow a commander and his standard. As the army of the adversaries of God and good,

---

[1] *Summa Theologiæ*, 3a, VIII, 3.

[2] There is occasionally a passage which one must overlook: e.g. 2a 2æ, LXIV, 2, 3, where criminals are compared to diseased members of the body. Here the Saint falls unwittingly into the common jargon of his age, but it would be altogether wrong to think that his considered social ontology is visible in such a formulation.

[3] 1a 2æ, LXXXI, 1; 3a, VIII, 1.   [4] 3a, VII.

the wicked are indeed a coherent company, but their coherence is relational only, not substantial as that of the human or animal organism.

However, while there are irreducible differences between body physical and body social, it is yet possible to subsume the two under one and the same concept. The Saint describes a body or organism in one context[1] as 'a multiplicity organised into unity on the basis of different activities and functions'. This wide definition clearly covers the social structure as well as the structure of flesh and bone. It makes them, not identical, but sister phenomena. True, the concourse of different activities and functions in the body social is never as close and smooth as it is in the body physical. But this is, after all, a distinction merely in degree and not in essence: and, what is more, it is a distinction which it is in our power to reduce. The basic pattern of co-operation and co-ordination is the same in both cases, and if comparative disorder disgraces most societies, it is, in principle, possible to overcome it step by step until it gives way to comparative order, until chaos is replaced by cosmos. The more we cease to be selfish and become social, the more we cease to be sinful and become saintly, the more will unity gain over diversity, and the more will the body social come to resemble the body physical. And even if complete harmony, or quasi-organical integration, is practically unimaginable down here below, we can well imagine it, with Saint Thomas, to reign in the communion of saints, that happy company of heaven, from which selfishness—the agency which sets men against each other and keeps them apart—has finally departed. Although an element of metaphor remains and must remain, that community of love can truly be likened to a body, the body of Christ; indeed, we are unable to envisage its essence otherwise than under this simile, for in our earthly experience we encounter nothing alive that would be so fully one as a living organism. In this way, organic integration remains the end of all social existence: not a fact, but a norm; not a reality, but an aspiration; not something that we have and hold, but a hope that is conceived in faith and may come to be born of charity.

[1] 3a, VIII, 4.

III

ORGANICISM
The Positive Form

COMPARED TO its normative rival, the positive or positivistic form of sociological organicism is a far more straightforward theory. Herbert Spencer, whom we propose to study as its leading representative, expressed its gist in a lapidary form by a simple question and answer: 'What is a society? A society is an organism' (pp. 465 and 467 of *The Principles of Sociology*, vol. I, ed. 1877). No distinction here between fact and norm, Is and Ought. Like so many of his kind, Spencer had in his mind a black-and-white, night-and-day picture of the difference between pre-scientific and scientific thought. The thought of, say, Aristotle and St. Thomas Aquinas was pre-scientific, and that is tantamount to saying useless, precisely because it concerned itself with the ideal as well as with the real. Spencer's own theories, on the other hand, were scientific, and therefore the undeniable truth, because, in the most radical fashion possible, they excluded that which is not from their field of vision, and looked only at that which is: at reality, in all its naked and unadorned factualness. This is why the label 'positivists' (in a wider sense) was proposed for the members of this school, and why they wore it proudly. Yet the meaning of the little word 'is' in the statement that society 'is' an organism cannot but appear problematic. Is it to be taken in its narrowest, most literal, signification? Or are we allowed to give it a somewhat wider, more metaphorical meaning? What does Spencer really suggest when he asserts that society *is* an organism, what he seems to suggest—or perhaps only that society is something *like* an organism? Truth to tell, Spencer found it convenient to remain in between these two possible poles of interpretation. His aim certainly was to edge as near as possible to the former alternative, which was, so to speak, the more positive and factual of the two: but he found it impossible to get rid of the metaphorical element altogether. What makes his tomes, so Victorian in outlook, and so musty in smell as all Victorian volumes are today, much more interesting than they otherwise would be, is his laborious attempt to convince, not only his readers, but even himself, that his basic assertion could be sustained. It is not at all surprising to find him so anxious to demonstrate the truth of his thesis. More was at stake than simply a problem of social theory. His whole philosophy, his monism, was proved hollow if different areas or aspects of reality could be shown to follow different laws.

Spencer attempted to achieve his object by two complementary methods. He tried first to prove that there are more similarities between body social and body physical than meet the eye; and, that done, he did his best to show that those dissimilarities between the two which meet the eye, are in fact more apparent than real. In pursuit of the former argument, he submits 'that growth is common to social aggregates and organic aggregates ... Living bodies and societies so conspicuously exhibit augmentation of mass, that we may fairly regard this as characteristic of them both' (p. 467). There are always more cells in an organism after it has been in existence for a while; there are always more men in a society after it has had time to develop. Already at this first step, the critical reader cannot help revolting against Spencer's 'inductions'. Superficially, no doubt, the fact that both body physical and body social increase in size during their evolution (or rather during part of their life-span) may create the impression that the two phenomena are akin to each other; but on a more analytical view of the matter it soon appears that such an impression is misleading. The multiplication of cells in the body physical is a spontaneous, more or less automatic, process which the will of man can neither speed up nor slow down: but the multiplication of men in the body social, and especially the rate at which it takes place, is vitally dependent on human willing. Even the fact that the growth of a population is the result of a physical drive, and to that extent an outworking of natural laws, does not really abolish the essential difference between the two kinds of growth. The least that must be said is that the desire for sex-satisfaction coalesces with, and is inhibited and sometimes enhanced by, specifically human, that is to say specifically volitional value-pursuits—the desire for a high standard of living, for instance, or for prestige, or for the securing of children's allowances where such are paid. When the Code Napoléon introduced the principle of free divisibility, i.e. decreed that every child should in future have an equal *per capita* share of his father's land, in opposition to the traditional custom, which gave all the soil to the eldest son and allotted to the other heirs merely monetary payments, it soon changed the 'law of multiplication' among the peasant population of France. The truth is that growth and growth may be two very different things. '*Si duo faciunt idem, non est idem*', said the Romans: when two do the same thing, it is not the same thing. This is a clear case in point.

But Spencer is not satisfied with saying that both physical and social organisms grow. If he had gone no further, he would at least have had external fact on his side, for the world's population has, through history, moved from record to record. What he asserts is that even the *modes* of growing are identical. And this, given his basic position—positivistic organicism—is no frivolous, but rather a necessary extension of the argument. For if both physical and social evolution obey the same laws, then their similarity must go far beyond the purely statistical fact of numerical multiplication. Indeed, it must be an all-embracing similarity, a full coincidence. Aware of this, Spencer pushes his investigation boldly forward, but already his second step shows the profoundly unrealistic nature of his whole approach. 'The growth of individual and social organisms are allied in another respect', he writes. 'In each case size augments by two processes, which go on sometimes separately, sometimes together. There is increase by simple multiplication of units, causing enlargement of the group; there is increase by union of groups, and again by union of groups of groups' (pp. 482/3). This second form of evolution he calls compounding and recompounding, and he claims that it is traceable, in essentially parallel phenomena, in both the vegetable, the animal and the human kingdoms, in the individual as well as in the social sphere. 'Plants of the lowest orders are minute cells . . . By clustering of such cells are formed small threads, discs, globes etc. as well as amorphous masses and laminated masses. One of these last, called a thallus when scarcely at all differentiated, as in a seaweed, and a frond in cryptogams that have some structure, is an extensive but simple group of the protophytes first named. Temporarily united in certain low cryptogams, fronds become permanently united in higher cryptogams: then forming a series of foliar surfaces joined by a creeping stem. Out of this comes the phænogamic axis—a shoot with its foliar organs or leaves. That is to say, there is now a permanent cluster of clusters. And then, as these axes develop lateral axes, and as these again branch, the compounding advances to higher stages . . . Social growth proceeds by an analogous compounding and re-compounding. The primitive social group, like the primitive group of physiological units with which organic evolution begins, never attains any considerable size by simple increase . . . The formation of a larger society results only by combination of these smaller societies. . . . This process may be seen now going on among various uncivilized races, as it once went on among the ancestors of the civilized races. Instead of absolute independence of small hordes, such as the lowest savages show us, more advanced savages show us slight cohesions among larger hordes . . . After such compound societies are consolidated, repetition of the process on a larger scale produces doubly-compound societies, which, usually cohering but feebly, become in some cases quite coherent' (pp. 483 —486).

Spencer does his best to adduce historical illustrations of these laws of growth and their operation. Have not the Iroquois merged in a grand league under which there are five nations, under which again there are 'severally' eight tribes? Has not the one-time empire of Egypt grown out of small independent states which in turn have grown out of a great number of tribes—and so on, and so forth? Vainly does Spencer try to impress the critical reader with this display of learning—its mortal weakness is obvious. First of all, a comparison of the development of the higher cryptogams with the origin of a large-scale empire like ancient Egypt is absurd in itself, and manifestly so; secondly, the historical evidence adduced is all doctored: Spencer reproduces such facts as suit his book and suppresses such as refuse to fit in with his pre-conceived scheme; and lastly, a law of nature worthy of its name is not established by the quoting of one or two appropriate instances. It must explain the whole of reality, and this is not conclusively shown by Spencer; indeed, this vital proof is not even attempted.

The next two steps in Spencer's argument are best taken to-gether, and between them they mark his closest approach to sound reasoning. Both physical and social evolution show increasing differentiation and—*pari passu*—integration of the bodies con-cerned. 'While they increase in size they increase in structure. A low animal . . . has few distinguishable parts; but along with its acquirement of greater mass, its parts multiply and simultaneously differentiate. It is thus with a society. At first the unlikenesses among its groups of units are inconspicuous in number and degree; but as it becomes more populous, divisions and sub-divisions become more numerous and more decided' (pp. 467/8). In the body physical, brain-cells become divided, both in structure and in function, from other cells; in the body social, the same happens to the intellectuals, call them what you will, who rise above the common herd, form a class of their own, and increas-ingly perform the work which appears their own. This growing differentiation, which makes for diversity, is connected with a parallel progressive integration, which makes for, and guarantees, unity. Brain and stomach and arms are very different from each other—as different as medicine men, field workers and warriors. Yet in either case, the differentiated parts, as bodily 'organs', co-operate for the benefit of the whole. 'Evolution establishes in . . . both [body physical and body social], not differences simply, but definitely-connected differences . . . The parts of an inorganic aggregate are so related that one may change greatly without appreciably affecting the rest. It is otherwise with the parts of an organic aggregate or of a social aggregate. In either of these the changes in the parts are mutually determined, and the changed actions of the parts are mutually dependent. In both, too, this mutuality increases as the evolution advances' (p. 469).

As already hinted, we have here reached the point at which what justification there is for the comparison of body physical and body social can be seen to the best advantage. Organism and society coincide, to some extent at any rate, because both are systems of differentiated and integrated structure and function. The biologists bear witness to this fact when they speak of a 'physiological division of labour'—when they use a simile taken from sociology in order to elucidate a physical phenomenon. 'This division of labour,' Spencer writes, 'is that which in the society, as in the animal, makes it a living whole'. And he continues: 'Scarcely can I emphasize sufficiently the truth that in respect of this fundamental trait, a social organism and an individual organism are entirely alike' (p. 470). It is impossible, at this juncture, to dissent from Spencer's essential submission. And yet—

Once again, as in our discussion of growth, we must press two criticisms against Spencer, even the Spencer who has hold of an important truth. The one is that he does not go underneath the surface similarity; the other is that he widens the area of similarity until it covers phenomena—or rather appears to cover phenomena —which are in fact proofs of dissimilarity. The first point is easily made by simple reference to that basic trait of man—selfishness or self-preference. If all taxpayers would send their contributions for the upkeep of government to the Inland Revenue offices with the same unquestioning willingness and punctuality with which the corresponding parts of the physical organism send nutritive currents to the organs of control within their system, the Spencerian comparison would appear altogether rational, nay, almost impregnable. But they do not. And because they do not, because the tax inspector has to fight the tax contributors all the way, a comparison between body physical and body social is really out of the question. Or rather, a comparison between the body physical and the body social, *as it actually is*, is out of the question. For we may usefully compare the body physical with the body social *as it might be*. We see at this point, as in a flash of lightning, the tremendous superiority of normative over positive organicism. Positive organicism, if we concentrate on its strength and forgive or forget its weaknesses, can be said to have recognised one salient truth—the fact that a society lives by divided and integrated labour. But normative organicism has understood two related, if not easily reconciled truths—the fact that a society lives by divided and integrated labour, and the further fact that integration is imperfect here, that the interests of the parts are backed by stronger vital forces than the interest of the whole.

This is an outsider's criticism of Spencer's position. But he himself controverts it, simply by gross, almost ridiculous, exaggeration. When attention is concentrated on the great fact of the

division and integration of labour, it can be sensibly and truth-
fully asserted that societies and organisms have an essential trait
in common. But Spencer refuses to concentrate on this great fact;
he refuses to concentrate at all and tries to show that many traits
are common to organisms and societies, great and small. The very
lay-out of his text is significant. Because physiologists distinguish
in the physical body a sustaining, a distributing and a regulating
system, he thinks he must make these three concepts into his
three central chapter-headings, as if the institutions of a society
could be neatly docketed under these terms. And in each chapter,
he then presents us with an inventory of the details of the physical
organism, adducing at each step the concrete social phenomena
which he fancies to be their homologues, as if this were the most
natural procedure for the description of the body politic. It is
well-nigh unavoidable that this should lead to ludicrous results.
Here it is impossible to do more than adduce one example of his
deplorable (if often ingenious) tendency to equate the two systems. The reader can find plenty of others in part II of volume I
of *The Principles of Sociology*, if he has time to waste.

Our example is taken from Spencer's §232. It considers the
evolution of physical and social 'organs'. 'The formation of
organs in a living body proceeds in ways which we may distinguish as primary, secondary, and tertiary,' Spencer writes, 'and,
paralleling them, there are primary, secondary, and tertiary ways
in which social organs are formed . . . In animals of low types the
secretion of bile is carried on not by a liver, but by separate cells
scattered along in the wall of the intestine at one part. These cells
individually perform their function of separating certain matters
from the blood, and individually pour out the products. No
organ, strictly so-called, exists; but only a number of units not
yet aggregated into an organ. This is analogous to the incipient
form of an industrial structure in a society. At first each worker
carries on his occupation alone; and himself disposes of the product to the consumer. The arrangement still extant in our villages,
where the cobbler at his own fireside makes and sells boots, and
where the blacksmith single-handed does what iron-work is
needed by his neighbours, exemplifies the primitive type of every
producing structure . . . By two simultaneous changes, the incipient secreting organ of an animal reaches that higher structure
with which our next comparison may be made. The cells pass

from a scattered cluster into a compact cluster; and they severally become compound. In place of a single cell elaborating and emitting its special product, we now have a small elongated sac containing a family of cells; and this, through an opening at one end, gives exit to their products. Hence results an integrated group of more or less tubular follicles, each containing secreting units and having its separate orifices of discharge. To this type of individual organ, we find, in semi-civilized societies, a type of social organ closely corresponding . . . In mediæval France handicrafts were inherited; and the old English periods were characterized by a like custom. . . . The related families who monopolized each industry formed a cluster habitually occupying the same quarter. Hence the still extant names of many streets in English towns —Fellmonger, Horsemonger, and Fleshmonger, Shoewright and Shieldwright, Turner and Salter Streets, and the like. And now, on observing how one of these industrial quarters was composed of many allied families, . . . we see that there existed an analogy to the kind of glandular organ described above, which consists of a number of adjacent cell-containing follicles having separate mouths' (pp. 497-500).

It is, no doubt, justifiable to expect of the social theorist a certain amount of imagination, alongside the rationality on which his work has to be based. But that imagination should, surely, remain linked to his rationality and not be allowed to break away from it and to defy it. Yet is a comparison between the Salter Street in an old, medieval city and a sack of follicles inside the guts of John Citizen still rational? To put the question is to answer it in the negative. Still, worse is to come, for Spencer does not hesitate to compare a modern industrial town to an animal liver. 'A third stage [of] the analogy may be traced', he asserts. 'Along with that increase of a glandular organ necessitated by the more active functions of a more developed animal, there goes a change of structure consequent on augmentation of bulk. If the follicles multiply while their ducts have all to be brought to one spot, it results that their orifices, increasingly numerous, occupy a larger area of the wall of the cavity which receives the discharge; and if lateral extension of this area is negatived by the functional requirements, it results that the needful area is gained by formation of a cœcum . . . Thus is at length evolved a large viscus, such as a liver, having a single main duct with ramifying branches running throughout its mass. Now we pass from the above-described kind of industrial organ by parallel stages to a higher kind . . . The master [manufacturer] grew into a seller of goods made, not by his own family only, but by others; and with the enlargement of his business necessarily ceased to be a worker and became wholly a distributor—a channel through which went out the products . . . of many unrelated artizans . . . until at length . . . came the factory: a series of stories, severally containing a crowd of producing units, and sending out tributary streams of product that join before reaching the single place of exit. Finally, in greatly-developed industrial organs, such as those yielding textile fabrics, arise many factories clustered in the same town, and others in adjacent towns, to and from which, along branching roads, come the raw material and go the bales of cloth . . .' (pp. 500 and 501). Spencer can hardly believe that anybody could be so obtuse as not to see that Manchester or Concord is a kind of liver, while a liver is something like Concord or Manchester!

All this is merely a sad confirmation of the old experience that even a good cause can come to grief when its defenders try to drive it too far. But we have as yet only dealt with one prong of the argument: the demonstration of coincidences. We have still to look at the other: the disposal of discrepancies. Two of them stand out in bold relief and peremptorily demand attention: the fact that a society is discrete, while a body is concrete; and the fact that every member of society has consciousness and sensitivity, while in the body both are concentrated in the brain. The first of these dissimilarities Spencer attempts to dissolve, but the second he finds himself unable to dispel. And so, in the end, the laboriously built-up structure of his positivistic organicism comes crashing to the ground.

When we say that a society is discrete, while an organism is concrete, we mean very simply that the 'members' of the former are free to move about as they see fit, while those of the latter are held in by skin or pelt and must move together. Confronted with this circumstance, Spencer tries two arguments in order to defend his thesis of the coincidence of society and organism, arguments of very different complexion and character. The one is the worst he could have used, the other the best. We shall start with the bad move, and then let the good move, in fairness, save as much of the theory as can be saved.

An organism, Spencer points out, is far less concrete than it looks, while society is far less discrete than might be imagined. 'The physically-coherent body of an animal is not composed all through of living units' (p. 475). There are not only the protoplasmic layers which alone are fully alive; there are also cartilage, tendon and connective tissue, which are of low vitality. In so far as these semi-vital and almost un-vital parts are interspersed between the fully-vital units, the latter do not really cohere: even a physical body is therefore loose-textured, however close-textured it may appear to the untutored eye and mind. On the other hand, 'the social organism, rightly conceived, is much less discontinuous than it seems . . . As, in the individual organism, we include with the fully living parts, the less living and not living parts which co-operate in the total activities; so, in the social organism, we must include not only those most highly vitalized units, the human beings, who chiefly determine its phenomena, but also the various kinds of domestic animals, lower in the scale of life, which under the control of man co-operate with him, and even those far inferior structures the plants, which, propagated by human agency, supply materials for animal and human activities . . . Since the physical characters, mental natures, and daily activities, of the human units, are, in part, moulded by relations to these animals and vegetals, which, living by their aid, and aiding them to live, enter so much into social life as even to be cared for by legislation, these lower living things cannot rightly be excluded from the conception of the social organism. . . . When, with human beings, are incorporated the less vitalized beings, animal and vegetal, covering the surface occupied by the society, an aggregate results having a continuity of parts, more nearly approaching to that of an individual organism; and which is also like it in being composed of local aggregations of units of various lower degrees of vitality, which are, in a sense, produced by, modified by, and arranged by, the higher units' (pp. 476 and 477).

This is a foul argument, and Spencer knew it. He is rather disingenuous at this point. He puts the considerations which we have summarised forward in order to extract from them what strength they hold and what help they can give; but he puts them forward, not as his own, but as somebody else's views, thus dissociating himself from them: 'One who thought it needful,

D

might argue . . .'; 'he might urge . . .'; 'he might say . . .'; 'he might show . . .' etc. There are before us, so to speak, two Spencerian selves in conflict with each other, a commonsensical self and a doctrinaire one, the latter trying to make him cross a Rubicon, the former warning him not to be so rash. To the critical student of the history of ideas, the hesitation displayed here must needs appear as a virtue. As we shall see in Chapter V, others rushed across the river and landed on the side of down-right absurdity.

After the silliness of §220, the sanity and insight of §221 acts like a breath of fresh air on a sultry afternoon. Spencer rightly points out in this paragraph that physical or local contiguity is not really the essence of organic wholes, but rather the functional interdependence, the mutual connectedness, of their parts. A society may be organic in coherence, even though each of its members has the capacity of independent locomotion, provided only that these members co-operate on the basis of divided and integrated labour, i.e. on the basis of an organic pattern. The following sentences can be repeated without misgivings; they harbour the heart of the matter; and though Spencer may have fancied that they prove the coincidence of body physical and body social, they show in reality to what extent there is indeed coincidence, and to what conflict and divergence: 'Though coherence among its parts is a prerequisite to that co-operation by which the life of an individual organism is carried on; and though the members of a social organism, not forming a concrete whole, cannot maintain co-operation by means of physical influences directly propagated from part to part; yet they can and do maintain co-operation by another agency. Not in contact, they never-the-less affect one another through intervening spaces, both by emotional language, and by the language, oral and written, of the intellect. For carrying on mutually-dependent actions, it is requisite that impulses, adjusted in their kinds, amounts, and times, shall be conveyed from part to part. This requisite is ful-filled in living bodies by molecular waves. . . . It is fulfilled in societies by the signs of feelings and thoughts, conveyed from person to person. . . . The mutual dependence of parts which constitutes organization is thus effectually established. Though discrete instead of concrete, the social aggregate is rendered a living whole' (pp. 477, 478).

These few lines contain and convey the essence of a sane and moderate organicism, of a positivistic organicism at that. And in the context in which they are presented, there is nothing that would spoil their message. Unfortunately, there is another context in which Spencer's besetting sin, his monism and materialism, his undue literalness in handling the body-metaphor, makes itself again felt and turns once more sense into nonsense. In §253, the 'internuncial agencies' of body physical and body social are compared, and Spencer cannot resist the temptation to draw a parallel between the nerve-strings in the one and the telegraph wires in the other. Both show "molecular continuity' (p. 557). Indeed, both show many essential similarities, similarities which can be traced down to the last technical detail. 'From great social centres diverge many large clusters of wires; from which, as they get further away, diverge at intervals minor clusters, and these presently give off re-diverging clusters; just as minor bundles of nerves on their way towards the periphery, from time to time emit lateral bundles, and these again others. Moreover, the distribution presents the analogy that near chief centres these great clusters of internuncial lines go side by side with the main channels of communication—railways and roads—but frequently part from these as they ramify; in the same way that in the central parts of a vertebrate animal, nerve-trunks habitually accompany arteries, while towards the periphery the proximity of nerves and arteries is not maintained: the only constant association being also similar in the two cases; for the one telegraph wire which accompanies the railway system throughout every ramification, is the wire which checks and excites its traffic, as the one nerve which everywhere accompanies an artery is the vaso-motor nerve regulating the circulation in it. Once more, it is a noteworthy fact that in both cases insulation characterizes the internuncial lines . . . Though in the aerial telegraph-wires insulation is otherwise effected, in under-ground wires it is effected in a way analogous to that seen in nerve-fibres. Many wires united in a bundle are separated from one another by sheaths of non-conducting substance; as the nerve-fibres that run side by side in the same trunk, are separated from one another by their respective medullary sheaths' (pp. 557/8). If we see Spencer in §221 for a moment at his best, we have him in §253 at his usual worst. From the height he had attained, he has sunk down again into his habitual materialistic obscurantism. For what else is §253 but a continuation of the nonsensical attempt to show that society is 'really' a kind of beast, sprawling before us across the ground?

In view of all the hard work which Spencer has put into the construction of his sociological theory, it must have cost him a good deal—indeed, it may have caused him some pain—to abandon it in the end. Yet this is precisely what he does. There is, he admits in the penultimate paragraph of the decisive chapter, 'a cardinal difference' between the 'two kinds of organisms'. 'In the one, consciousness is concentrated in a small part of the aggregate. In the other, it is diffused throughout the aggregate: all the units [of society] possess the capacities for happiness and misery, if not in equal degrees, still in degrees that approximate' (p. 479). If Spencer had consistently thought out what this means, he would have torn up the pages he had written before. For what exact, non-metaphorical comparison can there be between an organism controlled by one, and a pseudo-organism consisting of innumerable brains? But Spencer does not want to think all this out. He is still too much befuddled by his monistic creed, by his spurious scientism. How befuddled, can be seen from his attempt—which he well knows to be unconvincing—to find even for the differentiation between sensitive or nerve-cells and insensitive or body-cells a kind of homologue in the social system. 'There are, indeed, slight traces of such a differentiation", he writes. 'Human beings are unlike in the amounts of sensation and emotion producible in them by like causes: here great callousness, here great susceptibility, is characteristic. In the same society, even where its members are of the same race, and still more where its members are of dominant and subject races, there exists a contrast of this kind. The mechanically-working and hard-living units are less sensitive than the mentally-working and more protected units' (p. 479). This means, if it means anything, that cabinet-ministers, being part and parcel of the brain of the body politic, are more apt to feel pleasure and pain than coalminers—a statement which few will be prepared to accept as a scientific truth, and which nobody would have repudiated with more passion than Herbert Spencer, the arch-individualist and near-anarchist, himself, if he had found it in a book by another pen.

The truth is that Herbert Spencer has here come to the end of his tether. Reality has caught up with him and confronted him with an irreducible contrast between body physical and body social—a 'cardinal difference', as he candidly admits. Vainly does he try to push the unwelcome recognition aside by calling it 'a digression rather than a part of the argument'; vainly does he call on the reader to 'return and sum up the various reasons for regarding a society as an organism' (p. 480). The great admission has been made: a society is many rather than one; the individual lives within it may be interrelated and so constitute an 'accidental whole' in the sense given to the term by St. Thomas Aquinas, a quasi-organism; but they *are* individual lives and therefore they cannot be said to cohere like a 'substantial whole or true organism'; in other words, it cannot be maintained that they constitute a whole of the kind which we find exemplified in the organism of flesh and blood. For this reason, Spencer's 'Inductions of Sociology' present a poetical rather than a sober and scientific picture of the social system. Few writers have ever made the work of their critic so easy and led themselves so completely *ad absurdum* as this great champion of positivistic organicism in sociology.

IV

ORGANICISM
Secondary Forms

IN THE conception of society as an organism, actual or potential, we have before us the primary forms of realistic (as opposed to nominalistic) thinking in the social sciences. But the same holistic approach has also generated some secondary forms of organicism. We can characterise them by saying that they are remotely rooted in the conviction that a society is a unity rather than a multiplicity, but that they eschew the simple identification of body physical and body social which is the core of the primary incarnations of the same basic philosophy. The distance from the organismic doctrine in the narrower sense of the word can be greater or smaller and more obvious or less so: it is all a matter of degree. Here we cannot go too far outward towards the perimeter because our aim is to describe ideal types and not to identify trace influences. Yet one example of a really remote relative of doctrinaire organicism may, nay must be given, if for no other reason than in order to show that our tripartite division of social thought into realistic, nominalistic and mediating or processual covers, to all intents and purposes, the whole broad field. Perhaps surprisingly, the best example at our disposal is the social philosophy of Karl Marx.

How, it may be asked, can Marxism be regarded as a variant of organismic conceptions, if organicism is inclined to emphasise the integratedness and even the harmony of the social order, while Marxism stresses its internal disharmony and disintegration? Three considerations can be pitted against this rhetorical question which seems to bear a definite, but a wrong answer in itself. The first is a reference to that 'historical materialism' or 'materialistic conception of history' on which everything Marx ever wrote, said or did was squarely based. For what is the essential submission of that theory? It is the thesis that the culture of a society is a superstructure which rests on, or rather grows out of, that society's socio-economic life which forms its substructure. What else is this doctrine but an assertion of the living unity of a social system? How near we are here to the organological mode of thinking can be seen, if we formulate the whole idea in the following words: a society (a body politic) must produce its physical life, must eat, before it can produce its mental life, can think; therefore the production of physical life must be prior to, and decisive for, the production of mental phenomena. Admittedly, this manner of putting the matter is crude, but it is none too different from the words which Friedrich Engels spoke by the graveside of his friend.

Secondly, there is no need to identify society as a whole with the organic unit. Class may be so identified and interpreted. The grand design behind the greatest Marxist book of this century, Georg Lukács' *Geschichte und Klassenbewusstsein* (1923), is the demand to bring the subjective consciousness (or ideology) of the proletariat into line with its objective position and tasks in contemporary reality and progressive history—in other words, to achieve here harmonious adjustment, essential coincidence. In fact, however, even internally-divided, class-ridden and class-riven society is, to some extent, interpreted as a unity by those who stand in the genuine Marxist tradition. The antithetic worldviews of the hostile classes are conceived as couched in terms of the same fundamental conceptions; under capitalism, for instance, in terms of economics. Precisely this was the reason why Marx turned, in his later life, away from philosophy and towards political economy: the proletarian (dynamic) version of the laws of the economy had to be propounded and pitted against the bourgeois (or static) ideologies of the defenders of capitalism. It was as if two brothers, one older, one younger, one in a posture of defence, the other in an attitude of attack, were at grips, and not two complete strangers with nothing to say to each other.

Thirdly and lastly, what is the aim of all Marxism—of Marxism as a theory, as well as of Marxism as a movement—but the establishment of a fully harmonious social order in which men would co-operate with the same unproblematic and unconscious matter-of-factness as do the organs of a physical organism? What is the last reason for all the hatred of, and assault on, capitalism as the highest form of class society, but the fact that it is not an integrated and happy and harmonious social system? Rightly considered, Marxism is a specifically modern and highly individual, yet at the same time by no means untypical form of normative organicism.

This brief glance at Marxism can teach us two things: firstly, that by a proper analysis it is possible to find even in markedly unorthodox theories the basic, though often merely implied, conceptions which link them to one of the three orthodox traditions which we have distinguished. And secondly, that the variations on the three themes are very wide, so wide in fact that it may be difficult at times to discover the common theme in and underneath a given variation. A descriptive history of social thought would have to be concerned to reveal all the wealth of past theorizing; an analytical book like the present, on the other hand, is justified in pointing to the recurrence and ever-presence of certain fundamental cores in it. Its function in the study of the development of the social sciences will be a limited one, comparable perhaps to the task which anatomy has to fulfil in the study of man. Anatomy describes what is underneath the individual incarnations of human life, incarnations of which each is, in a sense, unique. It does not do justice to the riches of form which the body can and does display. The beauty and ugliness of the flesh is not discoverable in the skeletons it investigates, and a ravishing figure looks to it very much like an indifferent or even a repulsive one. But that does not mean that anatomy has nothing to give: it draws attention to the undeniable and important fact that behind the incomparable there hides the comparable, behind the specific the typical, and that an x-ray view will reveal structural similarities where the natural eye can behold nothing but dissimilar phenomena. Books on Marxism, for instance, would be far more interesting, and above all far more penetrating than they usually are, if they paid attention, not only to the dazzling surface of the system, but also to the hidden thought-structure which this surface covers —if they looked in it for a traditional theme, and not only for a never-before-encountered individual performance.

Returning from this expedition into the border country to the fields and gardens nearer home, we must look first of all at the theories of social instinct or instinctual gregariousness which can be understood as attempts to improve on positivistic organicism. As our account of Spencer has shown, the most awkward fact which this theory has to face is the discrete character of social aggregates. If this apparent discreteness is admitted, the whole argument falls to the ground; but if it is denied, the 'ligatures' which link men inside the 'body social' have to be identified, and this is difficult to do without falling into absurdity. Here the concept of social instinct can help. It teaches that body physical and body social are both coherent bodies, but that nature has secured this coherence in the latter case by means and methods different from those employed in the first. In the first instance, the cells cohere through intercellular substance, in the second the individuals cohere through instinctual ties. These ties are not visible, but they are real none-the-less. Above all—and this is the point that needs stressing—they are not man-made. They are not like the mental ties of which the third sociology is thinking, ties which human creativeness has added on to man's native endowment and internalised in him through education. No, these ties are not as precarious as that. The theory of social instinct is very definitely a variant of holism—society is *ab initio* a unity rather than a multiplicity, and not a multiplicity that would have to be made, through constant effort, through a socialising process, into a kind of unity. Sociability is born with us, with our bodies: it is biotic and not cultural.

One of the most persuasive protagonists of this doctrine was Wilfred Trotter, whose book *Instincts of the Herd in Peace and War*, first published in 1916, but written some years earlier, proved something of a best-seller in its day. Trotter does not deny that a fierce struggle for survival is going on in the universe, but he submits that the forces of life have created 'protective enclosures' inside the area of primeval war—walled-in gardens as it were, from which the law of the jungle is excluded. The term has to be used in the plural, for there are two such enclosures or gardens—the body physical and the body social. 'The animal kingdom', Trotter writes, 'presents two relatively sudden and very striking advances in complexity and in the size of the unit upon which natural selection acts unmodified. These advances consist in the aggregation of units which were previously independent and exposed to the full normal action of natural selection, and the two instances are, of course, the passage from the unicellular to the multicellular, and from the solitary to the social' (ed. 1942, p. 18). The two steps taken by nature, and inside nature, were, so it would appear, strictly parallel. The only difference concerns a technical detail: the binding agency through which the aggregation of units is secured and perpetuated.

What happened when single cells coalesced into multicellular bodies? There was loss and gain, with the gain decidedly outweighing the loss. 'In the multicellular organism individual cells lose some of the capacities of the unicellular — reproductive capacity is regulated and limited, nutrition is no longer possible in the old simple way, and response to stimuli comes only in certain channels' (*ib.*). Using metaphorical language, Trotter speaks of 'sacrifices' on the part of the cells: their freedom, so we may perhaps also say, using language hardly more metaphorical, is curtailed. But there is ample compensation: compensation describable by one simple word, the word security. 'There is now allowed a greater range of variability for the individual cells, and . . . variations . . . which were not immediately favourable would now have a chance of surviving.' 'Looked at in this way, multicellularity presents itself as an escape from the rigour of natural selection, which, for the unicellular organism, had narrowed competition to so desperate a struggle that any variation outside the straitest limits was fatal, for even though it might be favourable in one respect, it would . . . involve a loss in another' (pp. 18/19). What a chance of development! No wonder the forces of life availed themselves of it, and availed themselves of it to the full!

There are, however, inherent and necessary limits to this possibility. Aggregation leads to organisation and organisation means complication. But complication is problematic. For a while it pays: as the economists express it, there is at first a law of increasing returns. But from a certain point on, the situation changes. Increasing returns give way to decreasing returns. Organisation and complication may be a good thing: over-organisation and over-complication, as we all know, are not. Therefore the evolutionary effort in this direction, the direction of body-building, had to come to a halt. Yet nature was not baffled for long. She continued to push on, though she varied her techniques. After joining individual cells into inclusive organisms, she began to join individual organisms into inclusive societies. And again there was the same situation as before: loss and gain for the associated units, with gain decidedly outweighing the loss. Again there was a curtailment of freedom on the part of the individuals, over-compensated by the provision of security. Hence the two moves in the direction of pacification were strictly parallel, nay near-identical. For what signifies the secondary fact that the newly emerging social organism is integrated by means of mental rather than material ties? Not very much. Both are products of the same vital process, the process of evolution; both are therefore essentially natural. Society, the body social, is no less securely integrated than our frame of flesh, the body physical.

The argument is certainly ingenious. But whether ingenious or not, the decisive question is: is it true? Or, more narrowly formulated: is the social habit of man really underpinned by a live instinct? If so, society must be pronounced a whole in the sense of philosophical realism. Both mechanicism and the third sociology are then null and void, and must surrender to the superior insights of biological science.

For Trotter, there could be no hesitation in this matter. 'Gregariousness is a phenomenon of profound biological significance . . . a definite fact of biology which must have consequences as precise and a significance as ascertainable as the secretion of the gastric juice or the refracting apparatus of the eye' (pp. 20/21). Unfortunately his own book provides strong indications that sociality, as found in man during the period usually called history, is not, or at any rate no longer, an instinct that could be compared to other natural tendencies such as the secretion of the gastric juice, or mechanisms such as the refracting apparatus of the eye.

Only two of these indications will be presented here, the strongest two. In various contexts Trotter calls self-preservation, nutrition and sex the primitive instincts in man, and to them he adds gregariousness, which may not be a primitive, but is to him certainly a proper, instinct. Yet he is forced by the facts to acknowledge that there is a profound distinction between the first three natural drives and the last. This is what he writes: 'If we look in a broad, general way at the four instincts which bulk largely in man's life, namely, those of self-preservation, nutrition, sex, and the herd, we shall see at once that there is a striking difference between the mode of action of the first three and that

49

of the last. The first three . . . have in common the characteristic of attaining their maximal activities only over short periods and in special sets of circumstances, and of being fundamentally pleasant to yield to. They do not remain in action concurrently, but when the circumstances are appropriate for the yielding to one, the others automatically fall into the background, and the governing impulse is absolute master. Thus these instincts cannot be supposed at all frequently to conflict amongst themselves . . . The appearance of the fourth instinct, however, introduces a profound change, for this instinct has the characteristic that it exercises a controlling power upon the individual from without. In the case of the solitary animal yielding to instinct the [resulting] act itself is pleasant. . . . With the social animal controlled by herd instinct . . . the deed, being ordained from without, may actually be unpleasant, and so be resisted from the individual side and yet be forced instinctively into execution. The . . . herd instinct at once introduces a mechanism by which the sanctions of instinct are conferred upon acts by no means necessarily acceptable to the body or mind' (pp. 48 /49). It is almost incredible to see a man so blind as Trotter proves himself at this point. To say that a mode of action is ordained from without, does not fit into the general system of instinctual behaviour, is painful, and is resisted by the individual concerned, is, to all who have preserved their rationality and freedom of judgment, tantamount to saying—indeed, to saying four times over—that it is not instinctual. But Trotter has not preserved his rationality and freedom of judgment. He is the prisoner of an irrational belief, namely that all human conduct is determined by body-bound instinct. One wonders whether Trotter has ever experienced, or even heard of, education, whether he has ever seen a child before its training had become effective— or, indeed, whether he has ever looked critically upon himself and his own conduct. How much 'gregariousness' would there be without the internalisation of folkways in early life and continued social control throughout life? How spontaneous is altruistic action—*any* altruistic action? It is almost ridiculous—it is certainly delusory—to call it natural (in any sense of the word). Trotter himself quotes St. Paul: 'I delight in the law of God after the inward man; but I see another law in my members warring against the law of my mind and bringing me into captivity to the law of sin which is in my members'. These words, so profoundly realistic, can never be blended into an instinctual, i.e. monistic-materialistic interpretation of human sociality. They are conceived in the spirit of dualism and idealism—that 'idealism of freedom' which we have shown to be the complement and companion of the third social philosophy. What Trotter interprets as a conflict between nature and nature, is in reality a conflict between nature and culture, between natural spontaneity and cultural norm.

What one must hold against Trotter, though, is less that he underestimates the effect of culture than that he misunderstands the operation of nature. He blithely assumes that the so-called gregarious instinct shows itself in contradictory forms. What does the moral genius do when he preaches brotherliness? He obeys the promptings of instinct. What do the masses do when they reject his preaching? They obey the promptings of the same instinct. 'Human altruism is a natural instinctive product', Trotter writes, but on the very same page we read: 'Herd suggestion opposes any advance in altruism'. 'This', he adds, 'is a remarkable instance of the protean character of the gregarious instinct and the complexity it introduces into human affairs. . . . We see one instinct producing manifestations directly hostile to each other—prompting to ever advancing developments of altruism, while it necessarily leads to any new product of advance being attacked' (p. 46). It is not necessary to insist that the direction in which an instinct drives should be absolutely fixed and univocally determined, though normally this will be so. It can be imagined that instinctual urges become flexible, though it must be added at once that this will happen only to a being which has, as it were, stepped out of nature. But that an instinct should become self-contradictory is unimaginable. For what is the vital function of instinct? Surely, to produce, without hesitation, appropriate action. But here we have conflict, doubt and difficulty, and consequently the inhibition of action, appropriate or otherwise. To be in this quandary is precisely the curse—and the privilege—of a creature whose behaviour on the stage of life is no longer fixed by the dictates of natural law. Incidentally, it is by no means so that Trotter's critic must of necessity assume that sociality is entirely without basis in nature or even instinct. All he need urge is that the gregarious instinct in man, if it once existed, has become vestigial—a slight tendency which has to be developed and under-pinned by the forces of culture, but would, by itself, be insufficient to control the imperative demands of the 'primitive', or rather selfish, instincts of self-preservation, nutrition and sex. Trotter badly overshoots the mark if he asserts that sociality is not only based on, or remotely rooted in, instinct, but that it is—still is— as fully instinctual as the avoidance of hurt and pain or the pursuit of food or of sexual satisfactions.

A second indication of the mortal weakness of instinctualism in sociology occurs later in the book. On p. 102, Trotter discusses 'the social habit in animals' and says that 'there seems to be an inverse relation between its completeness and the brain power of the animal concerned'. In other words, the more social a creature, the less brainy; the less social, the more brainy. This observation is borne out by experiment; social wasps, for instance, prove less resourceful when placed in a difficult position (for instance a glass) than solitary wasps. Trotter utterly fails to grasp the implications of his own remark. Is it not clear that the most intelligent of all animals, namely man, must be expected to be also the least social?—the least social at any rate of all the species which nature has predetermined for a social mode of existence. This was the conclusion of a far more powerful thinker than Wilfred Trotter, Henri Bergson, whose *The Two Sources of Morality and Religion* (1932) rests on an incomparably sounder understanding, not only of culture, but even of nature.[1] As Bergson points out in his fascinating book, nature would never give a being both fully fledged instinct and fully fledged reason, for if she did so, she would only undo her own work. Instinct and reason are as near-contradictory as slavery and freedom: where the one dwells, the other cannot have its home. Animal societies and human societies are, not similar, but contradictory experiments in sociality: animal societies experiments in determination, human societies experiments in liberty. The pattern on the basis of an anthill is provided by nature ready made: the pattern on the basis of a human association or community has to be made by those who belong to it. And as this is so, we cannot, strictly speaking, say that society is prior to the individuals. Even a study of instinct, therefore, goes to prove that positivistic organicism is not a social philosophy that can be sustained. Trotter, certainly, has not improved on Spencer as he hoped to do. His concept of innate gregariousness is, for all its apparent plausibility, as little

[1] On Bergson, cf. Stark, *Social Theory and Christian Thought*, 1959, pp. 175–200.

capable of explaining the coherence of human societies as Spencer's cruder doctrine of social tissue.

While the emphasis lies, with Trotter, on the whole with social peace, in Ludwik Gumplowicz, author of *Rasse und Staat* (1875) and *Der Rassenkampf* (1883),[1] it rests entirely on social war. Yet Gumplowicz, no less than Trotter, is a representative of one of the secondary sub-varieties of positivistic organicism. True, his law of life is not a law of progressive pacification, but a law of abiding conflict. Wherever we look, he claims, we find unremitting hostility, attempts at mutual annihilation. Whether we look at the 'sidereal process of nature' which shows us star pitted against star, or at the chemical process of nature which shows us element pitted against element, or at the vegetal and animal process of nature which shows us the sexes in continuous tension, every-where we behold as the basic reality the mutuality of attack and defence between heterogeneous factors and forces. In view of the unity of nature, and man's place in nature, we cannot expect anything at all different (so Gumplowicz asserts) in the human sphere either. But if the reader of Gumplowicz's books were, on the basis of speculations of this kind, to form the impression (which would be by no means unreasonable) that all this is meant to lead up to a theory of competition, of a war of all against all, in the sense of a struggle between individuals for position, property or power, he would be disabused before long. The individual, he would soon enough find, does not exist for Gumplowicz. The 'heterogeneous elements' of the social realm are for him the races, the continuators of the subhuman anthro-poid hordes which, in the course of evolution, have crossed—as units—the borderline between animality and humanity. It is an error, Gumplowicz says in criticising Lotze, to regard individual human beings as the real elements of the process of becoming. 'In the social process of nature'—the reader will know how to appreciate this term!—'it is not individual men but the social groups which must be regarded as the [decisive] elements. In history we must look, not for the regularly recurring actions of individuals, but rather for the regularly recurring movements of the [primal] groups'—their movements in accordance with natural law (*Der Rassenkampf*, ed. 1909, p. 39).

[1] On Gumplowicz, cf. Stark, "Natural and Social Selection", in *Darwinism and the Study of Society*, ed. Michael Banton, 1961, pp. 49–61.

Now, when we attempt to see history, in Gumplowicz's materialistic, Darwinian manner, as a process plying between collectivities, what sort of 'natural law' does it reveal to us? Gumplowicz is convinced that he has found and formulated it. 'We are lucky', he says, 'to be able to present a formula concerning the mutual relationship of the heterogeneous ethnic elements—or groups different by descent—which cannot be denied to possess perfect, almost mathematical authority and universality because it shows itself always and everywhere, in past and present, in the most undeniable manner. This formula runs, very simply, as follows: each more powerful ethnic or social element strives to make the weaker element, which lies in its sphere of influence or comes to enter it, subservient to its purposes. This thesis concerning the relationship between the heterogeneous ethnic and social elements', Gumplowicz adds, 'bears in itself the key to the solution of the whole riddle of the natural process of human history' (*loc. cit.*, p. 154).

In support of this grim sociology, Gumplowicz points triumphantly to the recorded facts: war, war everywhere. The temple of Janus is never closed. And he points with even more insistence to the origins of the state, such as we can observe it, over and over again, in protohistory. When does a state arise, in other words, when does a society become organised? Only after the conquest of a weaker group by a stronger. Gumplowicz studies Egypt, Babylonia, Assyria, Persia, India, China, Phoenicia, Israel, and Europe—the picture is always the same. The state is simply the mechanism created by the conquerors for the permanent suppression and better exploitation of the conquered. *Vae victis!*

Our concern here is not with the realism, or lack of realism, of this view of history; it is exclusively with the thesis at the bottom of it, that the groupings clashing in protohistory were natural or nature-made hordes or herds, rather than man-made communities: that society is—at least originally—a whole, a real whole, in the manner in which the anthill or the beehive or the wolfpack or even the human body is a whole. The scholar and the scientist will be reluctant to speak with too much assurance on this point. In the half-darkness of the early ages, few facts stand out and can be clearly seen. But one consideration may perhaps be pressed. Even though many primitive clans think of themselves as one in blood, closer investigation has shown more than once that this is fiction rather than fact, an 'ideology' as we have come to call conceptions of this kind. To adduce but one example: the so-called kin-groups of Arabia in the days of the Prophet appear to have been in reality groups of mixed descent, partly due to the fusion of smaller units, and partly widened by the inclusion of alien individuals.[1] The idea of common ancestry, widespread as it is in primitive times, far from being always the effect of an antecedent natural coherence is in truth much more often the cause of an emergent and subsequent socio-cultural coalescence.

Be this as it may, the social philosopher is less interested in societies as they once were, or may have been, than in societies as they now are. And so far as these latter are concerned, Gumplowicz himself admits that they do not rest on common blood, and that they are made by man rather than by nature. It is true, he claims, that the old racial dividing lines are still visible, especially in social stratification, the upper classes of today being the conquerors, the lower classes the conquered, of the years of yore. But he recognises that the modern nation is a decreasingly natural and increasingly cultural formation. To the basic social process—conflict and conquest—he adds a second social tendency, that of amalgamation, and all he says makes it clear that this new phenomenon is not natural, but cultural. How is it that the races coalesce? They coalesce through three developments: the coming of a common language, the emergence of a common religion, and finally through intermarriage or blood mixture. Gumplowicz himself insists that the last-named (physical) cause of coalescence is as yet weak. But this must, surely, mean that the modern nation rests predominantly on linguistic and religious foundations. It is, in consequence, not a natural unit, but a cultural one. Gumplowicz has abandoned his pristine theory. Society is the product of human effort, of history, and not the outcome of blind objective forces, of nature.

There is evidence that this discovery pained the scientist in Gumplowicz, especially when it led to an estrangement with his

---

[1] Cf. W. Montgomery Watt, *Muhammad at Mecca*, 1953, p. 17; *Muhammad at Medina*, 1956, pp. 78 *et seq.* and 153. Dr Watt kindly informs me that the following literature is also relevant: W. Robertson Smith, *Kinship and Marriage in Early Arabia*, ed. 1903, pp. 8 *et seq.*; I. Goldziher, *Muhammedanische Studien*, 1889/90, I, pp. 97 *et seq.*; F. P. W. Buhl, *Das Leben Muhammeds*, German ed., 1930, pp. 25 *et seq.*; C. A. Nallino, *Raccolta di Scritti*, 1939/48, III, pp. 72 *et seq.*

student and friend, Ludwig Woltmann.[1] But, as a true scholar, he preferred truth to consistency. 'I have given up the strictly anthropological concept of race', he confesses, 'and use the term . . . more for social groups which form, not an anthropological, but a social unity . . . In the course of the social development of humanity, we have occasion to observe sentiments of closer belonging together, of warmer sympathy . . . which have a basis different from the physical foundation studied before. . . . Briefly expressed, we see that there are, besides the factors which appear to us natural, also some cultural ones which produce . . . syngenetic feelings and . . . solidarity' (pp. 196, 243, 244). It is hardly necessary to add anything to these words. The doctrine that society is a pre-existent and therefore 'real' entity held together by natural bonds, is to all intents and purposes relegated to the dimness of a distant past, and what stands in the lighted circle of the present appears, and is admitted to be, a cultural formation, neither prior nor posterior to human effort, but rather at one and the same time its producer and its product.

The interesting protagonists of organicism whom we have studied in this chapter and the last, were all, not only 'realists' in social philosophy, but at the same time also evolutionists. This frequent association between organicism and evolutionism does not betoken a necessary coincidence of the two views: Aristotle and St. Thomas Aquinas were convinced that the organisational lay-out of a society more or less tallies with, or at least more or less approaches to, the pattern of co-ordination characteristic of the physical organism, but they saw both body physical and body social (as indeed the whole of reality) in rather static terms. Still, there is a certain inner kinship between organicism and evolutionism which is apt to assert itself in societies that have become aware of the flow of things, of the developments taking place in both the natural and the human realms. For it is the property of living things to grow, and if society is a living thing in the sense of organicism, and especially in the sense of positivistic organicism, then it, too, must exhibit the phenomenon of growth. We are face to face here with one of the most striking disagreements between sociological organicism and sociological mechanicism. If the social order is likened to an equilibrium system, to the kind of tension between independent energies of which the balance

[1] Cf. *Der Rassenkampf*, ed. 1909, pp. 196–198 (footnote).

of a pair of scales is the simplest exemplification, then it is almost certain to be interpreted in a non-historical and unhistorical spirit. An equilibrium has no history; its laws do not change with the centuries. The formal equations in which it can be described are of timeless validity, as all purely quantitative propositions must be. Rational mechanics is a branch of mathematics and its students glory in the fact: those social theorists who wanted to model sociology on rational mechanics were quite unwilling to admit the reality of developmental change, for it would have made all their endeavour *ab initio* impossible. We shall see, when we come, in a later chapter, to the discussion of Vilfredo Pareto, how much of his thinking is merely a sustained attempt to conjure away the flow of time, to transmute the organisational lay-out of society into something like the pattern of co-ordination characteristic of a parallelogram of forces. In sharp contrast to this, the organicists of the last two hundred years have, to a man, tended to put society into history, not to take it out of it. Still, there has been a difficulty. If we say, with Spencer, that both physical and social bodies grow, we have manifestly made only a half, and not a whole, comparison, for physical bodies decay after a while, whereas social bodies appear to go on for ever. The concept of social or societal death has recommended itself to few organicists, though some, like Lilienfeld, come near to it. Others have shied away from it. Hegel, for instance, compares the oriental empires to the childhood of our race, Greece to youth, Rome to manhood and modernity to old age, but old age means maturity to him and not senile decay. There were, however, a few bolder spirits who drove the organismic simile to its logical conclusion and asserted that if a society is an organism, it must not only undergo evolution, but also involution: it must not only evince growth, but also beginning and end, birth and death. Of these radicals we shall briefly discuss Konstantin Leontiev whose book *Visantism i Slavianstvo* ('Byzantinism and the Slavs') came out in 1873. Nikolai Danilevsky had expounded similar ideas earlier on, and Oswald Spengler was to revive them later: but nowhere do we find them so clearly stated as in Leontiev, a writer of considerable power.

Leontiev asserts that the history of a nation takes it through three successive phases. First there is considerable rudeness and crudeness; then there comes about a period of flowering, a cultural acmé; and in the end decay sets in, followed by dissolution.

This sequence is not fortuitous, but necessary. During the ascending part of this life cycle, there is an ingathering of forces, a build-up of vitality; it is this, and this alone, which makes possible the splendid efflorescence of the middle years; but the vital store, the fund of energy, so slowly accumulated, is quickly dispersed, and, indeed, overdrawn, at the height of life, so that exhaustion must supervene: it all happens in accordance with a biological law. Who would not see that Leontiev's three phases are simply childhood, manly maturity, and old age? The history of societies is for him like the life-story of individuals. It is centred around a grand climacteric to which everything leads up and from which everything leads down, until death closes the chapter and night descends on the scene.

This whole conception of history is clearly an inference from the basic equation of organicism, body politic=body physical. Leontiev tried to demonstrate that it is more than that, a realistic picture of what had happened and was going to happen, borne out by the facts themselves. His prime example is Europe. The barbarians of the great migrations are the childhood of this cultural organism: simplicity and vitality are the key-notes. The feudal order is the age of maturity. It lasts from roughly the ninth to the eighteenth centuries. Refinement prevails and cultural creativity culminates. The French Revolution then marks the onset of downward development, disease and decay. Creativeness disappears and its place is taken by vulgarisation and vulgarity.

This scheme fits far more neatly into the organismic pattern of thought than might at first be supposed. For the evolutionists, increasing differentiation has always been the hallmark of upward development. But in the class society of the Middle Ages and early modern times, European society reached its highest social differentiation: king and serf were far more distant from each other socially than either barbarian chief and barbarian clansman, or a constitutional government and its constituents. What seemed to Leontiev the supreme proof of the fact that the tide of life had turned, was the appearance and the success of egalitarian movements, such as liberalism and socialism. Progressive democratisation meant to him advancing involution. Just as, after 50 or so, the male and the female body come again closer to each other, after years of divergent development, and this is a sign of senility, so, after 1789, the fading of the contrasts between class and class, man and man, signifies that society is on the road to ruin. Characteristically, Leontiev's hatred of liberalism is even greater than his condemnation of socialism. Socialism at least means order, means organisation: it is to that extent more in line with his organismic, holistic, totalitarian inclinations. Liberalism, however, with its adjuncts, democracy and individualism, is nothing to him but the harbinger of death and decomposition.

Not many words are needed in order to prove that this whole conception of history is untenable, not to say absurd. Leontiev's doctrine, like that of Gumplowicz, like that of Trotter, and also like that of Spencer, tries too mechanical a transfer of biological modes of thinking to social reality. Their patent errors ought to teach the social philosopher that he must do his own work, and not expect the natural scientist to do it for him. But, radical as they were, there are even more extreme organicists than these four men, and as they can serve as yet better examples and warnings, we shall now give them a passing glance.

V

ORGANICISM
Extreme Forms

A LREADY OUR study of Herbert Spencer has brought us into contact with applications of the organismic principle which can fairly be called extreme. The assertion, for instance, that we must distinguish in the social system a sustaining, a distributing and a regulating apparatus, because the body physical shows, according to the physiologists, these three structures, is an extension of biological concepts beyond their proper sphere which may, nay must, be called less than reasonable. But others were prepared to go much further still, and they definitely crossed the dividing line between reason and unreason. In a way, it would be more charitable and christian not to speak of them at all, for to speak of them means, however we formulate their ideas, to expose them to ridicule. Yet it would be wrong to pass them by without a word. Let us agree that they present us with a caricature, and not with a fair picture, of organismic sociology. The fact remains that looking at a caricature is highly instructive, more instructive even than looking at a realistic portrait. It is the essence of the caricature to exaggerate the characteristic features of its object and thereby to force them on our attention. Any weaknesses which the extreme organicists exhibit, can be charged, if with diminished force, against all organismic-holistic sociology. A book that would serve the cause of truth must not flinch from the task, unpleasant though it be, of bringing them out: it must be like the good diagnostician who exposes unhealthy growths where he finds them, and like the good surgeon who cuts them out.

An early example of the grotesque exaggerations of which sociological realism is capable, is Johann Caspar Bluntschli's book of 1844, *Psychologische Studien über Staat und Kirche*.[1] The second chapter discusses the 'nature and relationship of state and church' and is summed up, in Bluntschli's own words, by the following statements: 'Both state and church are constructed on the model of the organism of the human race, but . . . in a different fashion and direction; the state [represents] the male, the church the female element'. 'The church does not resemble the male; she is, like woman, essentially of a receptive, suffering and passive nature' (pp. 39/40). How passive, one is inclined to ask, was the nature of that Islamic *umma* which swept across the world like wildfire and left death and destruction in its trail? But it would be vain to discuss Bluntschli's ideas as if they were in any sense of the word scientific. His is simply an abstract conception that has run riot and that must be treated like any other pathological phenomenon.

Undeterred by any self-criticism, Bluntschli uses the distinction between state and church as male and female as a key to the understanding of historical development. At first, in the Asiatic empires, state and church are little distinct, as little distinct as are baby boys and baby girls. But then, slowly, they differentiate. 'While the children at first lived and played together, the fully formed maiden turns shyly away from the young man. The sex organs now reach full development; the relations of the sexes become, from this point onward, entirely different' (p. 43). Among the Jews, who represent the adolescence of humanity as the Asiatic empires do its childhood, Moses stands over against Aaron, king against high priest, state against church, yet the separation of the 'sexes' is not yet complete. 'Boy and girl go now more frequently their own ways, and the contrast of their natures becomes more noticeable' (p. 50). In Greece we get the beginning maturity of the race, and physiological conceptions again explain the historical facts. 'The ecclesiastical organisation is more mature than the political institution. In the same way the girl ripens earlier than the boy. The sexual organs of the former are sooner developed than those of the latter. The youthful breasts begin to swell; and the unfolding virgin turns into a beauty. Beauty was the soul of the cult of the Hellenes . . .' (p. 54). Rome is the phase

[1] *Psychological Investigations concerning State and Church.*

of young manhood. The state, conscious of its virility, pre-dominates. 'The thought of dominion, of powerful domination, of *imperium* early made its appearance, as an uncontrollable driving energy, in the manly character of the Romans, forming the inspiring spirit of the institutions of the Roman state. . . . Does not the life-history of the individual show a similar phenomenon? . . . Is the youth not also filled and driven by a glowing stream of psychic life? . . . He wants to hold the world in his embrace.' But he cannot succeed. He has not the necessary knowledge and experience. And he has not yet the right relation to womanhood. The Roman state 'did not understand the necessity of a church; it [should we translate: he?] did not grasp her quiet ways; egoistic and worldly as he was, he took no notice, in his youthful exuberance, of the more gentle sister. But how could the state reach perfection without the complement and the contrast of the church? The law of the duality of state and church is rooted in the very nature of man. It cannot be disregarded' (pp. 58–61).

It would clearly be a waste of time and effort to follow this nonsense step by step. Only a few more choice passages from the later discussions to round off the picture. The papal bid for world power was 'unnatural', as unnatural as a woman's bid for domination would be. 'The subordination of the state to the church, as the popes desired it, would have been just as unnatural as the subordination of a husband to his wife in the household' (p. 86). Before the Reformation, the church turns into a very naughty young lady. 'Taking more and more interest in external things and finding in them her enjoyment and her glory, she gives in the end the impression of an empty-headed and forward *coquette*' (p. 81). But, of course, there is a happy ending to the story. In spite of all misunderstandings, the lovers come together in holy wedlock. 'In this [present] age . . . which corresponds to the half-way mark between ascending and descending human life . . . the male state will reach full selfhood and achieve a [sound] understanding of himself and of the church. Then the two great powers of humanity, state and church, will appreciate and love each other, and the august marriage of the two will take place' (p. 87). In view of all this, it is perhaps not unnecessary to remind the reader that Bluntschli was one of the most respected scholars of his day.

Nor must we think of him as an isolated figure. Far from it! He is essentially the representative of a type, and wide-spread type at that. Another spokesman of the same basic convictions was Albert Schäffle, whose enormous work, *The Structure and Life of the Body Social*,[1] published in four sizeable volumes between 1875 and 1880, announces its creed already on the title page. The subtitle runs: 'An encyclopædic sketch of a real anatomy, physiology and psychology of human society, with special reference to the national economy considered as the social process of digestion.' In order to be quite fair to Schäffle, it must be emphasised that he is well aware of the fact—which he states and restates on many occasions—that the ties which bind men to each other in society are mental and not physical ties, and that, in so far as this is so, the comparison between body physical and body social does not apply. In this respect, Schäffle was not the extremest of the extremists; others, like Pavel von Lilienfeld, of whom we shall speak in a minute, went even further than he. René Worms characterises their difference by saying that to Schäffle society was merely an organised, whereas to Lilienfeld it was a fully organic system, an *organisme concrète*, with *concrète* as the operative word.[2] In theory, the contrast no doubt existed; in practice the borderline was vague from the very beginning and tended increasingly to fade out. The whole difference, such as it was, reminds one of the subtle theological discrimination between predestination and prededetermination. Like many Calvinists faced with this alternative, Schäffle professed the milder, but in fact propagated the wilder, doctrine.

In one passage, this pioneer of scientism in sociology expressed himself in the following terms: 'The coherence of the social tissues is not of the same kind as that of the organic tissues. No uninterrupted occupancy of space is observable so far as the personal and property substance [of society] is concerned, while in the organic body cells and intercellular parts form a solid object . . . It is not forces . . . like cohesion, adhesion, or chemical affinity which effect coherence and co-ordination in the body social, but mental forces which are capable, by dint of the physical powers of their instrumental apparatus, to establish a far-reaching spiritual and bodily connection and co-operation between spatially separated

---

[1] *Bau und Leben des socialen Körpers: Encyclopädischer Entwurf einer realen Anatomie, Physiologie und Psychologie der menschlichen Gesellschaft mit besonderer Rücksicht auf die Volkswirthschaft als socialen Stoffwechsel.*
[2] Preface to Lilienfeld's *La Pathologie Sociale*, 1896, p. VII.

elements' (p. 286). This somewhat stilted passage, needless to say, conveys sound common sense. Unfortunately, the very next paragraph takes back what has just been conceded, namely that a comparison between a physical and a psychic unity is, strictly speaking, impossible. 'All this', Schäffle writes, 'does not amount to an essential difference between social and organic tissues. Even in organic and inorganic nature we do not find a [unitary] link that would hold the bodies together, but the proper forces of the innumerable elements, which attract and bind each other mechanically and chemically in characteristic and constant types of cohesion, act as innumerable ties. The social tissues are in exactly the same case' (*ib.*).

If we try to be generous, and at the same time to penetrate to the conceptions which really matter, we may, and to some extent even must, admit that the physical non-contiguity—the spatial separation—of men in society does not, by itself, make it illegitimate to speak of the social order as based on organic, or quasi-organic, cohesion. Men may have the capacity of individual locomotion, but that does not mean that they may not or do not move in concert and concord. We have seen that even St. Thomas Aquinas allows that one definition may be made to cover both the co-operation of physical organs and that of men considered as social functionaries. The real contrast between the two forms of life lies somewhere else. It lies in the fact that physical organs are forced to co-operate for the benefit of the whole, while social "functionaries" are free to place their own interest above that of the community and very often, not to say regularly, do. Differently expressed: while men, in so far as they fufil social functions, may be compared to cells in so far as they fulfil organic functions, the cell is restricted to that role whereas man is not: he can play his own game. A comparison, in order to be sound, must, like a true equation, make sense if you read it from either side. But this is precisely what we cannot do here without drifting into absurdity. It may be possible to equate a working member of society with a working limb of the body physical, but it is impossible to equate a normal—i.e. a normally working—organ with a normal—i.e. normally selfish—person. What nonsense it would be to speak of a self-seeking kidney or a scheming spleen or an egotistic liver! Yet Schäffle tries to make out that the functioning together of the elements of society follows exactly the same absolute laws as the functioning together of bodily elements. In his opinion, the social whole is made in the very same way as organical and mechanical wholes. He sees, or rather concedes, neither the independence of the individual nor the contingency of collective life. Everything is as it must be. This is the conviction in which his extremism, his extreme materialism, has its centre. 'The collective . . . motions of the body social', he says, 'are middle resultants of much more complex and varied partial motions. Even to these resultants applies the law of movement in the direction of least resistance . . . The lines which legislation (*das Recht*) prescribes for the movement of society are in the last analysis merely the lines of the direction (*der Richtung*) of least resistance in which the contradictory individual movements, which have met, have merged themselves. Politics can in a certain sense be regarded as the great art of the daily finding of those directions of least resistance in which numerous antagonistic special forces fuse. The conscious social movements tend in exactly the same way in the direction in which nature and art, soil and society offer least resistance as do the unconscious mechanical movements of organic and inorganic nature. . . . Nothing prevents us from explaining the course of social history according to the laws of mechanics and to recognise in human society a (much more complicated) play of the same tendencies and forces which unfold themselves within organic and inorganic reality' (pp. 23 *seq.*). These sentences allow us to look deeply into Schäffle's mind. They show that his repeated insistence on the spiritual nature of the ties which bind men to each other in society means nothing, nothing at all. The social pattern coincides, in the full sense of the word, with the physical patterns of nature, animate and even inanimate, as if it were not man-made. The most that Schäffle really admits is that the social pattern is somewhat more complicated than those physical patterns. But a difference in complication is merely a difference in degree. It is assuredly not a contrast in kind. We must remember this as we go over to a study of the detail: Schäffle's comparisons try to uncover identities, not parallels. The formula *mutatis mutandis* may be used, but in a very restricted sense only. The laws of society are laws of nature. It is all as simple as that.

It is to the identification of the coincidences between body physical and body social that Schäffle's vast work is devoted.

Now, 'the simplest elements of the bodies of the higher species of plants and animals . . . are the cells and the intercellular substances interspersed between them' (p. 33). The first task of the social scientist must therefore be the identification of the social cell. Now, there can be few who would not, on hearing the term 'social cell' and trying to imagine what it might mean and stand for, think immediately, almost automatically, of the individual. The individual would indeed appear to be to the body social what the cell is to the body physical: the living part which, with its likes, constitutes the living whole. Pavel von Lilienfeld took precisely this view.[1] But Schäffle is an out-and-out anti-individualist. He is a sociological realist and a collectivist *à l'outrance*. Individuals do not exist for him: the person is an abstraction, not a reality. 'There is no such thing as an individual that exists absolutely for himself, any more than there are single cells . . . Any anatomical, physiological and psychological study of social facts which proceeds by empirical methods shows us, not "psychic" individuals, but institutions and individuals working within institutions, i.e. social organs, tissues, and tissue parts at work, which are, without exception, composed of persons and property, as the members, tissues and tissue parts of organic bodies are, without exception, composed of cells and intercellular substances . . . Not Robinson Crusoe, that badly overworked concept of traditional sociology, but the primal family is the starting-point of the evolutionary history of the body social . . . The body social uses its . . . elements, men and things, in characteristic connections, combinations and forms of motion. In it, there are no isolated persons —or pieces of property, but both exist only as integral parts of personal communities and as integral parts of total masses of property or wealth, i.e. social institutions. The simplest social unit, the family, without which no person can come into being, grow up and produce offspring, in other words the social cell, is already an articulated whole of persons and pieces of property . . . ' (pp. 588, 276, 214, 53). What Schäffle here suggests is no less than that all reality is a reality of social formations and that, in studying society, we may just as well forget about the individual. It surely is not necessary to criticise conceptions of this kind.

[1] This, of course, does not make Lilienfeld an individualist. Witness the following sentence: 'The primary source of all human socialisation is the reflex action of the social nerve system in its parts and as a whole' (*La Pathologie Sociale*, pp. 18 and 19).

The family, then, is the ultimate element of social reality beyond and beneath which the social scientist does not need to search for further entities. And that family is like a particle of flesh with a modicum of blood in it. 'The family has all the traits of the tissue cell . . . It is manifest that every fundamental trait of the structure and function of the organic cell is repeated here' (p. 57). Schäffle is not satisfied with saying this once. He has to repeat this 'truth' twice on the same page!

Once the family is thus identified with the cell, further absurdities follow as a matter of course. 'In the social as in the organic body, the preventive and the repressive protective tissues are wide-spread, and as inner and outer protective tissues are to be found in the latter, so also in the former . . . Without exception, we also find in all social organs a third kind of tissue which looks after the intake and outflow of the materials of regeneration and nutrition from and to the channels of economic production and circulation and secure a normal digestion on the part of all the elements of the organ or organic part concerned. This institution is the household. It is to be compared to the capillary tissues of the animal body. The great social digestive apparatus, in other words, the national economy, the production and circulation of commodities, leads in the end to as many households as the body social has organs and every organ independent tissues and tissue elements' (p. 324). One can sense behind these sentences the monstrous materialistic metaphysics of Herr Schäffle: society is a superorganism which eats and digests and excretes food like any other organism. Lest this mentioning of excretion be thought an unduly harsh criticism and an unforgivable exaggeration on the part of the critic, one more quotation should be added here, comment being superfluous: 'If we compare the social digestion carried out through persons with the vegetable and animal [processes of] digestion [occurring in physical organisms], the great similarities of the two strike the attention at once. Primary production marks the starting point, the ejection of human corpses and material waste (*Menschen-und Güterleichen*) the end point of external social digestion' (p. 335).

But a body consists not only of cells, it also has in it intercellular substances, and these the social scientist must identify as well. What, for instance, about the bone structure which gives coherence to the physical organism? 'The immobile part of settlement'—Schäffle presumably means the lay-out of streets and houses and roads and so on—'could be compared to the animal skeleton and the bone and gristle tissue, the mobile outfit [of a society] to the ligaments which fix the soft parts to the skeleton and to each other, and the science of the moveable equipment could be put into parallel with the science of syndesmology' (p. 327). Schäffle even manages to find homologues to such protective tissues of the animal body as hair, nails and horny skin: he mentions 'analogically in the body social' roofs, coverings, wrappings, fences, walls, clothes, even picture-frames and book-covers . . . (p. 329). Generally speaking, he equates the intercellular substance of the body social with society's material equipment, just as he equates the cell with its human personnel. 'The national wealth', he explains, constitutes 'partly intercellular substance, in so far as it is the medium of the social union of persons in collectively carried-out vital activities, partly intra-cellular substance, in so far as its substance is the inner domestic property of the families and individuals . . .' (p. 56). Wherever we turn, the appropriate correspondences stare us in the face!

One more quotation, to show the true extremism of Schäffle's positivistic organicism: 'The collective property in literature, works of art, roads, transport undertakings, defensive institutions, institutional buildings, public works equipment is similar to the circulating, solvent and protective material which serves the organic body by means of liquidity, softness, elasticity, the chemical counterbalancing of destructive affinities and in other ways. The analogy of an organic mass of property of the cells in the intercellular materials with the social institution of a mass of property in tools, coverings, means of transportation and collective arrangements of all sorts can hardly be overlooked' (p. 94).

It is a great temptation for the student and critic of Albert Schäffle and his whole school to string one quotation to the other and add one amusing detail to the next. Who would not like to smile and to evoke smiles? But this temptation should be resisted. We should try, instead, to understand how he endeavours to get around the fact, so awkward for the retailers of the body metaphor, that consciousness in the body physical is concentrated in the brain, whereas in the body social it is dispersed among all the 'cells'. The trick by which this difficulty is removed is certainly ingenious though it is no less unreal than the rest of his argument. We must, he says in substance, distinguish, both in the body physical and in the body social, conscious and unconscious movements. The brain deals with specific vital problems of which it has to take cognisance, but of the normal functioning of the inferior organs it is completely unaware. Who of us knows when, or how, the liver produces bile or the intestinal muscles move the mass of food we have eaten from mouth to body exit? It is exactly the same with the social brain, i.e. the government. It, too, has to attend to certain vital concerns which have forced themselves on the collective consciousness, but remains completely unaware of the business activities of the social cells, enterprises and households, who carry on the needful processes of nutrition, secretion, procreation, and so on. 'Even the movements of the animal organism,' Schäffle writes, are, 'to a large extent, unconscious reflex motions, carried out by the subordinate spinal and sympathetic nerve centres. The situation is no different in the body social; only a part of all social business activity (motion) enters its central sphere of power, the state' (p. 67), i.e. becomes conscious in the collective brain. Otherwise the social cells simply work away on their own in that same darkness of unconsciousness which also surrounds the goings-on among the physical cells in our bellies.

Once again we see what Schäffle's aim really is: to remove all discrepancies between society and organism, as the prestidigitator spirits away the rabbit which he has just shown, for a fleeting moment, to his audience. In the end, society appears as a kind of beast which feeds on nature as a cow browses on a meadow: 'Social, like all other life, is a millionfold interaction of the living body with its external conditions of existence . . . The land is the substratum of the body social and the primal source on which social digestion continuously draws, and into which it throws back its waste materials' (pp. 553 and 78). What an image of society Schäffle conjures up! Social reality is not the meeting and mixing, the co-operation and the contest of innumerable men—it is a kind of monolith, all the more monstrous for being endowed with life.

Two more points of detail, in order to show just how deep sociological realism—that mock metaphysic—has bitten into the thought of this man. One is his handling of culture, the other his discussion of the pros and cons of socialism. If he had really believed, as he pretends to believe, that social life is shot through by spirituality, he would not have endeavoured to show knowledge, science and art as aspects of the physiology of the body social, as concomitants of its physical processes. But this is precisely what he does. The 'communication of ideas' is to Schäffle 'a social nerve vibration' (p. 86). In another context he is still more specific. 'Ideas are not diffused by a single impetus as are circular waves [in the water] which travel further and further outwards, but by the independent communication from person to person and institution to institution. In the same way, the physiologists conceive the spreading of the nervous current as a communication from one centre of ganglia to another. In each of these the current may receive impetus as well as inhibition. We can observe every day that the same thing happens in the case of communication within the body social' (p. 408). The following passages are doubly characteristic: on the one hand because they show how quickly Schäffle descends from his sham-idealism into his very real materialism, into a conception of social life which transfers to sociology the conceptions of a narrow and, as it were, technical physiological materialism; on the other hand, because they assign physiological parallels even to such social and indeed moral principles as the principle of publicity, the duty laid on public administration to carry on its activities, for instance the placing of governmental contracts and the appointment of new civil servants, in the full light of day. 'Publicity, in the proper sense of the word, is an intellectual openness, effected by means of the exchange of symbols, between larger and smaller masses of the body social. In the organic body, too, there appears to exist, in various gradations, public relations and areas of communication between the elements of the organic members and parts, sustained by the nervous system, and here, too, mutual openness, mediated by the nerves, constitutes the pre-condition of the psychic vigour of the whole and the mutual intercourse of the organic elements . . . The abolition of publicity can be roughly compared to an . . . excision, from the organic body, of all the nerve-fibres which serve the psychic co-ordination and super-ordination of the bodily parts' (pp. 446 and 448). The institutions of intellectual effort can be called both 'social tissues' and 'psycho-physical tissues'. 'They consist of sensitive parts serving observation and motor parts affecting execution, of connecting threads of sensation and motor excitation, of centres of thinking, valuing and deciding corporate activity, in exactly the same way as the animal nervous tissue consists of sensitive and motor nerve connections and nervous centres' (p. 59). In view of statements of this kind, it means very little if Schäffle occasionally admits that neurology furnishes no analogue to such socio-economic techniques as book-keeping.

With regard to the question whether private property or socialisation affords a better basis for social life, Schäffle propounds two rather irreconcilable opinions, calling socialism impossible in one context and possible in another. What interests us here is not the contradiction of the two passages concerned, but, on the contrary, the common element in them: the discussion of the whole issue in terms of biology. 'Without . . . the provision of all those kinds and quantities of commodities which are necessary for the performance of the functions of the family,' we read on pp. 215/16, 'the family itself cannot exist, and hence the millionfold cellular regeneration, renewal and preservation of the body social itself would cease. Therefore the abolition of family property and of the inheritance of all the instrumental wealth which is specifically appropriate to a given family must be regarded as an idea that goes against nature.' It would cut across and inhibit 'the nutrition of cellular tissue'. 'Yet it is thinkable', says p. 248, 'that, in social digestion, just as in organic digestion, intake, processing and circulation of the means of subsistence should be entrusted to central collective organs, and that all other organs, tissues and tissue cells should draw their special incomes directly from the collective product, as this happens through the digestive, circulatory and vascular systems of the organic body.' The inner conflict in Schäffle's mind which comes to the surface when these two passages are confronted is much more interesting than might at first be supposed. To a man of Schäffle's age, background and upbringing, socialism cannot, initially and in itself, have been particularly attractive. But the whole logic of his organicism, which is, as we are trying to show, a form of anti-individualistic, collectivistic thinking, forced him in the direction of a state-socialism which would give to society more of that close integration which is so characteristic of the body physical.

One of the most absurd, nay ridiculous implications of an extremist organicism is the idea that society, being a body like other organic bodies, can also fall ill like other organic bodies. Here, once again, Schäffle slides into absurdity, in spite of occasional spells of sanity. 'Only in the body social, and not in the organic body, can there be a revolt against the essential order . . ..of a coherent system of several members', he says in one of his rare rational moods (p. 598). But he is more himself when he expresses himself as follows: 'It seems that the same applies to the pathological phenomena of society as to organic diseases . . . Virchow, with his cellular pathology, has had a revolutionary influence on medical science by tracing illnesses and restorative processes to transformations inside the cells. By dint of an unconscious pathology and therapy of social life, politicians and political scientists, too, have, since time immemorial, described the ailing of family life as the source of the deepest and most widespread social ills. Mass infection of the individual cells, for instance by proletarisation or luxuriousness, loss of vitality or sexual excesses, is the worst that can happen to a body politic. The whole body is in the gravest danger, when the cells in general contract disease' (pp. 722 and 257).

With this sort of nonsense, Schäffle was by no means alone in the field. He had a great competitor in absurdity, Pavel von Lilienfeld, whose tome *La Pathologie Sociale* appeared in 1896 with the blessing of no less a sociologist than René Worms. As Schäffle, and Lilienfeld himself in his earlier work, *Gedanken über die Socialwissenschaft der Zukunft*,[1] published in five volumes between 1873 and 1881, had endeavoured to show the coincidence of the laws of healthy society and the healthy body physical, so *La Pathologie Sociale*[2] tried to demonstrate the strict parallelism between physical disease and socio-economic trouble. After all that has been said, it would be a sheer waste of time, space and effort to enter more deeply into Lilienfeld's 'analyses' which are as deeply irrational as they are superficially scientific. Yet a short sample will be instructive, and that for two diametrically opposed reasons: on the one hand because it will show, once again, that there is a lot of nonsense in these ravings, and on the other because it will also show that there is, after all, a little sense in them.

Like Schäffle, Lilienfeld, too, believes that Virchow's insights are both scientifically sound and analogically transferable to social

[1] *Thoughts concerning the Social Science of the Future.*
[2] *Social Pathology.*

reality. 'According to Virchow,' Lilienfeld explains, 'there is no essential and absolute difference between the normal and the pathological state of an organism. Deviation from the normal state consists, according to Virchow, only in this, that a cell or a group of cells evinces an activity outside the appropriate time, outside the appropriate place, or outside the limits of excitation prescribed by the normal condition. The pathological state of an organism always implies therefore either an aberration with regard to time, or an aberration with regard to place, or an aberration with regard to the active energy of the simple cell. In this manner, a heterology is, according to Virchow, always either a heterochrony, or a heterotopy, or finally a heterometry . . . As every individual illness derives from a pathological state of the cell, just so every social malady has its cause in a degeneration or abnormal action of the individual who constitutes the elementary anatomical unit of the social organism. Equally a society, attacked by sickness, does not present us with a condition which would be, in principle, different from that of a normal society. The pathological state consists merely in this, that an individual or a group of individuals manifests an ill-timed or an ill-placed activity, or one which shows over-excitement or lack of energy' (*loc. cit.* 21 and 24).

In sum, Lilienfeld asserts that there are three diseases of the body social—heterochrony, heterotopy, and heterometry. What exactly does he mean? Taking his conceptions out of the language of fake scientism and translating them into that of sociology and common sense, we can explain what he thinks with the help of the following illustrations. If there is a society which is modern in every respect, where, for instance, rational modes of action are applied wherever possible, and in that society there remains a pocket of traditionalism, that is, an area into which modern, rational methods have not yet penetrated, then that area is in the condition of heterochrony. The society concerned will become 'healthy' only after the time-gap, or time-lag, between its modern and its not-so-modern sector has been closed. Writing about these things, one is constantly tempted to express them in organismic similes: phrases like 'one sector limps behind' or 'one sector is out of joint with the rest' tend to form themselves, as of their own volition, in one's mind, and try to push themselves into, and to flow out of, one's pen. This alone shows that organicism has a deep root, and that its basic metaphor is not altogether absurd, even if its votaries make it so.

Now for heterotopy: if there is a society of some size, where one town is decaying, because, let us say, its industries have become antiquated, and where another town is expanding, because its particular lines of production are booming, and if there appears to be overpopulation in the former place and underpopulation in the latter, we are confronted with the abnormal condition of heterotopy. The people are in the wrong place (like lymphatic tissues, Lilienfeld says, which have formed in the brain where they should not be). Here health will be restored by transferring the excess cells to the area of deficiency.

Finally, heterometry. It may happen to a state that its civil service is overgrown (another organismic simile has slipped into our text!)—that it is out of proportion to the part of the population which is productive in the narrowest sense of the word. This would be an 'unhealthy' situation. Or it may happen that the civil service is insufficiently developed or starved (more organismic language)—that it is so poor that it cannot fulfil its proper 'function' in the 'life of the whole'. In either case, we have heterometry, or lack of adjustment. The proper therapy in the first case would be the transfer of the supernumerary bureaucrats to the industrial sphere, and in the second case a shifting of hands in the opposite direction. Health would only be achieved when the deployment of the vital forces had reached coincidence with the needs of the 'organism' as a whole—when every 'organ' has that endowment of energy, and only that, which it needs in order to fulfil its part in the economy of the whole.

The sound, if simple, sociological insight which hides behind this silly wall of big words, is not too difficult to find. Surely, what Lilienfeld wants to say, and says in a deplorably artificial and round-about way, is that a society, if it is to be what it can be, *ought* to have *harmony*, internal harmony. It is altogether natural, as we have seen, to use the body-metaphor for the characterisation of this aimed-at harmonious or 'healthy' state: yet nothing but nonsense will be generated if a poetical (if useful) trope is transmuted into a philosophical truth. The concept of social pathology, to which organismic sociology had to lead because of its own inner logic and dynamism, is in the last analysis an ethical-political and not a scientific-positivistic construct. Men like

Lilienfeld and Schäffle, for all their pretended materialism, were in reality idealists, whether they knew it or not. They pursued one of the two great social ideals, the ideal of community, of firm social integration, of happy human co-operation, which in turn grew out of one of the two great social philosophies, the philosophy according to which society is, essentially, not many, but one. In so far as this is the upshot of all their voluminous writings, and in so far as the issue is much more openly and directly confronted by the older, the normative protagonists of sociological realism, like Aristotle or St. Thomas, than it ever was by the newer, the sociological realists of the nineteenth century, the work of these positivists marks a retrogression and not a progress in the history of sociological thought.

VI

EXCURSUS
Classical Anthropology

THE TRUTH, or otherwise, of a theoretical principle cannot be reliably determined without taking into account its reflection—one might almost say, its performance—in practical research. What we want to know is the degree of realism which can justly be ascribed to the theory in question. But realism, or the lack of it, does not fully show itself in abstract discussion: the concrete results to which an idea leads when it is applied to the data of experience reveal much more. Here as everywhere, the tree can best be known by the fruit it yields.

Now, it is an undeniable fact that the organismic principle has powerfully appealed to one set of realistic researchers and greatly aided them in their task, namely the social anthropologists. Confronted with many phenomena which at first sight appear strange, nay ridiculous—for instance the widespread custom called *couvade* according to which the father must take to his bed while his wife is delivered of the child—they have invariably tried to come to a proper comprehension by seeing the puzzling pieces of behaviour as part and parcel of a wider, interlocking system of culture, and asking what possible function the mysterious actions to be explained can conceivably have within the common life. The fundamental idea which guides the effort is clearly the conviction that a social system can meaningfully be described as a unity—a unity within which every element can shed light on every other because they are all organically—or, as it is usually expressed, functionally—related.

Indeed, if we survey the development of social anthropology as a whole, as Robert H. Lowie has spread it out before our eyes in his book *The History of Ethnological Theory* (1937), we see that functionalism has had only one major competitor, namely evolutionism. To the scholar working in this field, functionalism and evolutionism are certainly alternatives between which he must choose: they appear as contrasting because the one is based on a 'synchronic', the other on a 'diachronic' approach; i.e. because the one stresses the coexistence and co-ordination, the other the succession and mutual displacement, of phenomena. Yet the social philosopher will be right in insisting that both belong to the same general tradition, the tradition of sociological realism or organicism. It is organic wholes like the human body which show functional integration, and it is organic species, and they alone, which evince evolution. Herbert Spencer stood for both theories at the same time. Among ethnologists, the most radical protagonist of the diachronic principle was Lewis H. Morgan. His tendency was to distinguish stages of development with the help of single traits, for instance the appearance of bow and arrow or the introduction of iron tools. To that extent he was assuredly not an organicist. 'But actually,' Lowie tells us, speaking of Morgan's periods and sub-periods, 'Morgan characterised them by a whole series of features, so that major inventions appeared as the correlates of such and such economic activities, social customs, and political institutions. Thus he offers a comprehensive scheme of cultural wholes . . .' (p. 56). In other words, even he is, to a large degree, a holist, an organicist, and a functionalist.

In any case, however great the inroads were which evolutionism made, during the nineteenth century, into anthropological thinking, it is functionalism which accompanied it throughout its history and became the acknowledged orthodoxy. Lowie is inclined to regard Boucher de Perthes as the father of the science from whose 'discoveries . . . emanated . . . the sudden flood of light' which gave it life (p. 254; cf. pp. 7 *et seq.*). But 'Boucher de Perthes was, in modern parlance, something of a functionalist', so that functionalism was present from the word go. Now, the same label can equally be applied to other pioneers. Bastian 'argued that a science of mental life must take cognizance of ethnographic data, because the "individual's thinking is made possible only by his functioning in a social group"' (p. 36);

'Fustel de Coulanges' . . . position is militantly functionalist: institutions are declared unintelligible except in their context' (p. 40); Bachofen, 'like Fustel de Coulanges . . . is emphatically a functionalist in rejecting the study of a single aspect of civilization and especially in connecting social stucture with religious practice' (p. 43); in the same way, 'Maine was a functionalist in treating phenomena not as discrete, but as interrelated' (p. 53). As for McLennan, he is to be classed as predominantly an evolutionist. And yet Lowie says of him: 'Here is another pioneer with a marked functionalist bias . . .' (p. 47).

Coming nearer to our own age, the first major figure that confronts us is R. R. Marett. He, too, 'clearly forestalls contentions latterly supposed peculiar to the functionalist school' (p. 111). We can give substance to this assertion by quoting another competent observer: for Marett, says E. O. James in his *History of Religions* (1956, pp. 206/7), 'the business of myth . . . like that of religion in general, [in other words] its function, is to restore confidence in crises and to maintain the stability of the existing régime . . . Magic . . . is [likewise] a means of asserting optimism, of giving hope in the face of adversity . . . In short, however institutions may have arisen and developed, it is possible to discover by a careful investigation of their actual function in a living community their value in supplying spiritual power to help and heal by means of faith, and to facilitate the living together of its members in an orderly arrangement of social relations, quite apart from the truth or falsity of the beliefs held and the rites performed'. This, surely, is functionalism of the purest water. The theory thus stands at the threshold of the present, as it dominated the thinking of the past.

Crossing this threshold, we find more-or-less prominent elements of functionalism-organicism in Eduard Hahn, Franz Boas, Fritz Graebner, Wilhelm Schmidt, Richard Thurnwald, Ruth Benedict and many others. There is no need to speak in detail about them all. Only a word about Franz Boas, perhaps the most influential of this group. He, too, 'has consistently preached the totalitarian view of culture' and upheld 'the postulate that cultures are not mere aggregates of separate elements but integrated wholes'. 'As early as 1887 we find him warring against the curatorial practice of synoptic museum exhibits, because if a specimen is isolated "we cannot understand its meaning".

A rattle, for instance, may be a musical instrument or an implement of ritual; two objects identical in outward appearance may thus have vastly different connotations. "The art and characteristic style of a people can be understood only by studying its production as a whole". To this conception,' Lowie tells us (p. 142), 'Boas has steadfastly adhered', and his adherence to functionalism is all the more significant as Boas was anything but a rash system-builder; indeed, he was the soberest and most factual investigator that can well be imagined. And yet he found functionalism realistic and enlightening.

As can be seen, the organismic principle informs the whole history of social anthropology. At first, it is there merely in solution; but at long last it becomes compact and concrete, a consciously defined and defended position. This happens around 1922, the year when, in a strange but significant coincidence, A. R. Radcliffe-Brown published *The Andaman Islanders: A Study in Social Anthropology*, and B. Malinowski his *Argonauts of the Western Pacific*. With Radcliffe-Brown and Malinowski functionalism achieves the status of a classical doctrine. Both have left us in no doubt about their creed. Radcliffe-Brown formulated it above all in two brief papers: 'On the Concept of Function in Social Science' and 'On Social Structure',[1] Malinowski in his posthumously published book *A Scientific Theory of Culture* (1944), and also in his Introduction to H. I. Hogbin's *Law and Order in Polynesia* (1934).

Lest the bracketing together of these two men should arouse misgivings among social anthropologists in the technical sense of the word, let us quickly indicate that we are aware of the broad ditch which divided them. Malinowski has accused Radcliffe-Brown of a 'tendency . . . to eliminate the biological element from the functional analysis of culture', whereas in his opinion each and every aspect of culture corresponds to some fundamental drive 'of the human organism'.[2] The contrast between the two attitudes is sharp: it is one thing to say that the institution of marriage satisfies sex, i.e. a natural need, and quite another thing to say that it expresses a cultural striving, i.e. fits into a cultural scheme. For Malinowski human society is turned towards, and in its forms is dependent upon, extra-cultural determinants;

---

[1] Reprinted in *Structure and Function in Primitive Society*, edd. E. E. Evans-Pritchard and F. Eggan, 1952.
[2] Introduction to Hogbin, pp. xxxvii/xxxviii.

for Radcliffe-Brown it is, so far at any rate as its characteristic forms are concerned, very largely autonomous and its determinants are intra-cultural. Philosophically, the two thinkers are far from each other. Still, organicism has always comprised a more materialistic and a less materialistic wing, and for this reason it is permissible to group Malinowski and Radcliffe-Brown together as fellow-functionalists. Lowie, while insisting that 'the resemblances between the two English scholars should not be over-rated', yet writes—and this is decisive: 'They share with each other—but also with Boas, Bachofen, and Fustel de Coulanges—a concern with the interrelation of the several elements within a given society' (*loc. cit.*, p. 230). When Lowie says of Malinowski that 'others have either preached or practised the faith; he has done both' (p. 240), he is making a statement which can be applied with equal justification to Radcliffe-Brown.

Of the two doctrines, that of Malinowski is by far the less sophisticated. He is inclined simply to equate functionalism and social anthropology, nay, functionalism and social science in the widest sense of the word. 'Any small contribution I may have made,' he says in the essay 'The Functional Theory' contained in *A Scientific Theory of Culture*, 'consists in writing out and pinning the label of functionalism on an existing body of doctrine, method and interest' (p. 147). This sounds extremely self-effacing and modest, but is in reality a claim to stand and speak for the only possible approach. Evolutionism and diffusionism appear to Malinowski as sad deviations from the obvious truth. 'The selection of such phenomena as the classificatory system of kinship terms and the handling of it as a survival . . . shows how, by neglecting the functional analysis of vital linguistic phenomena, Morgan misdirected anthropological research for generations. Again, Graebner, rigging up a false or puerile analysis of culture in order to lay the foundation of what he regarded as a fool-proof world-wide diffusionism, has created an anti-functional approach of first-rate imbecility' (p. 149). These are strong words, but Malinowski means every one of them. Wherein, then, have we to find the cardinal error of a man like Graebner? 'He . . . assumes that it is possible to isolate single items from their cultural context', and in particular 'he defines . . . form as completely disconnected from function'. But 'form is always determined by function' and a truly scientific explanation of social reality must contain 'an appreciation not merely of isolated facts but of essential relations' (148/9).

Closely considered, Malinowski's functionalism reveals two aspects, two layers as it were, one above the other. The first is expressed in the 'general axiom' that 'culture . . . is an integral in which the various elements are interdependent' (p. 150). We realise that in Malinowski's mouth this is no vague and empty assertion when we learn that the three constituent 'elements' are artifacts, group organisation, and symbolism, parts of reality which indeed always exist and coexist, but between which the bonds of integration are by no means always manifest. Every society has tools such as hammer and tongs, group organisation such as clan or tribe or nationhood, and symbols such as words. The characteristic submission of Malinowski, by which he reveals his underlying doctrinaire organicism, is that the interdetermination of these phenomena is such that no scientific study of any of them is possible unless it is undertaken in conjunction with the study of them all. 'It is impossible to isolate the material aspect of social behaviour, or to develop a social analysis completely detached from symbolic aspects . . . The totality of a cultural process involving the material substratum of culture, that is, artifacts; human social ties, that is, standardized modes of behaviour; and symbolic acts, that is, the influences of one organism on another through conditioned stimulus reflexes; is a totality which we cannot cut up by isolating objects of material culture, pure sociology, or language as a self-contained system . . . The three dimensions of cultural reality enter at every step of the process . . . A concept of disconnected items . . . is useless' (pp. 152, 154, 149).

This is the configurational and purely cultural aspect of Malinowski's theory. To it he adds (and this, above all, distinguishes him from Radcliffe-Brown) a more materialistic thesis. In a revealing passage which is clearly aimed at Radcliffe-Brown, though the name of the antagonist is not mentioned, Malinowski expresses himself as follows: 'Functionalism would not be so functional after all, unless it could define the concept of function not merely by such glib expressions as "the contribution which a partial activity makes to the total activity of which it is a part,"[1]

---

[1] These words are taken literally from a paper by Radcliffe-Brown, first published in the *American Anthropologist* in 1935 and now reprinted in *Structure and Function in Primitive Society*. Cf. *ib.*, p. 181.

but by a much more definite and concrete reference to what actually occurs and what can be observed . . . Such a definition is provided by showing that human institutions, as well as partial activities within these, are related to primary, that is, biological, or derived, that is, cultural needs . . . Functionalism would have no true claim to deal with culture in its fundamental aspects, such as educational, legal, economic, or pertaining to knowledge, primitive or developed, and religion, unless it were able to analyze and thus define each, and relate them to the biological needs of the human organism' (p. 159).

Malinowski takes the materialistic creed implied in these words very seriously. Even all the thought and all the art which has developed around the concept of survival after death is said to be '. . . related to some deep biological craving of the organism' (p. 174)—or rather, with becoming doubt, 'perhaps' so related, i.e. related to our body, rather than freely produced by our mind. Generally speaking, he calls it an 'axiom in the science of culture . . . that every cultural achievement that implies the use of artifacts and symbolism is an instrumental enhancement of human anatomy, and refers directly or indirectly to the satisfaction of a bodily need' (p. 171).

This driving forward of the functional principle of analysis until a biotic need of the human organism is reached, which thus appears as the end of ends, will work quite well for a stretch of the way, even in the study of social facts and social forms. It is all very simple and plain-sailing so far as the family is concerned. 'The function of the family is the supply of citizens to a community' (p. 168). It is, of course, also the satisfaction of the sex drive, the philoprogenitive drive, if there is such a thing, etc. The connection with biotic need is obvious here. Still, even with regard to the family, Malinowski's materialism soon runs into a difficulty which is present even though he refuses to take notice of it. The very next sentence reveals it: 'Through the contract of marriage the family produces legitimate offspring . . .' Can the production of *legitimate* offspring really be called a *biotic* need, a need of the human organism? Would not the production of non-legitimate offspring equally well satisfy the need for the satisfaction of sex and parental emotion, and the provision of new human material for the continuation of the stock of the community? To raise these questions is to answer them in the affirmative.

But if the narrowness of Malinowski's materialism becomes obvious already here, in the study of inter-sex relations, when we deal with a form of life common to man and the animals, how much more manifest must it become when we go over to the consideration of a form of life which is specifically and exclusively human? What is the biotic function, for instance, of the clan? 'The function of clanship,' Malinowski writes, 'I see in the establishment of an additional network of relations cutting across the neighbourhood groupings and providing a new principle in legal protection, economic reciprocity, and the exercise of magical and religious activities. The clan system adds, in short, to the number of those personal bonds which reach across a whole tribe-nation, and allow for a much wider personal exchange of services, ideas and goods, than would be possible in a culture organized merely on the basis of extended families and neighbourhood groups' (*ib.*). One can agree that the clan thus characterised has a function—but is it a function in relation to natural need? Is the clan, as a social institution, really natural and necessary? Malinowski himself has to concede that it is not. 'Clans are obviously an additional, one might say, supererogatory type of internal differentiation', he admits on the next page, and he adds the very pertinent question: 'Can we speak of a legitimate need for such differentiation, especially when the need is not ever-present; for not all communities have clans, and yet they go on very well without them?'

Confronted with this query, Malinowski to all intents and purposes abandons his materialism—abandons what we have called the second layer of his functionalist philosophy. 'In cultural evolution,' he writes, 'we might introduce the concept of the struggle for maintenance, not of individual organisms nor yet of human groups, but rather of cultural forms' (p. 170). With this modification of his opinion, his position becomes, at any rate so far as 'certain wide, separate institutional groups' are concerned, identical with that of Radcliffe-Brown. The 'concept of function in this sense', he defines as 'a contribution towards a more closely knit social texture'. But this definition is practically the same as that of Radcliffe-Brown criticised and rejected on page 159—'the contribution which a partial activity makes to the total activity of which it is a part'. The matter is important for us because it shows, in a new way, that functionalism-organicism is sound so long as it is understood in a non-materialistic sense, and that it is no longer so as soon as it ceases to be cultural and becomes naturalistic—that it is sound so long as it is handled in the spirit of Aristotle and St. Thomas Aquinas, and not in that of Spencer or Trotter or Schäffle or Leontiev.

But this is somewhat by the way here. What concerns us in our present context is not so much the truth or error of the attempted subordination of social norms to natural needs as the fact that even this second limb of Malinowski's theory is clearly a manifestation of underlying holistic, organismic, integrational conceptions. For what is it that is asserted? Essentially this: that as society is, internally considered, an interlocking system, so it stands revealed, in an external view, as an integral element of a wider interlocking system, that of nature, the background and absolute basis of all human life, in which its 'function' is to subserve vital needs, as its own integral elements subserve, on their own level, the foreground and more relative necessities of society and culture. Differently expressed: as 'culture is . . . a system of objects, activities, and attitudes in which every part exists as a means to an end' (p. 150), so the physical universe, too, is a system in which every part, without exception, and hence also society and culture, exists as a means to an end and must be understood, by the observing scientist, in and out of this functioning and subservient—'instrumental'—position. Whatever else one may hold against Malinowski, one thing is certain, namely that he is consistent in what he says, and that he takes his functionalist theory to a logical conclusion. Indeed, one may assert that it is precisely his consistency which leads him into error, for he drives his principle forward until territory is reached to which it can no longer be said to apply, the territory of culture in the narrower sense of the word, of non-instrumental culture, which is dominated, not by physical necessity, but by values conceived in freedom—the territory of human autonomy.

As we have seen all along, it belongs to the inherent logic of the functionalist—i.e. the organismic—position and constitutes, so to speak, its philosophical core, to play up the social whole and to play down the individual part, to consider that 'society is before the individual'. This aspect, too, becomes clearly articulate in Malinowski's text. 'No single item of material culture', he asserts, 'can be understood by reference to an individual alone; for wherever there is no co-operation, and such cases are hard to find, there is at least the one essential co-operation which consists in the continuity of tradition. The individual has to acquire his personal skill and the knowledge behind it from a member of the community already acquainted with skills, technique, and information; and he also has to receive or to inherit his material equipment" (p. 151). This may be only a very moderate, undogmatic and commonsensical statement of sociological realism, but it is sociological realism all the same. There can thus be no doubt about the fact that Malinowski must be set down as a member of the 'realistic' school of social philosophy.

The case of Radcliffe-Brown is far more interesting than that of Malinowski. On the intellectual level, his position was determined by two great influences: the influence of Georg Simmel and the influence of Emile Durkheim. As will be shown later on, both Simmel and Durkheim can (though with considerable reservations) be assigned to the third or 'cultural' school of social philosophy. Accordingly we find at times statements in Radcliffe-Brown which assert the independence of social life from physical determinants and, by implication, the autonomy of the social sciences. For instance, we read in the Introduction to *Structure and Function:* 'It is by reason of the existence of culture and cultural traditions that human social life differs very markedly from the social life of other animal species. The transmission of learnt ways of thinking, feeling and acting constitutes the cultural process, which is a specific feature of human social life" (p. 5). In spite of such insights, however, Radcliffe-Brown, like so many of his colleagues in modern times, has shown a strong tendency to lean on the natural sciences. The only question was—to which side would he lean? To the side of a mechanistic or to the side of an organological philosophy? To the side of philosophical nomin-alism and individualism, or to the side of philosophical realism and holism? The initial influences must have been about equal, for Simmel had a bias towards nominalism and Durkheim towards realism. It is highly significant that the Durkheimian influence won over that of Simmel. Radcliffe-Brown, though, of course, an Englishman, is treated by Lowie in the chapter called 'French Sociology', so much did his general attitude resemble that of the largely realistic, organismic Durkheim school.

Owing to his acquaintance with, and appreciation of, Simmel, Radcliffe-Brown at times expressly rejects organismic ideas.

Some anthropologists, he points out, regard societies 'as being in some sense or other discrete real entities'. But this is wrong. 'My own view is that the concrete reality with which the social anthropologist is concerned in observation, description, comparison and classification, is not any sort of entity but a process, the process of social life. . . . The process itself consists of an immense multitude of actions and interactions of human beings, acting as individuals or in combinations or groups' (pp. 3 and 4). If this were really Radcliffe-Brown's conviction, his working creed, we should have no right to speak of him in this chapter. But after this polite bow to Simmel, he entrusts himself, practically without reserve, to Durkheim, whom, with Montesquieu, Comte and Spencer (three other organicists)[1] he acknowledges as his master (cf. p. 14). After this theoretical acknowledgement of the individual, his independence and importance, he treats societies consistently as substantive wholes—so much so that Malinowski thought himself justified in accusing him of a 'tendency to ignore completely the individual'.[2] The key-conception with which he operates is definitely that of the social system.

It is interesting and highly instructive to observe how Radcliffe-Brown, unbeknown to himself, shifts progressively from the middle ground mapped out by Simmel towards the organismic-holistic position. The use of the term social system, he tells us, is based on the realisation 'that in a particular form of social life there are relations of interconnection and interdependence, or what Comte called relations of solidarity, amongst the various features' (p. 5). Interdependence is a stronger word than interconnection, and solidarity is a much stronger expression still. In other words, the unity of social life is increasingly emphasised, the fact of diversity increasingly forgotten. No wonder that it is not long before the principle of functional analysis is formulated: 'The theoretical significance of this idea of systems is that our first step in an attempt to understand a regular feature of a form of social life,[3] such as the use of cheques, or the custom by which a man has to avoid social contact with his wife's mother, is to discover its place in the system of which it is part' (p. 6).

[1] Concerning the first of these, whose alignment with the organismic tradition is not so generally admitted as that of the other two, cf. my book *Montesquieu: Pioneer of the Sociology of Knowledge*, 1960, *passim*.

[2] Cf. *Introduction to Hogbin*, p. xxxviii.

[3] *Sic*. Should the text read: "or a form of social life"?

This functionalism is to Radcliffe-Brown far more than merely a heuristic principle which could help to explain strange phenomena, but would have no philosophical significance. It is, on the contrary, very definitely the expression of a basic philosophical attitude, of adherence to 'realistic' philosophy. From the concept of social system he advances to the concept of social structure, and this is thought of as lasting, i.e. as relatively independent of the individuals who make it up. 'One of the fundamental theoretical problems of sociology is that of the nature of social continuity. Continuity in forms of social life depends on structural continuity, that is, some sort of continuity in the arrangements of persons in relation to one another.' Such structural continuity exists, and because of it the death of individuals does not alter the life of societies. 'A nation, a tribe, a clan, a body such as the French Academy, or such as the Roman Church, can continue in existence as an arrangement of persons though the personnel, the units of which each is composed, changes from time to time.' On reading these words, one is immediately reminded of one of Spencer's favourite arguments: the cells of the human liver die off and are replaced by others which are continually being born, while the liver itself never stops working; in the same way, the civil servants staffing the Treasury retire and others are continually being appointed, while the Treasury itself never ceases to function; hence social 'organs', just like physical ones, are immortal—a supreme proof that they are 'more' than the units which compose them. But we need not bring in Spencer here in order to prove that Radcliffe-Brown has embraced the organismic faith. His own words—the words immediately following—show that he has taken his stand by the side, not only of the Durkheimians, but even of the Spencerians: 'There is continuity of the [social] structure, just as a human body, of which the components are molecules, preserves a continuity of structure though the actual molecules, of which the body consists, are continually changing' (p. 10[1]).

In order to be able to appreciate the full meaning of these sentences, it will be expedient to remind ourselves of the way in which Georg Simmel deals with the self-same phenomenon. For him, continuity is a matter of inflow and outflow and of their statistical relationship. If the influx of new members and the wastage of old members is rapid and copious, continuity of life

[1] Cf. pp. 192 *et seq.*

G

is in his opinion not to be asserted, however much the outward form of the organisation or group concerned may remain un-altered. Only if the influx of new members and the outflow of old members is slow and gradual, will it be permissible to speak of true continuity, because only then will the characteristic traditions of the organisation or group be able to survive. If we take, for instance, an army officers' club and watch its develop-ment during war-time when many old members are killed off and many new members are brought in, we shall invariably find that its culture has undergone subtle transformations, even though outwardly there is little change, the club house and its furniture remain, etc. etc. Compared to Radcliffe-Brown's attitude, there is a far higher degree of individualism about Simmel's definition of continuity. Simmel's definition concentrates attention on the parts, not on the whole; and what is even more decisive philo-sophically, it is based on quantitative modes of thought—number of comers-in in relation to number of goers-out—not on concepts such as function which are essentially qualitative, precisely because they are holistic-organismic.

Radcliffe-Brown's second concept, that of social structure, thus reveals him as even more of a sociological realist than his first concept, the concept of social system. But his third technical term—social function—is even more radically anti-nominalistic. In developing it, he openly identifies himself with those who equate body physical and body social. 'In reference to social systems and their theoretical understanding', Radcliffe-Brown writes, 'one way of using the concept of function is the same as its scientific use in physiology. . . . It is this use of the word function that seems to me to make it a useful term in comparative sociology' (p. 12). And, later in the book: 'I would define the social function of a socially standardised mode of activity, or mode of thought, as its relation to the social structure to the existence and continuity of which it makes some contribution. Analogously, in a living organism, the physiological function of the beating of the heart, or the secretion of gastric juices, is its relation to the organic structure to the existence or continuity of which it makes its contribution. It is in this sense that I am interested in such things as the social function of the punishment of crime, or the social function of the totemic rites of Australian tribes, or of the funeral rites of the Andaman Islanders' (pp. 200/201).

At the time when these words were spoken—in 1940—the physiological analogies used were already under a deep shadow; the days of Spencer, when they were accepted as enlightening, seemed a long way off. Yet Radcliffe-Brown is disinclined to apologise for their use; indeed, he asserts their legitimacy: 'In using the terms [social] morphology and physiology, I may seem to be returning to the analogy between society and organism which was so popular with medieval philosophers, was taken over and often misused by nineteenth century sociologists, and is completely rejected by many modern writers. But analogies, properly used, are important aids to scientific thinking, and there is a real and significant analogy between organic structure and social structure' (p. 195).

Such theoretical utterances are characteristic. Simmel must have been very far from Radcliffe-Brown's mind when he made them. Yet there are other passages, which are, if possible, even more characteristic of him, because they are not meant to be programmatical, but show his philosophical realism in action, so to speak. One of the most revealing occurs when our author tries his best to do justice to the individuality of the individual. This is what he writes: 'Every human being living in society is two things: he is an individual and also a person. As an individual, he is a biological organism, a collection of a vast number of molecules organised in a complex structure, within which, as long as it persists, there occur physiological and psychological actions and reactions, processes and changes. . . . The human being as a person is a complex of social relationships. He is a citizen of England, a husband and a father, a bricklayer, a member of a particular Methodist congregation . . . and so on' (pp. 193/4). In other words, he is a body and he is a role-complex. Now, the copula 'is' which Radcliffe-Brown himself uses here—'he *is* a biological organism': 'he *is* a citizen of England'—is highly significant. He does not say: a man *has* a body or he *plays* a role. This form of words is avoided because it implies a third element, namely the true self, which neither *is* a body but *has* a body, nor *is* a role-complex but *plays* roles. Am I really no more than body on the one hand, actor on the social stage on the other? Am I not a substantive ego in the Cartesian sense, the sense of *cogito ergo sum*? Is Radcliffe-Brown not presenting us with a version of Hamlet without the Prince of Denmark? Simmel, and other sociological nominalists, would certainly suggest that he is doing just that.

Lest we be accused of over-subtlety, of artificially interpreting harmless words as incriminating evidence, let us quickly append one more passage which is clearly anti-individualistic. 'Social structures are just as real as are individual organisms', we read on p. 190. 'A complex organism is a collection of living cells and interstitial fluids arranged in a certain structure; and a living cell is similarly a structural arrangement of complex molecules. The physiological and psychological phenomena that we observe in the lives of organisms are not simply the result of the nature of the constituent molecules or atoms of which the organism is built up, but are the result of the structure in which they are united. So also the social phenomena which we observe in any human society are not the immediate result of the nature of individual human beings; but are the result of the social structure by which they are united.' These words flow from the very depths of sociological realism. Common sense—and the 'third' sociology—insist that it is as true to say that the individuals make society as it is to turn this statement round and say that society makes the individuals. But for Radcliffe-Brown (as the words just quoted clearly prove) the latter assertion is far more true than the former, and for that reason he is and remains a typical organicist.

One important proviso remains to be made. Radcliffe-Brown's organicism resembles that of St. Thomas Aquinas more than it does that of, say, Lilienfeld, in that he is inclined, not simply to equate physical organism and social order, but rather to argue that they both are incarnations of a higher principle capable of producing differing forms of life. The organism, he tells us (p. 179), 'is *not* itself the structure . . . the organism *has* a structure'. This formula reveals a very important insight which men like Lilienfeld did not possess. Structure—in other words, ' a complexly integrated system'—can rightly be ascribed to both physical organism and social order, and for this reason Radcliffe-Brown's organicism cannot be said to be extreme and excessive, even though, with its emphasis on integration, it *is* organicism, an approach irreconcilable with the ' "shreds and patches" theory of culture' so often found in modern society and so repulsive to the student of primitive life, the functional anthropologist.

VII

The Truth-Content of Organicism

IN THE broad field of social studies, there is hardly anybody
who would have a better claim to be called a scientist than
the social anthropologist of today. Unlike the student of
contemporary society, he is forced, by the very nature of his
material, to describe it meticulously and minutely before he can
venture to put forward any tentative hypothesis, let alone any
explanatory thesis or theory. The strangeness of the facts with
which he has to deal is sufficient to ensure strict factualness on
his part. To this must be added the healthy reaction to the
premature system-building which characterised the earlier phases
in the development of the subject. The social anthropologist has
learnt that generalisations à la Morgan will never do, that reality
is too complex and too manifold to be explained on the basis of
partial and confined experience. This again has strengthened the
realism, the respect for the facts, which the subject-matter of the
science alone would seem imperatively to demand.

In view of this fundamental attitude, it is surely both suggestive
and significant that the social anthropologists have, almost to a
man, embraced the functionalist principle of explanation which is
essentially part and parcel of the wider tradition of organicism.
Could it be that they have given themselves to this theory, not in
spite of the facts, but because of the facts? Could it be that
'realistic' sociology contains a sound core, in spite of the extrava-
gances of some of its representatives such as Spencer and Trotter,
Gumplowicz and Leontiev? Could it be that what is needed is not
a different philosophy, not a more factual definition of society, but
merely a more careful use of metaphor, a more judicious application of the holistic modes of thought?

The social anthropologists themselves have always had the tendency to justify their functionalism, not on theoretical, but on pragmatic grounds, which is not surprising, considering the kind of men they are. Functionalism, they contend, works. Radcliffe-Brown speaks for all of them when he says that there is 'reason to think that we can advance our understanding of human societies if we investigate systematically the interconnections among features of social life'.[1] And he himself gives plenty of examples which bear out this contention. We shall present one of them in the briefest possible outline. If it convinces the reader that something can be achieved by the application of the functionalist principle to strange societal facts, much will be gained. Realistic sociology, discredited by the indiscretion of those who wanted to propagate it, may then regain our respect. The picture, repulsive when it is overlaid by spurious colours, may well appear attractive when it is cleaned.

Among part of the Ba Thonga people of Portuguese East Africa, a mother's brother's son is called a grandfather, even though this sort of cousin is often younger than the person who so refers to him. Nothing could at first sight be more mysterious than such a custom; yet Radcliffe-Brown makes it perfectly understandable, and he does so by integrating it into the totality of the social system under which these particular people can be seen to live.

The Ba Thonga, like many other primitives, regard the relation between a mother's brother and a sister's son as particularly close. The uterine nephew is an object of care and solicitude to his uncle; when he is sick, his uncle (on the mother's side) offers sacrifices on his behalf; he is also allowed to take certain liberties with his uncle, for instance eat the supper prepared for him, appropriate some of his cattle and other possessions etc. When the uncle dies, the nephew may claim part of the inheritance and sometimes even one of the widows. Comparable customs occur all over the world. Radcliffe-Brown instances Tonga and Fiji, islands very far indeed from the African home-land of the Ba Thonga.

How can all this be explained? As a good functionalist, Radcliffe-Brown leads us from the part to the whole, asserting, in true style, that 'it is a mistake to suppose that we can understand the

[1] *Loc. cit.*, p. 6. Cf. chapter V of *The Andaman Islanders*, 1922.

institutions of society by studying them in isolation without regard to other institutions with which they co-exist and with which they may be correlated' (*loc. cit.*, p. 17). If we want to explain the ties between sister's son and mother's brother, we may, for instance, receive a clue from the study of the ties between brother's son and father's sister because, different as they are, they are yet comprised in the same comprehensive pattern. 'So far as present information goes, where we find the mother's brother important, we also find that the father's sister is equally important, though in a different way. The custom of allowing the sister's son to take liberties with his mother's brother seems to be generally accompanied with an obligation of particular respect and obedience to the father's sister' (*ib.*). Here we have a kind of a key: the father's sister is respected or even feared because she is related through the father, the sterner parent, whose function is to discipline the child; on the other hand, the mother's brother is treated familiarly and even loved, because he is related through the mother, the more affectionate parent, whose function is to give the young care and comfort and emotional satisfaction. Linguistic usages sometimes confirm this interpretation: a father's sister may be called 'female father', a mother's brother 'male mother'. Distance to the former may be increased by the fact that she is a woman—for you have to respect the other sex; nearness to the latter may, on the parallel and opposite principle, be intensified by the fact that he is a man—for you may be informal with your own sex. All this is perfectly easy to understand. But the extension of the characteristic attitude to the father does not stop at the father's sister; it also takes in the paternal grandfather and indeed all the people on the paternal side, just as the extension of the characteristic attitude to the mother does not stop with the mother's brother but reaches the maternal grandfather and all the other folk on the maternal side. Even more: the circle on either wing is still further widened by the inclusion of the respective spirits of the departed. When sick, you appeal through your mother's people to your maternal gods, for they can be expected to be particularly sympathetic and ready to help. But this also explains, and quite naturally, why not only the mother's father, but also the mother's brother and even on occasion the mother's brother's son, my cousin, is called by me a grandfather. 'The person who must sacrifice on my behalf to my maternal ancestors is first my mother's father, then, if he is dead, my mother's brother, and after the decease of the latter, his son, who may be younger than I am. There is a similarity of function for these three relationships, a single general pattern of behaviour for me towards them all and this is again similar in general to that for [maternal] grandfathers.' Therefore, 'however absurd it may seem to us to call a mother's brother's son, who may be actually younger than the speaker, by a word meaning "grandfather" . . . the nomenclature is . . . appropriate' (pp. 29, 30). The puzzle with which we started out has thus found its solution.

This is, to say the least, elegant argument and plausible analysis. Does it confirm the thesis of realistic sociology that society is a unity rather than a multiplicity? It does so far as it goes, i.e. *so far as primitive communities are concerned*. In fact, with this important proviso, the implications of which we shall have to consider very carefully, it confirms philosophical realism in a double way: firstly, in the pragmatic sense because it shows that by treating such societies as integrated wholes, we reach solid insights; and secondly—and here we are going, it should seem, far beyond the claims of the typical anthropologists—in a material sense as well, for, properly understood, it reveals to us that such societies are in fact and in truth above as well as 'before the individuals who compose them', that in them the primacy of being belongs to the 'we' and not to the 'me', that only a realistic ontology does justice to their essential character.

No more need be said about the first of these points; the second merits all the closer attention. We can bring it out best by critically looking at Radcliffe-Brown's own summary of his analysis. 'The pattern of behaviour towards the mother', he writes, 'is extended with suitable modifications to the mother's sister and to the mother's brother, then to the group of maternal kindred as a whole, and finally to the maternal gods, the ancestors of the mother's group' (p. 27). This whole deduction is highly typical of modern man and his nominalistic modes of thought. There is first an individual and a relationship between individuals, with an appropriate pattern of conduct; and this is then generalised until it comprises, and regulates the intercourse with, a whole group. The personal appears here as primary, the collective as secondary and derived. But is it really like that that the primitive thinks and feels? Is it not rather the other way round? Is his mind not focused on a group within which an individual, and an individual relationship, only stands out as a special case? In other words, is the group ('my mother's people') not more primary, in the sense of more real, than the person (even the mother)? In a way, Radcliffe-Brown indicates just this, but in an all too unemphatic fashion. 'In primitive society', he says, 'there is a strongly marked tendency to merge the individual in the group to which he or she belongs' (p. 25). This statement is undoubtedly true, as everybody knows, but here again there is some modern nominalism in the background which spoils the formulation. Instead of saying that 'there is a tendency to merge the individual in the group', it would be better to say that there is a tendency not to let the individual emerge from the group. This would come far nearer to the facts. Primitive thought is realistic, not nominalistic; the group is apprehended as a unity, not as a collection of individuals; and in so far as this is so, the theses of holistic sociology (if freed from their obfuscating biological and physiological jargon) are true in relation to this world.

The contents of the last paragraph will, it is to be feared, come up against some resistances due to the current reaction against earlier unhappy theorising about primitive man. Is this not the old and exploded doctrine of primeval communism in a new guise? Has it not been shown, and that convincingly, that the individual is important even in simple societies? No doubt matters have often been crudely exaggerated. But if it is wrong to exaggerate a fact or feature, it is equally wrong to exaggerate the reaction to this exaggeration, to go too far in the other direction. (Radcliffe-Brown does not do this, as our last quotation shows.) It is neither permissible nor necessary to say that primitive man sees only the group and not the individual, just as it would be wrong to suggest that modern man sees only the individual and not the group. Part and whole are always together in the picture; the question is merely one of priority. In the primitive world, the established ontological principle gives primacy to the whole, not the part; in the modern world it is the other way round. Would Aristotle (a sober observer) have asserted that the whole is before the part if this statement had not corresponded to the facts as they still were in his day?

But we have a far better witness than Aristotle, or, for that matter, any philosopher. We have the witness of life. For part and parcel of most primitive life is the blood-feud, and the blood-feud is based on the ontology of which we are speaking—or rather on the reality of which this ontology is one of the reflections and manifestations. *We* operate with the conception of individual responsibility. If James MacDonald or Shean O'Shaughnessy have hurt us, we shall hate *them* or have the law on *them*. But the clansmen of history operated with the conception of collective responsibility. They said *a* MacDonald or *a* O'Shaughnessy (a carrier of Donald or Shaughnessy life) had hurt them and *all* of those who carried their name (i.e. embodied their life) were hated and fought. For us, the guilt attaches to a person and the group is not primarily involved; for them the guilt attached to the group and the individual was only involved consequentially. Is this not supreme proof of the fact that there are societies in which the 'we' ranks ontically and ontologically above the 'I'? It is not too much to say that the truth of realistic sociology, so far as such societies are concerned, is sealed by blood, and plenty of it.

One of the profoundest students of early societies, William Robertson Smith, has well spoken of the facts. 'If the slayer and the slain are of different kindred groups,' he explains in his classical book, *Kinship and Marriage in Early Arabia*, 'a blood-feud at once arises, and the slain man may be avenged by any member of his own group on any member of the group of the slayer. This is the general rule of blood-revenge all over the world . . . To determine whether a man is or is not involved in a blood-feud it is not necessary to ask more than whether he bears the same group-name with the slayer or the slain. The common formula applied to manslaughter is that the blood of such a *hayy* [or clan, indicated by a common patronymic] has been shed and must be avenged. *The tribesmen do not say that the blood of M or N has been spilt, naming the man; they say "our blood has been spilt".*[1] The call to vengeance is no doubt felt most strongly by the father, the son or the brother of the slain, and they may be more reluctant than distant cousins to accept a composition by blood-wit. But this has nothing to do with the principle of the blood-feud. No man who is within the group can escape responsibility merely because he is not a close relation of the slayer or the slain. If there is blood between Lihyan and Adi there is war between every man of Lihyan

[1] Our emphasis.

and every man of Adi till the blood is atoned for' (ed. 1903, pp. 25–27). If, in this way, 'kinship . . . among the Arabs means a share in the common blood which is taken to flow in the veins of every member of a tribe,' what can be more natural, nay irresistible, than to conceptualise this factual unity of the group by saying that it is *one body*? What more natural, too, than generally to think in terms of sociological realism?

Needless to say, a great deal more evidence for the fact that sociological 'realism' is realistic in closely-knit communities could be adduced, but it will hardly be expected.[1] One of these evidences, and not the least of them, is the predominance, for two millennia, of realistic modes of thinking, both in social philosophy and in philosophy generally. They would hardly have become orthodox —indeed, they would hardly have arisen—if they had not been in agreement with the facts of life. Aristotle and Plato were as much confronted with societies of which unity was more characteristic than diversity as were Malinowski and Radcliffe-Brown. In either case, there was the best possible reason for embracing organicism and functionalism—namely that they were true, though, as we must add, an exaggeration of the truth in so far as they claimed to be a universally valid social philosophy.

So long as social life remains closely knit, sociological realism remains in the saddle, and rightly so. True, the clan tends to disappear when nomadism gives way to permanent land settlement, but its place is taken by an equally 'real' social unity—the village community. Even the members of the medieval town were still regarded as 'one hand'—witness the fact that outsiders held all responsible e.g. for the debts of one. But as soon as the social bond loosens; as soon as individualism raises its head, other forms of social thought make their appearance. The Cynics and Cyrenaics

[1] Cf. my paper laid before the Fourth World Congress of Sociology at Stresa (1959) under the title "The Sociology of Knowledge and the Problem of Ethics" (*Transactions*, Vol. IV, pp. 85 *et seq*). What I am dealing with there (apart from some Greek conceptions) are the sacred traditions of the Judæo-Christian culture. Both the collective fall of mankind through Adam and its collective redemption through Christ presuppose a realistic philosophy of society, for only if the group is a substantial unity and not a multiplicity can the guilt of one and the merit of one immediately and necessarily involve all.—Cf. further my Aquinas Lecture of 1956, *The Contained Economy*, where the priority of social norms to individual actions in the Middle Ages is demonstrated with reference to the concept of "just price".— For a more general discussion cf. Paul Fauconnet, *La Responsibilité*, 1928, esp. pp. 67 *et seq*., and the ample literature there mentioned. Particularly apposite is the passage from Plutarch quoted on p. 89.

of Greece and writers like Marsilius of Padua in the Middle Ages betoken a dissolution of traditional social forms as much as they do a turn towards nominalism in social and general philosophy; indeed, their nominalism or atomism is merely a repetition, on the mental—the superstructural—plane, of the growth of individualism or atomism in the 'real' substructure of life. Diogenes in his tub, radical individualist and radical nominalist, symbolises them both.

Here again it is interesting to see how like causes have like effects in the case of the social anthropologists. As soon as they shift their attention from the type of society called by Tönnies *community* to the type of society called by him *association*, their theoretical conceptions begin to alter. Usually, they are not aware of these developments and their reason, but one of them, J. H. M. Beattie, has well explained what is taking place. In a brief but penetrating paper, he writes: 'The classical field studies of Malinowski and Radcliffe-Brown were undertaken among small island communities. Since it appeared that these societies were functioning in much the same way as they had always functioned . . . for these first intensive field-workers a synchronic, functional approach was wholly consistent with the nature of their social material . . . But so simple a recipe [as functionalism] proved . . . inadequate . . . for the understanding of the more complex western societies, to the study of which social anthropologists have recently turned. For it was plain that these were anything but integrated working wholes, and their complexity could not be adequately comprehended in so restricted a frame of reference. Theories and hypotheses associated with the functional approach have had, therefore, . . . to submit to review and revision.' There has arisen what Beattie calls a 'post-functionalist approach' and its coming has been 'to some extent conditioned by the changing nature of the living societies which anthropologists study.'[1] What has happened to British anthropology, then, is similar to what has happened to human thinking about society in general: when the underlying reality changed, thought changed as well; more concretely: when the underlying reality changed from community to association, thought changed concomitantly from sociological realism to sociological nominalism. Nothing could be less surprising or more appropriate.

[1] "Contemporary Trends in British Social Anthropology" in *Sociologus*, 1955, pp. 6 and 7.

It follows from all we have said that the organismic principle is within its rights if, and in so far as, it arises in the framework of, or has reference to, a closely-knit social structure in which the 'we' is ontologically more potent than the 'I'. But sociological realism has also appeared in societies which were anything but community-like in type—societies rent by conflict, characterised by a large measure of individualism, and in the throes of rapid change, societies, in a word, which cannot, by any stretch of the imagination, be compared to organically integrated wholes such as the human body. The example of Auguste Comte springs to mind at once. His lifetime from 1798 to 1857 was a period of the deepest social dislocations. He himself was never tired of bemoaning the 'anarchy' of contemporary existence. And yet he was a sociological realist of the purest water—a *positivistic* realist who not only demanded that society should be organised on the organic pattern, but asserted that it *was* so organised, *was* at all times a body like the body politic. Two questions arise from this fact: firstly, the question of origins, and secondly, the question of validity. How is it that mental structures appropriate to community could arise in associational society, and what can be their value, seeing that they do not, in their basic thesis, agree with contemporary life?

The answer to the first query is far simpler than might be imagined. When sociological realism has made its appearance in loosely-textured societies—and this has happened more than once —it was regularly the expression of a yearning for a more ordered and pacified social life. The theories concerned reflected, not the underlying facts, but rather the strivings to which the underlying facts gave birth. In other words, such forms of thought were, to some extent, indeed, as a rule to a large extent, ideological. Differently expressed: though Comte's theory is offered as a positive, i.e. scientific exposition of the facts, it is in reality a normative, i.e. ethical outline of an ideal. 'Ought' sentences in the subconscious have become 'is' sentences in the conscious mind, and herein consists the ideological character of Comtean sociology.

In the western world, philosophical realism has, since the victory of capitalism over feudalism, or association over community, twice made a determined bid for the domination of the social sciences: once in the twenties, and once in the seventies or eighties, of the nineteenth century.[1] Characteristically, both periods were crises of confidence, if we may so express it, in modern society; and characteristically, too, both were marked by a revulsion from democratic principles and a revival of authoritarian and aristocratic ideas.

The first of these movements, vaguely and vulgarly known as romanticism, was part and parcel of the aftermath to the French Revolution. As M. Gouhier has shown in the second volume of his great work, *La Jeunesse d'Auguste Comte* (1933-1941), nominalistic, mechanistic notions held the field up to 1789 and beyond,[2] while from 1815 onward there is a decisive swing towards realism and organicism. It is fascinating to see in detail, how, especially in France, the star of Newton begins to set, and at the same time the star of Lamarck to rise: how *la physique sociale* gives way to *la physiologie sociale*. Henri de Saint-Simon, Comte's master, becomes a different man in the course of time: 'Little by little,' we are told by Bouglé and Halévy in the introduction to their edition of *La Doctrine de Saint-Simon* (1924, p. 18), 'his old instinct for organisation gains the upper hand over liberal influences. He comes to the conclusion that a régime of absolute liberty fritters away all efforts, wastes all energies and multiplies antagonisms; absolute liberty is a negative idea . . .' 'After 1820,' M. Mauduit adds,[3] 'Saint-Simon . . . lays [ever] greater stress on the principles of order and authority . . . At the end of his career, Saint-Simon finally went so far as completely to repudiate liberty, which appeared to him as no more than disorganisation.' With this political reorientation, an intellectual reorientation went hand in hand, a fact of the greatest possible importance in our context. To quote M. Mauduit once more: 'At first, Saint-Simon admired especially the mathematical and physical sciences . . . and hoped to find in universal gravitation a means of systematising the world; later on . . . he treated mathematicians and physicists with contempt and ended by calling them *brutiers* because all they studied was inorganic bodies' (p. 147). Comte underwent exactly the same

[1] Cf. the text of my Woodward Lecture at Yale on April 1, 1958, published under the title "The 'Classical Situation' in Political Economy" in *Kyklos*, 1959, pp. 57 *et seq.*

[2] For an illustration cf. my study of the Girondist leader, Brissot de Warville, in *America: Ideal and Reality. The United States of 1776 in Contemporary European Philosophy*, 1947, pp. 80 *et seq.*

[3] *Auguste Comte et la Science Economique*, 1929, pp. 16 and 19.

evolution. Up to 1820/22 he was an orthodox liberal; then he turned away from liberalism and all it stood for, including the atomistic social theory associated and assorted with it: *réorganiser* becomes his watchword. A short passage in a letter to his friend Valat, dated Dec. 25, 1824, reveals as in a flash of lightning the whole tendency of his thought, together with its basic inspiration: 'Egoism will in the end lead to general dissolution' (*cit.* Mauduit, p. 30).

The only question which arises in this context is why the re-action to 'the philosophy of egoism' should have been so long delayed: between 1789 and 1820 or 1825, 30 or 35 years had passed, a whole generation had come and gone. The answer (at which we can do no more than hint here) lies in the fact that the new libertarian and individualistic society gets finally discredited only with the outbreak of the economic crisis which stretches from 1815 to roughly 1825 and becomes particularly sharp and distress-ing after 1818. There is evidence that the misery of the unem-ployed weighed heavily with Auguste Comte,[1] as well it might: there is a fear of freedom in him which leads not only to the demand for governmental measures of relief, but beyond it to a general condemnation of *laissez faire* and even to the assertion that the body social, when healthy, is as integrated as the body physical, and that a relaxation of the fibres here and there can be nothing but disease.

In the 'seventies, the situation was similar, as economic history can well show. After 1825, the voices of criticism become muted, though they refuse to be silenced altogether. Capitalism takes another stride, especially in connection with the railway boom. Freedom seems to work after all: there is bread-and-butter for a widening circle of men. At once sociological atomism is back in favour. The great economists Menger and Walras, in 1871 and 1874 respectively, preach anew the twin gospel of individualism and mechanism. But round about the latter date, the boom breaks. From then on to the year 1896, there stretches the un-happy period commonly known as the Great Depression, and it is accompanied with a renewed repudiation of capitalism or at least of competition, and with a renewed call for conscious inter-vention whose practical effects were increasing protectionism, cartellisation, Trade Unionism, the small family pattern and other

[1] Cf. Mauduit, *loc. cit.*, pp. 133 *et seq.*

elements and efforts at ordering and 'planification'. The detail does not belong to this place; suffice it to say that the broad intellectual tendency towards organicism observable in these years, a tendency noticeable above all in Emile Durkheim, is rooted in such strivings, fears and hopes, in the diagnosed sickness and recommended remedy of the age. Durkheim is not only the theoretician who asserts that social facts are so real that they can be treated *comme des choses*; he is also the student of that dread phenomenon of contemporary life, *l'anomie*.

Our analysis of the origin of organismic forms of thought in societies which are not organical in their mode of coherence gains powerful support from the fact that organicism, in one shape or another, has always been the ideology of conservative parties. Karl Mannheim has proved this in detail,[1] but proof is not really required, for if there is a fact which is universally known and universally acknowledged, it is this. The four greatest names in the history of conservatism in Europe are, as everyone agrees, Joseph de Maistre and Louis de Bonald in France, and Adam Müller and Friedrich von Gentz in Germany. All four grew up in that uneasy period which lies between the revolutions of 1789 and 1848; and if there is any difference between them and their contemporary Auguste Comte, it does not lie in the basic idea of their sociology. It rather lies in a double secondary feature: Comte was both more and less of an organicist than they were: less, because he thought that society as it happened to be, still needed transforming before it could achieve *la synthèse finale*, the final, lasting state of thorough integration, and more because that final state was conceived by him even more on the model of a hale and hallowed body natural than it was by them. But the proposition that society is and ought to be organical in coherence is common ground. This fact raises, in an acute form, the question of validity. If Comte, and to a lesser degree Durkheim, shared some of the values of men like de Maistre and de Bonald, Adam Müller and Gentz, was their thinking not as hopelessly contaminated as theirs—crudely speaking, should they not be excluded from the history of sociology and relegated to the history of

---

[1] Cf. esp. "Das konservative Denken" in *Archiv für Sozialwissenschaft*, Vol. LXII, 1927, pp. 68 *seq.* and 470 *seq.*, now also (in English translation) in *Essays on Sociology and Social Psychology*, 1953, pp. 74 *et seq.* Cf. further *Ideology and Utopia*, Engl. translation (any), pp. 197 *et seq.*

politics? It would be quite wrong to deny that both Comte and Durkheim, not to speak of all the others, were to some extent deflected from the straight and narrow path of scientific and scholarly objectivity by the practical preoccupations which filled their minds, and it makes no difference whatsoever to their case that they were not aware of the ideological element in their thought which welled up from the depth of their subconscious. But it would be equally wrong to jumble them together with the hackwriters of conservative interests. A scholarly attitude remains a scholarly attitude, even if it bears in itself a tendency which ought not to be there.

This healthy attitude will in the end assert itself against the disturbing ideological element, provided only that the will to truth is strong enough, as it undoubtedly was in the case of Durkheim. If the development of the Durkheim school is scrutinized, we find two complementary trends at work. The first is a retreat from radical organicism. As a young man, Durkheim talked very much like Herbert Spencer, using bio-logical and physiological jargon with as little judgment as he did. But later on the tone changes—not as much, perhaps, as it should have changed, but yet to a considerable degree. The mature Durkheim is not an organicist, but a member of the cultural school, though always very much on the right wing of that school. The second trend is even more significant in our context. It can be summed up by saying that from a sociologist, as the word is currently used, Durkheim turned into a social anthropologist. There is a long way from the study of suicide in contemporary France (1897) to the study of religion among the stone age people of Australia (1912). The philosophical realism of *Les Règles de la Méthode Sociologique* (1895) is far more applicable to Arunta society than to Parisian life; and it is also far more applicable to Parisian life after its re-interpretation in an idealistic spirit[1] than in its earlier, rather crudely materialistic version. The fact is that the older Durkheim, and even more his disciples such as Marcel Mauss, felt more at home in primitive society than they did in modern. We know why: in the study of primitive society they could feel solid ground under their feet, and this is the reason (a good scholarly reason) why they shifted to this field.

---

[1] The turning point was perhaps the essay of 1898, '*Représentations Individuelles et Représentations Collectives*'.

H

To sum up, then, theories like those of Comte and the younger Durkheim need to be treated with due care, perhaps even with suspicion, but they need not be condemned outright. A certain value-pursuit, conscious or unconscious, will regularly push a man in a definite direction, but the question is always, how far he is prepared to go: will he keep within the facts or pass beyond them? will he submit to the controls of reality or disregard and defy them? Only in the latter case will truth be irretrievably lost.

Even a practical-political aim will thus not necessarily be mortal to scholarship. Indeed, one can go so far as to say that its presence in or underneath a theoretical statement may be a sign of realism, in so far as the tendency in thought is also a tendency of life. Granted that some of Comte's and the younger Durkheim's thinking was wish-determined and not fact-determined, their wishes were forerunners of facts of the future: not valid at the time, their ideas were destined for validation, for self-validation. It is partly because of Comte's and Durkheim's teaching (among other factors) that society has recently retreated from individualism and advanced towards firmer integration, and in the measure in which this advance continues, will the philosophical realism—the realistic sociology—of these men gain increasing truth-value.

So much about organismic modes of thought which arise, where, strictly speaking, they ought not to arise, in societies which are not organically integrated, but merely on the way to organic integration. But there is yet a third case to be considered, besides that of organicism in accordance with, and organicism in anticipation of, the facts—the case of organicism against the facts. Herbert Spencer was born in 1820 and formed his decisive ideas around 1845, in the middle of a period of advancing individualism, not like Comte (born in 1798 and maturing around 1823) and Durkheim (born in 1858 and maturing round 1883) in a period of reaction to and revulsion from it. What can have induced this man to preach organicism, and what are the consequences of his incentive, whatever it may have been, on the value of his doctrines?

One thing is certain: it was neither contemporary life, characterised by rampant individualism and unbridled competition, nor yet a personal ideal that led Spencer to the kind of sociology which he retailed, for in politics he was so radical a liberal that he can almost be called an anarchist. What then was it? It must have been a strong influence as it conquered both theoretical observation and practical programme. The answer is not far to seek. Spencer wanted above all to be a scientist, and more particularly a scientist of the kind which was most in fashion and favour at the moment —a biologist. His day, let us not forget it, was the day of Darwin, the heyday of Darwinism. Spencer was out for prestige. And as he was in search of prestige rather than in search of the truth, he produced a system, the bulk of which is the reflection of an artificial model and not a reflection of actuality, of the facts as they were. If we may express ourselves in a somewhat stilted, but nevertheless technically correct way, we can say that both Comte's and Spencer's thought were ideologically distorted, but whereas Comte's was a macrosociological ideology, based on a value-striving of all society in his day, Spencer's was a microsociological one, the result (the none too respectable result!) of valuations (of the preferences and prestige-structure) inside a restricted circle, that of the intellectuals, and of a personal bid inside that circle, a bid for recognition. And for this reason, the value of his 'inductions' cannot be rated very high.

Will it be said that this is too harsh an estimate of Herbert Spencer? (—or rather of the Herbert Spencer who wrote *The Principles of Sociology*, for his *Principles of Psychology* reveal a far different mind and make him a forerunner of the cultural school.[1]) He himself has proved the weakness of his main doctrine in the most conclusive manner by virtually abandoning it, though far too late in the day.[2] When he says, in *The Man versus the State* (1884), that society is no more than 'the mutual limitation of activities', he speaks not only in his own authentic voice, the voice of the champion of individuality against social coercion, but also in the authentic voice of his time which had realised a higher degree of individualism than any earlier or any later age. But the statement that society is the mutual limitation of activities, implies a decisive rejection of realistic sociology: it is difficult to think of a neater formulation of the opposite principle, the principle of nominalism. Real are in this view only the individuals who limit each other: society is not a real—a substantial—entity. In the *Man versus the State*, Spencer has made his way to a sound appreciation of the contemporary facts; and in doing so, he has led us away

[1] Cf. my paper, already quoted (see p. 6), on Spencer, esp. pp. 519 *et seq*.
[2] For the detail, cf. again my paper, this time pp. 517 *et seq*.

from organicism and all it stands for to the threshold of the alternative theory, the theory which models sociology, not on biology, but on mechanics, the atomistic and contractual theory, to the study of which we must now turn.

PART TWO
Society as a Mechanism

VIII

MECHANICISM
The Normative Form

As we have seen, normative organicism, classically formulated by Aristotle and St. Thomas Aquinas, asserts that society is basically organic in design, but recognises at the same time that this design is nowhere fully carried out in reality. Society is indeed an organism, but an organism *in posse* rather than an organism *in esse*, as the medieval philosophers would have expressed it. Normative mechanicism is both its pendant and its counterpart. It is its counterpart because it maintains that society is a mechanically, not an organically, ordered and coherent entity: an equilibrium system rather than a kind of body, a multiplicity rather than a unity. But it is the pendant and parallel of normative organicism in that it admits that the laws of mechanics are not fully operative in social life as we actually find it, even though they are basic to it, that there are inhibiting factors which bring about that society is not what it ought to be and what it would be if 'nature' had her way. Where organicism sees empirical social life as an ascent towards quasi-organic integration, mechanicism sees it as a descent from quasi-mechanical balance. Where organicism demands that politics should push forward to that happy consummation, mechanicism calls for a great return, a return to the halcyon days of coexistence without coercion, which is presumed to have existed once upon a time and to have shown forth the true essence of human sociality. We can study this mode of thought in another pair of great philosophers, Rousseau and Kant. Curiously enough, their relation is not unlike that of

Aristotle and St. Thomas. Rousseau, like Aristotle, gives a clear, if somewhat diffuse presentation of the fundamental ideas. Kant, agreeing with him in the essentials, brings, like St. Thomas, the core conceptions of the theory into sharpest focus.

A good deal of Rousseau's doctrine is presented to us in the form of conjectural history; he himself speaks of a *histoire hypothétique des gouvernements*;[1] but we must not be put off by this curious mode of presentation. He is not really interested in what has been, but only in what ought to be: the past is merely a screen on to which he projects the image of his ideal and of a hoped-for future. It is, in Rousseau's case, no paradox to say that he means tomorrow when he speaks of yesterday.

Now, the fundamental assertion which Rousseau puts forward under the cover of fictitious history and political fable can best be expressed by an inversion of Aristotle's famous adage that man is a *zoon politikon*, a social being. To Rousseau he is essentially a solitary creature. The 'state of nature', which is supposed to open the history of mankind, is defined as 'a state under which men lived in isolation' (I, p. 359). Primal man was not caught, as we are, in the net of society. 'His neighbours were not to him what they are to us . . . He had no more commerce with them than with the other animals . . .' (*ib.*, p. 272). This is how Rousseau describes 'savage man': ' . . . wandering in the woods, without industry, without language, without settled domicile, without war and without entanglements, without any need of his neighbours as well as without any desire to hurt them, perhaps without ever knowing any one individually . . . subject to few passions and sufficient unto himself . . .' (*ib.*, p. 263).

Just how deep this individualism goes, can be seen from the treatment accorded to the family. Rousseau allows that it is a natural society (and the only one that is so), but he immediately takes back the better part of what he has conceded. Even the family is 'natural' only for a fleeting moment, namely while the children need their parents in order to survive. 'As soon as this need comes to an end, the natural bond dissolves . . . If they continue to remain united, it is no longer on the basis of nature, but on that of will; and the family itself is maintained purely by

[1] Cf. the end of the preface to the *Discours sur l'Origine et les Fondements de l'Inégalité parmi les Hommes, Oeuvres de J. J. Rousseau, Nouvelle Édition*, 1819, vol. I, p. 215. References are to this edition.

convention' (II, p. 111). *If* they continue to remain united; the word describes, so far as natural man is concerned, an exceptional rather than a real case. 'In that primitive state, having neither houses nor huts nor property of any kind, each slept where accident led him and often only for one night; males and females came together by chance, according to fortuitous encounter, occasion and desire, without language being very necessary for the expression of the things which they had to communicate to each other: and they turned from each other with the same ease. The mother suckled the children to begin with out of her own physical need ... As soon as they had the strength to seek their own food, they did not hesitate to leave their mother: and as practically the only means of finding each other again was not to lose sight of each other [in the first place], they soon came to the point where they would not even recognise each other' (I, pp. 242/43).

The whole idea of man revealed in these and similar passages stands in the sharpest possible contrast to sociological realism. According to Aristotle, men are meant for society; according to Rousseau, they are meant for solitude. Sometimes the point is put in a manner that can almost be described as brutal: 'Men are not made to be crowded together in anthills, but to be scattered over the earth', we read in *Emile*. 'The more they congregate, the more they corrupt each other. The infirmities of the body as well as the vices of the soul are the infallible effects of such too numerous association. Of all animals, man is the one least able to live in herds. Human beings crowded together like sheep would perish in a very short time. The breath of man is mortal to his neighbours; this is no less true in the literal than in the metaphorical sense' (VI, p. 60).

While this is not only unrestrained, but also unphilosophical language, we find in *Emile* also a passage which brings Rousseau's nominalism into sharp focus and formulation: 'Natural man is all for himself; he is the numerical unit, the complete absolute, who has no relation except to himself and his equals. Social man is merely a fractional unit which depends on a denominator, and whose value lies in his relation to the whole, which is the body social. The good social institutions'—Rousseau clearly uses the word 'good' here in inverted commas—'are those which know how best to denaturalise man, how to rob him of his absolute existence in order to give him a relative one, and how to transfer his ego into the common unity; so that each individual no longer thinks of himself as one but rather as part of that unity' (VI, p. 14). A 'natural' society can therefore be expressed by the formula $I_a + I_b + I_c + \ldots I_n$; it is a sum of irreducible units, and not an irreducible unit; it is a collection, not a *corpus mysticum*; it is one only in language, but not in reality.

In view of this historical account and philosophical attitude, it must be a matter of surprise to Rousseau that society exists. Perhaps it ought not to exist; but it does, and because it does, there is an *explicandum* for him, a problem which 'realistic', i.e. holistic-organismic, thought has no need to raise or to face. With becoming frankness, he admits that he is puzzled. 'It can be seen . . . from the small care which nature has taken to draw men together by mutual needs and to facilitate the use of language, how little she has done to prepare their social habit, and how little of her own she has put into their efforts to establish its bonds. Indeed, it is impossible to imagine why, in this primitive condition, a man should have been more in need of another man than an ape or a wolf of his like, nor, assuming the need of [the assistance of] one's neighbours, what motive could have induced others to comply, nor even, in the latter case, how they could have agreed about the conditions [of mutual aid]' (I, p. 250). Even more disarming is the following passage: 'Man is born free, and everywhere he is in chains . . . How has this change come about? I do not know' (II, p. 110).

Needless to say, Rousseau is not satisfied with this negative answer. He casts about for some explanation and tries several, the least unrealistic being along Malthusian lines.[1] The whole is no more than a pseudo-problem which Rousseau has brought on himself by his excessive individualism and his radically nominalistic sociology. What concerns us here is not the fantastic discussion of a historical evolution which never took place, but the spirit in which it is conceived, and this spirit is not only the spirit of individualism and nominalism, but also that of mechanism. Man abandoned solitude and fled into society (or rather, to use Tönnies' term, which is most appropriate here, into association) because a balance was disturbed, the balance between his individual strength and the difficulties with which life confronts him and with which he has to contend; and man was justified in

[1] Cf. esp. I, p. 366.

taking this step because, on balance, the loss account does not come up to the level of possible and actual gain, even though our view of the balance-sheet is somewhat distorted by subsequent developments due to human stupidity and wickedness.

First about the disequilibrium which initiated and necessitated the great change: 'I suppose men come to the point where the hostile forces which, in the state of nature, run counter to their preservation, gain the upper hand . . . over the forces which any individual is able to employ in order to maintain himself in that state. In that situation, the primitive condition cannot go on; and the human race would perish if it did not change its mode of life. Now, as men cannot create new forces, but only assemble and direct those already in existence, they have no other means of self-preservation than the formation, by association, of a sum of forces which might overcome the hostile influences [they are up against] . . . This sum of forces can spring only from the coming together of individuals . . .' (II, pp. 123/24).

It is the desire for self-preservation, then, *individual* self-preservation, that levers man out of solitude and propels him into society. Society is not a primary fact of the human situation, it is a secondary phenomenon that needs to be historically explained and—we are almost inclined to say: economically—justified. From a study of the pros and cons of the social state—the 'compensations' (II, p. 132) which man receives when he surrenders his freedom—it appears that the enterprise is, on the whole, profitable: 'Look for the motives which have led men, united by their mutual needs in the great society [of all mankind], to unite more closely still by means of civil society [i.e. in particular states], and you will find no other than that of making the possessions, life and liberty, of each member secure through the protection of all . . . All, born equal and free, surrender their freedom only for the sake of their advantage' (I, pp. 394/95; II, p. 111). The advantage or *utilité* of the last quotation is, of course, personal advantage and personal utility. Society is no more than a tool in the hand of the individual, and not the individual a cell in the body of society. For the rest, irreducible diversity, nay, irreconcilable conflict remains supremely characteristic of the social state: 'In the social state, one man's good is of necessity another man's evil. This connection lies in the nature of things and nothing could change it' (VI, p. 164).

All this is nothing, if not consistent nominalism. Rousseau

drives it forward as far as he can. But the very consistency with which he develops this position leads in the end to its collapse. The model of man and society which he has built up in his mind appears to him in the end unsatisfactory and unrealistic, and, without abandoning it, he feels constrained to modify it—to modify it by the introduction of a social bond stronger than self-interest and the balancing of self-interests. For a final assessment of the value and validity of nominalism as a social philosophy, this is a fact of supreme importance, comparable to the abandonment, at the eleventh hour, of realism by Herbert Spencer. The third or mediating sociology can draw great comfort from either event.

The social cement which, by the side of self-interest, Rousseau sees as part of the binding which holds societies together is the natural sentiment of pity, 'a natural repugnance to seeing any sensitive creature, and above all our fellow-men, perish or suffer' (I, p. 213). 'If our common needs unite us by [the bonds of] interest,' we read in *Emile*, 'our common sufferings unite us by [the bonds of] affection' (VII, p. 26). This is an important statement. It marks a step in the direction of instinctualism as represented in this book by Wilfred Trotter. In so far as pity is natural to, and inborn in, human beings, and in so far as it links man with man in the framework of society, society is not an artefact, but a natural growth; not only a convention, but also a reality; not a fiction, but a fact.

However, it is only a very short step in the direction of instinctualism that Rousseau takes. Once again, he retracts the better part of what he has conceded. First of all, fellow-feeling is to him a weaker sentiment than selfhood. In case of conflict, the former must yield (cf. I, p. 214). Secondly, pity is only a partial experience, not one that would extend to all human beings: 'It does not lie in the human heart to put oneself in the place of people who are happier than we are, but only of those who are more to be pitied' (VII, p. 30). And—thirdly—even the sympathy for those whom life has treated more harshly than it has ourselves is not unmixed with, perhaps we can even say, unspoiled by, a good dose of egoism: 'One pities in others those evils only of which one does not believe oneself exempt' (VII, p. 32). This statement echoes Calvinist conceptions, not to say Hobbesian ones. Rousseau's habitual insistence that man is born good must not be taken quite *au pied de la lettre*. Even harsher is the following passage: 'Pity is sweet because we feel, in putting ourselves into the place of him who suffers, the pleasure of not suffering as he does. Envy is bitter because the contemplation of a happy man, far from putting the envious person in his position, arouses in him a regret of not occupying it already. It appears that the former exempts us from the pains which he suffers and that the latter robs us of the good which he enjoys' (VII, p. 26). Finally, the reference to pity only increases the negative value-accent that lies, for Rousseau, on all social life: 'It is man's weakness which renders him sociable; it is our common miseries which lead our hearts towards humanity. . . . Every attachment is a sign of insufficiency . . . A truly happy being is a solitary being . . . We attach ourselves to our neighbours through the experience of their pains rather than through that of their pleasures' (VII, pp. 25, 26). On reading these words, one cannot but be reminded of Hobbes' notorious chapter XIII in the *Leviathan*: 'Men have no pleasure, but on the contrary a great deale of griefe in keeping company'. And though Rousseau does not accept the 'warre of every man against every man' as the natural condition of mankind, he is yet very far from seeing society kept together by any kind of innate goodness or social instinct: 'It is from the conjunction and combination which our mind is able to make of these two principles [self-preservation and pity] that . . . all the rules of natural law flow; there is no need to bring in the principle of sociability' (I, p. 213).

In spite of a natural tendency to commiserate, on some occasions, to some extent, with some of our fellow men, the social bond must—in view of all this—be explained, not along holistic, but along atomistic lines: convention is its origin, not nature. It is posterior to individual existence, not prior to it. In his educational novel *Emile*, there is a little story which gives us the gist of Rousseau's sociological theory in its simplest form. Emile, brought up in more or less the same way in which nature brings up her happiest children, the so-called savages, is of course a closed self, a self-centred and self-contained monad: 'He thinks of himself without considering others and finds it good that others should not consider him. He expects nothing of anybody and feels no obligation to anybody. He is alone within human society . . .' (VI, p. 411). However, this last sentence is metaphorical, not a statement of fact. Emile is emphatically not alone within human society. He cuts across the paths of others, and others cross his path. The result is conflict, or at least the danger of it. Little Emile, living out his play instinct, plants some beans and eagerly watches them grow. One day, arriving at the bed he has made, he finds them all gone and the earth turned over. Robert, the gardener, appears guilty of this apparent act of vandalism. But, when charged, he defends himself by attacking. Emile himself had committed an act of the kind he now complains of: when he had planted his beans, he had ruined the Malta melons which the gardener had started just there, at the very same spot. Here then we have a conflict situation such as Rousseau regards as archetypal for all human encounter, for all social life. Two rights, two equally good rights, face each other. How can their clash be resolved? How can a comparatively peaceful social life be secured? In one way only: by an amicable arrangement for the future, by a *contrat social*. 'Would it not be possible', the tutor (none other than our friend Jean-Jacques) says to Emile, 'to propose a settlement to Robert? Let him grant us a corner of his garden, so that we can cultivate it, under the condition that he shall have half of the produce.' This solution is accepted on both sides; peace is restored, or rather established; but underneath the contract there remains the tension of contradictory interests. 'Remember', says Robert, 'that I shall dig over your beans, if you touch my melons' (VI, pp. 150 *et seq.*).

Here, in a nutshell, we have Rousseau's whole social philosophy. 'The social order is a sacred right', a sacred institution, 'which serves as basis to all others', says the most classical statement of the doctrine, *Du Contrat Social*. 'Yet this right does not come from nature; hence it is founded on conventions' (II, p. 110). Julie d'Etang, Rousseau's ideal woman, asserts the same principle: 'All human society . . . is based exclusively on the faith of engagements' (IV, p. 86). Jean-Jacques and Emile, the ideal pair of friends, live according to it: 'We were never dependent on each other, but we always came to an agreement' (VI, p. 296). This is the best that men can do for each other. Even 'friendship . . . is an exchange, a contract like the others,' Rousseau assures us, though he admits that it is particularly sacred (VII, p. 54).

An interesting context in which Rousseau's individualism, atomism, contractualism, and sociological nominalism in general comes to the front is his discussion of the role of punishment in education. As is well known, he has gone down to posterity as the most determined condemner of the rod. 'Use the rod and spoil the child' was his opinion, as against that of the Bible. Pestalozzi, the mildest of all educators, was his disciple. Yet Rousseau's advice to grown-ups was to hit back, if the child hits them first, and to give as good as they get (cf. VI, p. 147). This recommendation is based on Jean-Jacques' deepest conviction, namely that all social life is a pattern of mutuality: the child has to learn this fact, or else it will be unfit for any social role whatever. The secret of human coexistence and co-operation lies in the adage of the Roman lawyers: *do ut des*, the adage which can be translated into homely English as *tit for tat*.

Now, this recognition leads us immediately deeper into Rousseau's thought: it leads us from his contractualism to his mechanicism. Clearly, a contract is only fair, and can only be fair, if the contracting parties are equal in strength—in other words, if there is a *balance of forces* at the basis of it. The good society is, properly speaking, an *equilibrium system*, within which individual counteracts and counterchecks individual, so that nobody can subdue his neighbour. If there is no such balance or equilibrium, all is lost: 'In the relations between men, the worst that can happen to one is to find oneself at the mercy of another' (I, p. 296).

Primitive society was an equilibrium system; present-day society is not. Yet all society ought to be. Hence Rousseau's programme for the future. Hence also the battle-cry of the French Revolution: *liberté, égalité, fraternité*. Translated into sociological language, this famous device can be interpreted as follows: if men are granted freedom, harmony will come about, provided only that there is equality at the same time. For if there is equality, men cannot harm each other, and liberty, far from leading to disorder, will lead to order—indeed, to the firmest kind of order that we can imagine, order on the basis of the laws of mechanics, physics and astronomy. Both Rousseau and his disciples were mechanicists, and both were normative mechanicists, regarding egalitarian, i.e. equilibrated society as a *desideratum* rather than a *factum*, an aim to be attained, not a value already enjoyed. The famous Dedication to the *Discours sur l'Origine et les Fondements de l'Inégalité parmi les Hommes* contrasts 'the equality which nature has established among men' with 'the inequality which they [themselves] have instituted' (I, p. 191). Here lies the diagnosis of all social ills, and here the recipe for a general and abiding cure. '*Retournons à la nature!*'

It is in this particular that the society of the past is so decisively superior to that of the present, and because of it we may proclaim it as the model of the future. 'Inequality is hardly noticeable in the state of nature . . . Its influence is almost zero.' The study of primitive communities demonstrates that 'men . . . are by nature as equal among each other . . . as the animals of all species' (I, pp. 267 and 209). The consequences of this real natural equilibrium of social or rather individual forces were as beneficial as the results of its abandonment and replacement by a fictitious unnatural law-book equality are disastrous: 'In the state of nature, there exists a *de facto* equality which is real and indestructible because in that state it is impossible that the simple difference between man and man should be great enough to make the one dependent upon the other. In the civil state, there exists a *de jure* equality which is chimerical and vain because the means provided for its maintenance'—the civil laws which defend the rich against the poor and the constitutional laws which defend the privileged against the people—'are themselves the causes of its destruction, and because the strength of the public hand, added to that of the strongest individual . . . undoes the kind of equilibrium which nature had established between them. From this basic contradiction flow all the others which can be seen in the social order between appearance and reality. The greater number will invariably be sacrificed to the smaller, public interest to private . . . ' (VII, pp. 60, 61).

How could it be otherwise? When the underlying equilibrium is lost, the social contract turns into its own caricature. 'Let us sum up in four words', Rousseau writes with a caustic pen, 'the social contract of the two estates [of today, the rich and the poor]: you have need of me because I am rich and you are poor; let us therefore come to an agreement: I will grant you the honour of serving me, on condition that you give me the little that you have left, for the trouble which I shall take of ordering you about' (I, p. 346).

As can be seen, the story Rousseau has to tell is a story of the fall: mankind forfeited its pristine happiness when it lost the one-time equilibrium of man and man. But where there is fall, there is also the possibility and the promise of redemption. The social contract must be re-drawn so that it strengthens rather than upsets the balance. Rousseau calls it 'a remark which should serve as a basis to the whole social system: that instead of destroying natural equality, the fundamental contract substitutes, on the contrary, a moral and legal equality for whatever physical inequality nature may have put between men, and that men, who may be unequal on the score of strength or intelligence, become all equal through convention and law. Under bad government, this equality is no more than apparent and illusory; it serves only to keep the poor man in his misery and the rich in his usurpation. In fact, the laws [of our perverted societies] are always useful to those who possess and detrimental to those who have nothing: from which it follows that the social state is only of advantage to men, if all of them own something, and none of them has too much' (II, p. 136).

There can hardly be a clearer formulation of Rousseau's programme than these words: clear not only in respect of its practical aim, but also in respect of its philosophical foundations. A good society is a society in equilibrium: equilibrium is only possible if each of the associates has as much power of assertion (and power in defence) as every other. This conviction appears again and again in Rousseau's works. In one context he calls *'médiocrité* . . . the true strength of a state' (I, p. 443). In another he writes as follows: 'With regard to equality, it is not necessary to mean by this word that the shares of power and wealth should be absolutely equal, but . . . that no citizen should be so rich as to be able to buy another, and none so poor as to be forced to sell himself. . . . Would you give coherence to the state? Bring the extreme positions as near to each other as possible: suffer neither nabobs nor beggars. These two status groups, naturally inseparable, are equally disastrous for the common good' (II, p. 175). And again: 'The greatest evil has already come to pass when there are poor who need to be defended and rich who need to be contained. It is only on the middle classes that the whole force of the laws become effective; they are equally powerless against the wealth of the rich and the misery of the poor; the former eludes them, the latter escapes them; the one breaks the net, the other slips through it. It is therefore one of the most important duties of government to prevent the extreme inequality of possessions' (I, p. 412).

No doubt, as a theoretical speculator, Rousseau operates with

I

what we now call a model, a mechanistic model, not unlike a pair of scales which get into equilibrium only if the weights on either side are equal. But he does not entirely forget the hard and fast facts of reality. He has (though he does not tell us so openly) a negative and a positive illustration of his theory: France and Geneva. Clearly, the following sentences refer to France, the country *par excellence* of social disequilibrium, where a rich nobility confronts a wretched peasantry: 'Men distributed unequally over the territory and packed together in one place while others are depopulated; the agreeable arts and industry in the narrower sense of the word favoured at the expense of the useful and hardworking crafts; agriculture sacrificed to commerce; the tax-collector made necessary by the bad administration of the means of the state; finally, venality driven to excess . . . so that even the virtues are on sale for money: such are the most obvious causes of wealth and misery, of the substitution of private for public interest, of mutual hate among the citizens. . . .' (I, pp. 412/13). Against this dreadful *ancien régime*, Rousseau holds the ideal, born of his mechanistic sociology or normative mechanicism, of a *nouveau régime* under which France would become a commonwealth of cottages. The reader can find the seminal ideas in chapter IX of book I of *Du Contrat Social*. What Rousseau demands is, in substance, a restriction of landed property to the size which corresponds, on the one hand to a man's needs of subsistence, on the other to his capacity of work.[1] If this principle were accepted, the large estates of the nobles would disappear; their place would be taken by the equal holdings of free farmers; society would get into a stable equilibrium underlaid by a balance of individual forces, and all would be well.

This social ideal Rousseau found to some extent realised in the city of his birth. Geneva had no great landowners and no poverty-stricken serfs: her citizens, practically all artisans, were much of a muchness. Julie's clever friend, *confidante* and cousin Claire grasps the point clearly on a visit to the city. Her language lets the mechanistic philosophy behind it shine through: 'Seeing the mutual action and reaction of all the parts of the state which keeps it in equilibrium', she writes, 'one cannot doubt that more art and true talent is used in the government of this small republic than

---

[1] The programme is identical with that of John Locke, Cf. Stark, *The Ideal Foundations of Economic Thought*, 1943, pp. 15 *et seq.*

in that of the greatest empires' (V, p. 225). But Rousseau speaks not only through the mouth of a fictitious character; he raises his own voice in witness. Remembering the far-off days when he had been an apprentice under the shadow of the *Bourg de Four*, he writes in his *Confessions*: 'Nothing would have suited my mood better, and nothing would have been better fitted to make me happy, than the quiet and obscure state of a good craftsman . . . such as that of the engraver's is at Geneva. This state [is] lucrative enough to yield an easy subsistence, and not lucrative enough to lead to opulence' (XV, p. 66). Knowing Rousseau as we do, we must be permitted to doubt that a modest middle class existence of this kind would ever have satisfied him. Did he not run away from home because he found it unbearable? But what is unacceptable as a piece of self-estimate and self-revelation, is highly significant as an indication of a social dream. Once again we find that 'the social state is only of advantage to men if all of them own something, and none of them has too much'; that everything depends on avoiding those extremes of fortune which unbalance even the most robust inter-human relationships; in a word, on that equality which means equilibrium, and which, through its internal tensions, keeps the mechanism of society in order as the mainspring does the works in a Geneva watch.

This whole philosophy of Jean-Jacques Rousseau, according to which the very antagonism between men will lead to their peaceful co-existence, if only equality will help them to keep each other in check, can well be summed up as a doctrine of the 'unsociable sociableness' of the human race. But this striking phrase is not Rousseau's; it comes from the pen of his ardent admirer, Immanuel Kant.[1] Kant shares Rousseau's basic sociological convictions, as St. Thomas Aquinas did those of Aristotle. But he improved on their formulation, and that in a double way. Firstly, he made it perfectly clear that their common opinion was a kind of mechanicism; and, secondly, he recognised, and made others recognise, that their mechanistic sociology was normative rather than positive, a picture of the good society rather than a picture of given society, a reflection of the great Ought rather than a mirroring of the sober Is.

[1] Cf. *Gesammelte Schriften*, ed. Kgl. Preussische Akademie der Wissenschaften, VIII, 1912, p. 20. On Kant in general, cf. my book *Social Theory and Christian Thought*, 1959, pp. 37 *et seq.*

Rousseau, as we have seen, often speaks in mechanistic terms, but they are to him hardly more than useful metaphors, a kind of poetry in prose. Kant, far more conscious of the importance and implications of words, knows full well that they betoken a very real kinship between the science of society as developed by Rousseau, and the science of mechanics as developed by Newton. Discussing, ostensibly, international peace, but, *sub rosa*, intra-national peace as well, Kant expresses the conviction that one day we may perhaps secure it through the 'principle of equality as between mutual action and reaction', in other words, through the establishment of a balance of power. Order will then be produced and perpetuated 'after the manner of an automaton'. Here, as everywhere, Kant regards it as our prime task, both as men of theory and as men of action, to comprehend 'the secret mechanism of the arrangements of nature', to find 'a law of equilibrium.'[1]

We have seen that Rousseau, in the style of his age, had chosen to put forward his nominalistic sociology and to preach his social ideal in the guise of hypothetical history. There is little harm in this foible, provided we know how to understand his true meaning, how to unwrap it from its fictitious coverings. Yet Kant felt, and no doubt rightly, that there is a certain danger in this mode of exposition after all. It may create the impression that the social contract is, in some sense of the word, a fact, as if concrete men had, once upon a time, met at a concrete place and arranged to put themselves under a common law. And even if this primitive conception is avoided, if the *contrat social* is conceived, in accordance with the lawyers' concept of quasi-contract, as an accord entered into, not consciously, but semi-consciously, not by express words, but by conclusive deed, there remains an element of the fictitious which is the better avoided in philosophical discussions. Kant therefore tried to get rid of it by pronouncing the concept of *contrat social* a 'regulative' principle. By this he means a principle which can serve as a test and touchstone of social institutions and enactments, rather than as their historical explanation. Do you want to know whether a piece of legislation is good or bad? Ask yourself if it would have been acceptable to all the citizens to whom it is meant to apply, in other words, if it *could* have become part and parcel of a social contract, *if* such

[1] *Loc. cit., Gesammelte Schriften*, pp. 26, 25, 29.

contract-making, such social ordering, were technically feasible. If yes, it must be unexceptionable; if not, it clearly sins against the most basic condition of a successful social life, the equal freedom of all under the law. We see from this re-interpretation of Rousseau's conceptions that Kant not only brings out their mechanistic character, but also the fact that they constitute a normative, rather than a positive, mechanicism.[1]

This, incidentally, is a point where we can see how true it is that extremes tend to touch. 'If a constitution is to be permanent', Aristotle had written over two thousand years before Rousseau and Kant, 'all the parts of the state must wish that it should exist and the same arrangements be maintained'.[2] This coincidence of view between the prime representative of normative organicism and the chief spokesmen of normative mechanicism is not really surprising. For however much they may have differed in their interpretation of actual social life, they agreed, as we all must, in their social ideal, the vision of a truly pacified and harmonious order of human coexistence.

[1] We cannot go here into the more complex question of the connection between Rousseau's doctrines and Kant's 'categorical imperative'. For a brief discussion, cf. my contribution to Vol. VIII of the *New Cambridge Modern History* (chapter III).
[2] *Politics*, 1270 b 20.

IX

MECHANICISM
The Positive Form

GREAT AS the differences are which divide normative and positive organicism, the contrast between normative and positive mechanicism is even greater. The reason for this lies ultimately in the dissimilar character of the natural phenomena with which the organical and the mechanical sciences are respectively concerned. An organically coherent system is not, in all its parts, univocally determined. Heart and liver, if they are to function together, must certainly be proportioned to each other, but there is some latitude—some possibility and permission of variation—on either side. Within rather elastic limits, deviations from the norm do not destroy the health and harmony of the whole. Indeed, it is doubtful to what extent we can speak of a norm here. Between proportion and disproportion, normality and abnormality, health and disease, there are many intermediate stages which make it impossible to divide Is and Ought too sharply from each other. It is different with mechanically coherent systems. There is no half-way house between balance and unbalance: equilibrium either exists, or it does not. And equilibrium is also, and always, describable in absolutely unambiguous, absolutely univocal mathematical formulae. Exactitude is therefore the key-note of mechanistic thought in the sense of thought that consciously imitates the mechanistic model. Playing upon words, we may say with good reason that positive mechanicism is apt to be more positivistic than positive organicism.

We can see how true this is on almost every page of Vilfredo

Pareto's monumental work, the *Trattato di Sociologia Generale*,[1] which lies before us as the most massive and impressive statement of the mechanistic conception of social life. Pareto is a fighter: what he fights for is radical factualness, what he fights against, wishful thinking in any and every sense of the word. Grimly determined to track down and expose the consequences of this most dangerous of all truth-destroying tendencies, mercilessly surveying the past history of the so-called social sciences from this point of view, he finds practically no theoretician who would deserve to be described as a scientist: all, all of them, were preachers, do-gooders, men of the pulpit rather than servants of the truth. What he writes about Aristotle is characteristic: 'Had Aristotle held to the course he in part [of his nature studies] so admirably followed, we would have had a scientific sociology in his early day. Why did he not do so? There may have been many reasons; but chief among them, probably, was that eagerness for premature practical applications which is ever obstructing the progress of science, along with a mania for preaching to people as to what they ought to do—an exceedingly bootless occupation—instead of finding out what they actually do. His *History of Animals* avoids those causes of error, and that perhaps is why it is far superior to the *Politics* from the scientific point of view' (§277). But Aristotle was a comparatively mild case: the ravages caused by the preaching mania are usually far worse. Pareto does not mince his words. He calls Rousseau's social contract a conception of 'utter inanity', and finds only one term sharp enough to characterise the Kantian categorical imperative—the term 'childish'! (§1503 and §1521).

Against the pseudo-scientific theories which have disgraced the past, Pareto pits his own ideal of a pure science which will serve the truth and only the truth. He demands that sociology should at long last become 'logico-experimental'. It should, first of all, become experimental, that is, experiential, factual, narrowly restricted to what is observable. It should, in other words, become as sharply divided from metaphysics as physics has been since Kepler and Galileo. And when the facts are elicited, described and docketed, they should be correlated and connected up by

---

[1] First published in 1916. English translation by A. Bongiorno and A. Livingston under the title *The Mind and Society* in 1935. Following established practice, our text refers to paragraphs, not pages.

purely logical methods, that is to say, by procedures which leave
as little room for error as the deductions and conclusions of the
logicians and the mathematicians whose chains of reasoning are,
and must be, beyond cavil. Only when these two basic conditions
are fulfilled will sociology cease to be what even Kant's social
speculations still were—'arbitrary assertions relating to altogether
fantastic things', a 'sort of metaphysical poetry' (§1521).

This ideal of a social science cleansed of prejudice must not
only be everybody's theoretical creed, but also everybody's practical pursuit. On this point there cannot be a moment's hesitation
nor yet a shade of disagreement. But if the desired end is to be
attained, the word prejudice must surely be taken in its widest
possible connotation. Now, prejudice has many forms, and Pareto
did not see them all. That is why he stumbled and fell. A science
of society can be spoiled in at least two ways: by letting a practical-
political, and by letting a philosophical, preoccupation turn you
from the truth; by preaching a certain social, and by preaching a
certain scientific ideal, instead of seeing the facts as they really are.
So far as the first pitfall was concerned, it is an understatement to
say that Pareto was aware of it. He was obsessed by it: he searched
for its manifestations with almost maniacal fervour. But, alas!, as
sharp-sighted as he was in one eye, so blind was he in the other.
What he really pursued was not a social science in agreement with
social facts, but a social science in agreement with physical, and
more especially mechanical, laws. He never stopped to think whether the ideal of a mechanistic sociology is not a contradiction in
terms, whether the differences between man and molecule are not
so great that it is impossible to compare them, let alone force them
into the same conceptual frame. Men *are* for him 'the molecules of
the social system' (§2080), power-points which push and pull until
a certain equilibrium is reached. Far from seeing reality as it is, he
saw it as it would have to be, if it was to fit into a preconceived
intellectual pattern, if it was to yield a mechanistic model and
interpretation. He may have fancied that he saw the facts, but in
fact he saw only fancies. His prejudice in favour of a scientific
ideal was bound to lead him as far away from the truth as the
prejudice of the others in favour of a social or human ideal. If
others propounded wish-determined instead of fact-determined
theorems, he also had his desire which determined him. 'My wish
is', he says before he even looks at the facts, 'to construct a system

of sociology on the model of celestial mechanics, physics [and] chemistry' (§20). And again: 'All the natural sciences to a greater or lesser extent are approximating the logico-experimental type. We intend to study sociology in just that fashion, trying, that is, to reduce it to the same type' (§68). Pareto's trouble was that he was trying too hard—trying by hook or by crook, as the saying goes—to reduce sociology to a kind of 'celestial mechanics, physics or chemistry'. It has been said of Spencer that his mind was like a magnet, picking out the iron which suited it, but leaving the other metals untouched. Pareto was just the same. Indeed, he was worse. For not only did he reject some evidence, but he falsified a large part of it so as to make it possible to manipulate it, to transmogrify society into a kind of mechanism. He who despised all metaphysics was an extreme metaphysician himself, basing himself, as he did, on the unproven and unprovable proposition that all reality is controlled by the same laws, and that these laws are the laws of rational mechanics. In view of this conviction, it meant little or nothing if he at times admitted that social facts are more complicated than physical and even economic ones (§2079), for this is only another way of saying that they are essentially the same.

The heartpiece of Pareto's *Trattato* is in paragraphs 2060–2104, which deal with 'the elements that serve to constitute society' and 'the state of equilibrium'. All that goes before leads up to them; all that follows is meant to make them secure. Basically, Pareto tells us, a social system is a system of interdependent elements. For a single moment, he seems to approach the organismic position: 'Something of the sort [of interdependence] is observable in animal organisms. The form of the organs determines the kind of life that the animal leads, but that manner of living in its turn has its influence upon the organs' (§2061). A little reflection will prove that this is not really organicism. For organicism, in the sense of holism, thinks, not in terms of parts, however interdependent, but in terms of totality; not in terms of organs, but of organisms. Apart from that, the very next lines show clearly that Pareto models his sociology, not on biology and physiology, but on mechanics and mathematics. 'In order thoroughly to grasp the form of a society in its every detail,' he writes, 'it would be necessary first to know what all the very numerous elements are, and then to know how they function—*and that in quantitative terms*.[1]

[1] Our emphasis.

It would, that is, be necessary to assign indices to the various elements and their effects . . . and they, being quantitatively considered, would be stated in the form of mathematical equations. The number of equations would have to be equal to the number of unknowns and would determine them exhaustively' (§2062). Pareto, who is nothing if not honest, immediately admits that we have no hope of finding the figures which we need; indeed, that we are very hard put to it if we want even to identify the elements involved; yet he insists all the same that, in principle, his approach is justified. But does his formulation really refer to a *social* system? Surely not. It is an *abstract* statement of the *general* conditions that determine *any* equilibrium. As such, it is no doubt correct. But how are we to get from this *abstractum* (as empty in itself as any mathematical formula) to the *concretum* of social life—any given social life—if we have no hope of determining the numerical indices which alone can put flesh on the dry bones? And is the difficulty of finding the figures merely a technical difficulty? Is it not likely, is it not at least possible, that our inability to give a quantitative description of the social system *in terminis* is due to the fact that it is not quantitative, not quantitatively determined?

However that may be, it becomes increasingly clear, as we read on, that Pareto does not talk about society at all, that he talks all the time of equilibrium in general. Take the following sentences: 'The real state . . . of the system is determined by its conditions. Let us imagine that some modification in its form is induced artificially. At once a reaction will take place, tending to restore the changing form to its original state as modified by normal change' (§2067). Clearly, a mechanical system will react in this way. If I have before me a pair of scales in balance and I touch one of the sides, the disturbance so created will after some swinging up and down give way again to the determined stable state. And if I change the weights in a more permanent way, a new equilibrium position will tend to come about and we shall have successive determined equilibrium positions of the scales. But do societies behave analogously? Have they, too, an inherent tendency to equilibration? Pareto does not prove it. He simply assumes that they do, that they must. Are the human forces that meet in a social system really quantitative after the fashion of physical energies? Pareto does not prove it. He simply assumes that they are. Here, where he reveals his central conceptions, Pareto speaks with the voice, not of the sociologist, but of the mechanician. In his early years, he had been an engineer, a bridge builder. He remained, in substance, the same sort of man when, later in life, he changed over to the social sciences.

But, of course, he tries to be a sociologist as well as a mechanician, and that must mean that he has to find human analogues, real or imagined, to the determinants of mechanical equilibrium. The job is by no means easy. For personal, as opposed to impersonal forces, appear to have at least two characteristics which would seem to put comparison altogether out of the question: it looks as if they were underlaid by freedom; and it looks, too, as if they were different from age to age, qualitatively different, and not merely different according to number, weight and measure. Pareto, with his sharp eye, saw that here lay his problem, that he had to argue these differences away if his mechanistic sociology was to be more than 'a sort of metaphysical poetry'. He had, in other words, to show that things are not what they seem, that underneath apparent freedom there lurks real determination, and underneath apparent history an abiding pattern, a congeries of forces that do not change.

This task is tackled in the two thousand or so paragraphs which precede the analysis of 'the state of equilibrium'. They occupy three vast volumes in the English edition, volumes brim-full of profound learning and profounder thought, but for all that no more than a prolonged effort at special pleading.

Pareto tries to achieve his purpose by making certain incisive and decisive distinctions. The first is that between logical and non-logical actions. Logical actions are rational actions. They have an aim which can be realised in the world as we know it; this aim is clearly envisaged; and the means chosen to secure fulfilment are appropriate. Non-logical actions, on the other hand, are irrational actions. They may have an aim which cannot be realised within the framework of space and time; or, if they have an aim which it is possible to realise, it may not be clearly envisaged; or, finally, the means chosen to secure fulfilment may be inappropriate. The mariners of ancient Greece knew two means of navigation: rowing with oars and making sacrifices to Poseidon. In so far as they rowed with oars, they acted logically; in so far as they made sacrifices to Poseidon, they acted non-logically. Subjectively, they may have seen their two methods as equivalent. Objectively, they were contrasting and, properly considered, mutually exclusive.

Logical action is characteristic of technology, science, and, to some extent, of economic life. In other fields, action is predominantly, not to say exclusively, non-logical. Anything that we do out of an inherited drive or in accordance with traditional custom is non-logical, and as these two incentives (instinct and habit) are the main determinants of our conduct, by far the greater part of our behaviour is irrationally caused and permeated by irrationality—by sentiment, as Pareto very often puts it, using a word which clearly contrasts with rationality, reason and logic.

It was, above all, this conception of the springs of human action which put Pareto into contrast to the earlier protagonists of mechanicism, such as Immanuel Kant. For Kant, man was a rational animal: irrationality was no more than an impurity, a thing of the past, and not necessarily a fact of the future. (For this reason he could think in normative terms.) For Pareto, man was an animal pure and simple, with only the slightest fringe of rationality to his nature. And irrationality was for him an abiding trait of man that would dominate all ages to come as it had dominated all ages before. (For this reason, any normative conception was out of the question for him; everything was as it had to be—the basic thought of positivism.) Pareto was inclined to believe that nothing connected him with a man such as Kant, but he was wrong. Both were rationalists, though rationalists with a difference. Kant was the hopeful rationalist of the rosy dawn of the capitalist (technological and economic) age; Pareto was the disappointed rationalist of the glaring noon. Both hankered after a world dominated by reason. The philosopher of the eighteenth century thought it was coming; the scientist of the twentieth knew that it was not. It was because Kant and Pareto were, in the depths, agreed, that both were led to a mechanistic conception of social life.

This comparison of the two great mechanicists may be something of an aside here, though it is an important one. What matters more in our argument at this juncture is the use to which Pareto puts his distinction of logical and non-logical conduct. Logical conduct may be something of a rarity, but in so far as it exists, it shows an area of human reality where all is determination and all is permanence. Taking pots and pans by the shortest route from the potter's shed to the market square is a typical piece of logical conduct. There can be no two ways of doing it, since only one line can be the shortest between two points; and there can be no historical variation either, because the shortest line is always the shortest line. Hence, where logical action is concerned, we can have excactly the same type of theoretical analysis as in mechanics and mathematics. A sociology dealing with it will be capable of making statements as objectively and eternally true as the proposition that twice two is four—and this is the reason why Pareto defines it and describes it with so much care.

Non-logical action appears to offer a far more knotty problem. For here all seems to be caprice, and everything different from age to age. The Romans adored Jupiter; we adore Science. The Romans gambled on auguries; we gamble on football pools. When we cross the dividing line between rational and irrational conduct, we seem to lose the solid ground under our feet. Can there be a science of what is indeterminate and ephemeral? Assuredly not, if by science we mean mechanics and mathematics. But, then, things are, in principle, if we are to believe Pareto, not really unpredictable and time-bound even here—they only look as if they were. Pareto claims that even this area of human reality will, properly analysed, yield us facts—determinate, determined, and timeless facts—which can be made the raw material of a proper science, and he proceeds again by his quasi-scholastic method, i.e. by making a radical distinction.

This second distinction, more daring than the first into logical and non-logical conduct, and more basic to Pareto's system than the other, is that between 'residues' and 'derivations'. A residue is what ordinary people would call a drive; a derivation is what, by an almost equally popular term, is often described as an ideology. If we take any socially relevant action, Pareto claims, we can split it into two parts, the action itself, the deed done, and the explanation of it which is its frequent accompaniment. The action itself, the deed done, is for Pareto, a typical materialist and hence a metaphysician *malgré soi*, something physical, and that in a double sense of the word. It is physical in that it comes out of our physis and manifests its drive-structure, its inherent tendencies; and it is physical in that it is observable in the physical world and works a change in it, in that it is kinetic, a force acting in a field of forces, no different really from the pushes and pulls studied by celestial and terrestrial mechanics. This action, this system of actions, is what the social scientist has to study and to understand. It is what mainly matters; it is the stuff, as it were, of social reality. Compared with it, the verbal aura with which we like to surround our actions is unimportant. It is secondary, it is mainly, nay, merely, embellishment. We are animals with a fringe of reason to our nature. As animals, we conduct ourselves in accordance with our physical propensities (the residues); as animals with a fringe of reason to our nature, we like to add a kind of explanation or justification (a derivation) to our actions. In our pride, we like to think that our mind controls our conduct; but this, Pareto maintains, is not so. We act first, and invent a 'reason' for our action afterwards. The word reason as here used must be put into inverted commas. For non-logical action, being by definition irrational, being based on sentiment, has no real reasons; it has only pseudo-reasons, and these we call derivations (or ideologies).

It is immediately clear why Pareto draws this whole distinction. He draws it in order to be able to develop a mechanistic theory of social life. If mind is only marginal in men, if men's behaviour is a manifestation of the mechanical forces inherent in them, if the intellect and the conscious will intervene only *post festum*, then we can have a mechanics of human interaction as we can have a mechanics of the high heavens where the sidereal bodies interact and strive for an equilibrium. By his (superficially) clever disjunction of residues and derivations, Pareto has thrown both freedom and history out of doors. Men can talk as they like, but not act as they like; men talk differently in different periods, but their mode of action is always in essence the same. And even if it changes, it changes simply because the subconscious, one could almost say sub-human, drive-structure changes (for instance through race-mixture and such-like physical events). It does not change because men would assert their freedom and steer history into new channels. They have very little freedom to assert; they cannot direct history, but are directed by nature. All these conceptions are manifestly unproven and unprovable metaphysical assertions, and they are none the more convincing for being labelled scientific.

Pareto cannot even expose his distinction between residues and derivations—the residues which remain when the verbal veil of outward actions is ripped off, and the derivations which, drawn from them, are wrapped round them—without betraying his ulterior motive—to get rid of freedom and history. Listen, for instance, to the following quotations. Theorizing, writing books, is regularly part and parcel of non-logical conduct. Now, 'theories in the concrete may be divided into at least two elements, one of which is much more stable than the other. We say, accordingly, that in concrete theories . . . there are . . . two principal elements (or parts); a substantial element (part), which we shall designate as a, and a contingent element (part), on the whole fairly variable, which we shall designate as b . . . The element a corresponds, we may guess, to certain instincts of man, or more exactly, men . . . and it is probably because of its correspondence to instincts that it is virtually constant in social phenomena. The element b represents the work of the mind in accounting for a. That is why b is much more variable, as reflecting the play of the imagination' (§798 and §850). A remains unchanged throughout history and therefore can yield statements as absolutely true as $2 \times 2 = 4$; b does not remain unchanged and would make a mechanistic-mathematical doctrine of man and society impossible, *if it were* important. But it is *not* important. 'Derivations . . . figure only as manifestations, as indications, of other forces that are the forces which really determine the social equilibrium.' They are merely the signposts which show where a certain push is aiming, not the energy which exerts the push. Nothing could be more misleading, we are assured, than to 'ascribe an intrinsic value to derivations and regard them as functioning directly as determinants of the social equilibrium' (§1403). Hence a is reality; a alone is reality; b is not. Pareto's argument has reached port.

Pareto, needless to mention, presents these considerations in as scientific a form as he can, but actually his argument reminds one of rather loose popular talk which is often heard. 'Human nature is always the same', people will say, 'human nature is the same the wide world over', etc. In statements of this kind, there is a basic ambiguity. Human nature can either mean the physical nature of man, his body and all that goes with it, and then the assertions concerned are very largely right; or it can mean the customary and habitual mode of human action, different from age to age and from country to country, and then they are very largely wrong. In Pareto there is no ambiguity, but that only makes his theory less realistic than even this popular talk. He simply does not allow for a mode of human action which is based on custom and habit. He sees only half of the facts, the half that suits him. The rest is defined out of existence. *Sic volo, sic jubeo.*

Pareto distinguishes six residues: the instinct for combinations, the tendency to combine and build up things, to create empires, for instance (class I); group persistences, the tendency to keep aggregates, once formed, in existence (class II); the need of expressing sentiments by external acts (class III); residues connected with sociality, e.g. the tendency towards enforcing social uniformity (class IV); integrity of the individual and his appurtenances, i.e. the individual's self-defence in the widest sense (class V); and sex (class VI). His volume II, where all this is discussed, is most impressive in size, and even his detractors have to admire his learning. But does he really distinguish six residues or quasi-instincts? Surely not. If sex is set aside, there are in point of fact only two. Classes I and III belong together: they represent the forces making for activity, for change. In the same way, classes II, IV and V belong together: they represent the forces making for stability, for resistance to change. Even this part of Pareto's analysis is really and basically an imitation of mechanics: classes I and III comprise the centrifugal, classes II, IV and V the centripetal tendencies in the social system. Sometimes the aping of mechanics becomes quite obvious. Thus Pareto writes at the beginning of the section dealing with group persistences: 'After the group has been constituted, an instinct very often comes into play that tends with varying energy to prevent the things so combined from being disjoined, and which, if disintegration cannot be avoided, strives to dissemble it by preserving the outer physiognomy of the aggregate. This instinct may be compared roughly to mechanical inertia: it tends to resist the movement imparted by other instincts' (§992). It is true that the social universe, like the physical, shows both tendencies towards change and tendencies towards stability, but this is very little out of which to make a system of sociology.

Still, this is not the worst. The worst is that 'residue' is, critically considered, no more than a label affixed to an action after it has been done. Does a man see a house on fire and run away from it? Residue number V; does he act in the opposite way and enter the house to save somebody or something? Residue number IV. Even in the latter case, there is no free decision to help, to fight down fear, to overcome animal instinct—oh no, for this would destroy Pareto's precious theory. Everything is due to different inborn quasi-instincts. Indeed if the house is the man's own house, both his flight and his bravery appear in Pareto's system as effects of the same quasi-instinct, residue number V; if the man runs away, he wants to preserve himself; if he does not, he wants to preserve his things ('appurtenances'). The one drive is here ascribed to two different, even opposite, manifestations. And this happens often. Does a man read naughty books? Residue number VI. Does he call for suppression of pornographic literature? Again residue number VI, says Pareto (cf. §1331). He might just as well tell us that there is no difference between +a and —a! Clearly, anything and everything can be done with such conceptions. The so-called residues are in reality no more than words, and this is why they can be so easily manipulated. They belong to the same class of fictitious entity as the many 'instincts' which psychologists at one time (now happily long past) invented—including a supposed instinct for cleanliness which even the man in the street knows to be conspicuously absent in little boys.

But Pareto is happy to have his residues, for now he can define his 'social equilibrium'. 'The sentiments or instincts that correspond to residues, along with those corresponding to appetites, interests, etc., are the main factors in determining the social equilibrium. . . . Speaking in general terms, suppose a society is being influenced by certain sentiments corresponding to the residue groups A, B, C . . . manifested through the derivations a, b, c . . . Now let us give each of those groups of residues a quantitative index corresponding to the intensity of its action as a group. So we get the indices a, β, γ . . . Let us further designate as S, T, U . . . the derivations, myths, theories, and so forth, that correspond to the residue groups, A, B, C . . . The social system will then be in equilibrium under the action of the forces a, β, γ . . . which are exerted approximately in the direction indicated by the derivations S, T, U . . . due account being taken of counter-forces' (§875 and §2087). Let anyone ask himself, how much these sentences tell him about social reality. If he is at all honest, his answer must be: nothing whatsoever. Pareto, always aggressive and supercilious, says of many other writers that their theories are 'pure verbiage', but his own empty cleverness deserves this epithet and label as much as their disquisitions do—or more. This is a case where one must say with the old proverb that he who lives in a glass-house should not throw stones.

However, let us be charitable and formulate our criticism in a more restrained way. What Pareto has done is, surely, this: he has taken reality and drained out of it human freedom and historical variability and thus gained a model which is amenable to treatment in mechanistic terms. The trouble is that this model bears no longer any recognisable likeness to social life as we all know it. In social life, as we know it, man is indeed activated by certain inborn drives, for instance, sex, as Pareto says, but these drives come up against culturally created, not naturally existing, norms which make up a system of social control and mould human activity until it is altogether different from animal (or molecular) motion. Sociology is less concerned with the instinct of sex than with the institution of marriage; and the institution of marriage *regulates* sex, disciplines it, controls it, and is thus part and parcel of the system of social control. This system of social control, secured by pressures and internalised by education, is something man (as creator of culture) has added on to, and superimposed on, man (as part of nature), and as it is the product of personal, and not of impersonal or physical forces, it is characterised by great plasticity. Different ages have carried on different experiments in living together, and we are free to try yet others today or tomorrow or at any time we like: and because this is so, neither freedom nor history can be disregarded by the student of man and society. They are not only real, but essential to human reality. What should we say of a physiologist who could talk of man as if he were a dead mechanism rather than a living organism? Yet this is precisely what Pareto does. He talks of man as if he were a molecule, and of society as if it were a parallelogram of dead forces and not a communion of living personalities. The price he has paid for his mechanistic model—his mechanical toy —is too great.

But the free variability of social life, observable in history, is not only a fact which can be held, from the outside as it were, against Pareto's mechanicism: it is a fact which asserts itself even inside it, so to speak. Great cataclysms like the French Revolution are simply there and cannot be disregarded. Pareto has to accommodate them within his scheme. But this is next to impossible, for he has denied the main causes of revolutionary change. Widening his concept of the social equilibrium, discussing what he calls 'the general form of society', Pareto finds that the following factors make a society what it is: its physical environment; its economics; its derivations; and its residues. There is nothing here that could explain a sudden upset: the physical environment is practically constant; the economic element is no less so: it is dominated and determined by the desire to maximise satisfactions, to achieve the greatest possible output from the smallest possible input, and this is an absolutely unchangeable endeavour on the part of economic man. Indeed, Pareto's economics is entirely what the Historical School called 'perpetualist' and 'universalist'. Economists have often discussed 'Pareto's law' developed in his *Cours d'Economie Politique* (1896/7). This so-called 'law' (it is, of course, nothing of the kind)[1] suggests that income distribution is by and large the same in all societies. Not only have everywhere few people high incomes and many people low incomes, but even the proportions involved are practically constant; in other words, the shape of the income pyramid, the degree of inequality, is permanent—a palpably untrue proposition. How great is the difference in this respect between the Britain of 1950 and the Britain of 1935—how much greater the degree of equality in the former year than in the latter! But Pareto does not see variability in economic life, and so he cannot use it for the explanation of social change. The derivations on their part do change, yet, as we have seen, they cannot explain anything. They are powerless, indicators of real forces, but not real forces themselves. So we arrive at the residues. These are indeed real; these are in truth the principal factors in the social equilibrium; but when it comes to the explanation of social change, they, too, fail us. For residues (i.e. inborn instincts) change extremely slowly, if they change at all, and therefore it would seem that they make for an abiding, not an evolving or revolving social pattern, that a dramatic event such as the French Revolution cannot possibly be explained with their help.

As the reader can see, Pareto has succeeded all too well in his attempt to abolish history. He is obliged to bring it in again after he has thrown it out. Elementary necessity forces him to account somehow for change within a theoretical framework which, being mechanistic, cannot really accommodate it. The solution which he offers is certainly ingenious, but it is altogether artificial. All it proves is that he cannot think in terms of history at all.

[1] For a brief discussion, cf. Erich Roll, *A History of Economic Thought*, ed. 1950, pp. 413 and 414.

Pareto's theory of change is known as 'the circulation of élites'. What a society is like, depends not on its people at large so much as on its governing class. If all those whom nature has fitted for domination showed the same basic drives, revolutions would not occur. But, as we have seen, drives—residues—are of two kinds. There is the kind described as class I (*plus* III), and there is the kind described as class II (*plus* IV and V). The former produces a type of man who is best characterised as a schemer. He lives by his wits; he plots and plans and chops and changes. The latter produces a type of man who is deeply conservative. He will live by brawn rather than brain, always ready to oppose innovation by force. If the governing group were composed of both class I and class II men, all would be well. But every governing group tends to close its gates to people who are evidently not their own kind. Thus there is apt to spring up a contrast, and in due course a conflict, between the 'governing' and the 'non-governing' élite. And this situation manifestly carries in it the seeds of revolution.

'Suppose a certain country has a governing class, A, that assimilates the best elements, as regards intelligence, in the whole population', Pareto writes. 'In that case the subject class, B, is largely stripped of such elements and can have little or no hope of ever overcoming the class A so long as it is a battle of wits. If intelligence were to be combined with force, the dominion of the A's would be perpetual . . . But . . . in the majority of cases people who rely on their wits are or become less fitted to use violence, and *vice versa*. So concentration in the class A of the individuals most adept at chicanery [class I men] leads to a concentration in class B of the individuals most adept at violence [class II men]; and if that process is long continued, the equilibrium tends to become unstable, because the A's are long in cunning but short in the courage to use force and in the force itself; whereas the B's have the force and the courage to use it, but are short in the skill required for exploiting those advantages. But if they chance to find leaders who have the skill—and history shows that such leadership is usually supplied by dissatisfied A's—they have all they need for driving the A's from power' (§2190). A revolution then ensues. And a revolution can, of course, also happen if the B's are in power and the A's are not. The mechanism of change will, in principle, be the same.

This, in briefest outline, is Pareto's explanation of sudden change in social life. What takes place is that the ins become the outs, and the outs become the ins. One could describe this as the see-saw theory of history. When the one side goes up, the other goes down, and *vice versa*. But if we spoke of a see-saw theory of *history*, we should be using a misnomer. For there is no real history here, no real development, there is only a rearrangement of pre-existing elements. A see-saw is the same kind of mechanism as a pair of scales. There can be a new adjustment of the scales or sides to each other; there can be change *inside* the system we call a pair of scales or a see-saw; but there can be no change *of* the systems so described. They are dead, not alive; they are static, not dynamic. They are, properly considered, not inside time at all, in so far as time implies change, as it must when the term is used in a historical (or even a biological) context.

It is not too much to say that Pareto's change is no change at all, but really repetition. His model of history is not one whit more realistic than his model of society. What happens in history is not that ins become outs and outs become ins, but that entirely new classes appear on the scene who initiate new experiments in social living. There is no circulation, but forward movement. There is no jumping from equilibrium position to equilibrium position, but constant flow and constant birth.

A mind like Pareto's, caught in the coils of mechanicism, cannot see this. The utmost it can achieve (and the utmost that Pareto did achieve) is to envisage change on the model of the movements of the figures on the chess-board. These figures can shift in relation to each other, and therefore a new look can come over the game. But underneath all remains as before. Nothing substantially new can enter in. Above all, the rules of the game remain unaltered. But this is not so in society. When evolutions and revolutions take place, there is not only a readjustment of positions, but also a redrafting of the rules. Every new society is, if we may so express it, a new kind of game.

Compared to Spencer's organicism, Pareto's mechanicism may, on the surface, appear more rational. In truth, however, the choice between them is that between Tweedledum and Tweedledee. One pair of distorting spectacles is no better, though perhaps no worse, than any other. What we need is to see straight.

X

MECHANICISM
Secondary Forms

I⊤ HAS been our endeavour to show that organicism has produced, not only some primary, but also some secondary manifestations, that is to say, theories which, without being—like
organicism proper—elaborations of the body-metaphor, yet belong within the same ambit of thought. We must now attempt to
do the same for mechanicism, and we shall again begin by looking
at a rather peripheral phenomenon, utilitarianism. Bentham's
relation to the mechanistic tradition is perhaps no more obvious
than Marx's to the organical; yet it is at the same time no less real.

In his *Essay on Political Tactics*, Bentham appears to condemn
all metaphorical language in the social sciences. His words are
so striking that they would almost deserve to stand as a motto
to this book: 'The imaginations of writers have been stretched to
give to political bodies the properties of different kinds of bodies.
Sometimes they are mechanical bodies; and then it is a question of
levers and springs, of wheelwork, of shocks, of friction, of
balancing, of preponderance. Sometimes they are animated bodies;
and then they have borrowed all the language of physiology: they
speak of health, of sickness, of vigour, of imbecility, of corrup-
tion, of dissolution, of sleep, of death and resurrection'. Such
'figurative language . . . is mischievous', Bentham writes. 'It
accustoms us to reason upon the most false analogies and gathers
round the truth a mist which the most enlightened minds are
scarcely able to penetrate.'[1]

[1] Cf. Stark, *Jeremy Bentham's Economic Writings*, vol. I, 1952, pp. 96/97.

These are golden words. But Bentham, unfortunately, does not keep the scales even. He condemns organicism, but he is far from condemning mechanicism, though he appears to avoid its metaphors. He defines, in the very same context, a body politic as 'an assembly or collection of individuals, inasmuch as they are found united together in order to perform a common act,' and this definition is pure nominalism. Indeed, in the next lines, he approaches very closely to the concept of *contrat social*: 'That which constitutes a political body, is the concurrence of many members in the same act. It is therefore clear that the act of an assembly can only be a declarative act—an act announcing an opinion or a will. Every act of an assembly must begin by being that of a single individual: but every declarative act, the expression of an opinion or of a will . . . may finish by being that of a body. "This", says Titius, "is what passes in my mind." "This is precisely what has passed in mine", may Sempronius equally say. It is, therefore, the power of agreeing in the same intellectual act which constitutes the principle of unity in a body.'[1]

In view of this attitude, it is hardly surprising that Bentham at times forgets his own warnings and slips into the language of mechanicism after all. 'Whatsoever . . . be the aggregate mass of the matter of good existing in the community in question,' he writes on June 9, 1816, 'it is the interest . . . of each member of the community . . . to have the whole of it. But . . . no one of them will ever find it in his power to give effect to this his abstract self-regarding interest. Each man's abstract interest finds in . . . the abstract interests of all the others so many counteracting interests . . . Thus it is that in urging him to the use, enjoyment and preservation with relation to what he has been accustomed to use, or to expect to have it in his power to use, as his own, the interest of each man performs the function of the mainspring of a watch: while in his endeavours to extend his occupation beyond the limits of his own property, he finds himself counteracted by as many conflicting interests as there are [men] in the community, performing, each of them, within its own field or sphere, the office of a regulator in that ingenious piece of mechanism.'[2]

---

[1] *Loc. cit.*, pp. 95/96.

[2] This passage, taken from the 'Political Deontology' papers, is not yet published. Cf. sheets 17 and 18 in box XV of the collection of Bentham manuscripts in University College, London.

But the mechanistic conception of society is far more to Bentham than an occasional embellishment of his books: it constitutes the very basis of his programme of social reform. He was deeply impressed by the fact that a penny or a pound means far more to a poor man than to a rich, and concluded from this that the ideal system of distribution would be strictly egalitarian. Egalitarianism, however, has a mortal weakness: it kills incentive. Only where a man can reap the reward of his efforts, only where his efforts can raise him above the common level, will there be a flourishing production—will there be anything to distribute. Therefore we must not insist on the maximisation of equality, for all its abstract excellence. But if we cannot maximise equality, we can at least minimise inequality and inhibit the tendencies towards it. This is what we should do. Bentham's over-all social programme was the gentle reduction of the rich, and the gradual raising of the poor, to the middling level. The first he wanted to achieve by the egalitarian treatment of inheritances: equal per capita distribution among all the children, which would mean the breaking up of accumulated masses of wealth. The second he endeavoured to bring about by the stimulation of savings, a subject to which he devoted his best thought. Thus his final aim coincided—not in the detail, of course, but in its outline—with that of Rousseau: a society of petty producers in which everybody could rise in the social scale, but only in accordance with his merit, and only within the framework of his life. The children were, in all regular cases, to return to a lower level, to start more or less where everybody else was starting. Such a society would be largely egalitarian as well as libertarian, and it would constantly renew that equality —that equilibrium of individual forces—which liberty was constantly tending to destroy. As can be seen, Bentham was in the last analysis as much of a normative mechanicist as Marx was a normative organicist.

Drawing nearer now to the main-stream of mechanistic thought, we propose to look first at an attempt to model the science of society on a special kind of mechanics, the mechanics of the heavenly bodies, *vulgo* astronomy. Henry Charles Carey pursued this possibility with much vigour (though with little common sense) in his *Principles of Social Science* (3 volumes, 1858–1859).

Like other protagonists of this point of view, Carey tells us that man is 'the molecule of society'. But, unlike others, he is inclined to emphasize the gregarious nature of man, even calling man 'of all animals . . . the most gregarious', and to that extent he recalls Wilfred Trotter. Yet, characteristically, he does not allow the existence of a social instinct. Man is born 'destitute . . . of the instinct that in other animals takes the place of reason'. What then holds men together in society? The answer is: 'the law of molecular gravitation' (I, pp. 41, 42).

By itself, this phrase might be no more than a metaphorical way of expressing the fact of sociality, but in Carey unfortunately it is more, far, far more. All the corollaries of the physical principle of gravitation are assumed by him to apply to social 'gravitation' as well. 'Gravitation is here, as everywhere else in the material world, in the direct ratio of the mass, and in the inverse one of the distance', Carey assures us. 'The greater the number collected in a given space, the greater is the attractive force there exerted, as is seen to have been the case with the great cities of the ancient world, Niniveh and Babylon, Athens and Rome, and is now seen in regard to Paris and London, Vienna and Naples, Philadelphia, New York, and Boston' (pp. 42, 43). Gravitation thus creates foci of human aggregation, and these are the human homologues of the heavenly bodies. 'Why is it,' Carey asks (a very apposite question!), 'that all the members of the human family do not tend to come together on a single spot of earth? Because', he answers, 'of the existence of the same simple and universal law by means of which is maintained the beautiful order of the system of which our planet forms a part. We are surrounded by bodies of various sizes, and some of these are themselves provided with satellites, each having its local centre of attraction, by means of which its parts are held together. Were it possible that that attractive power could be annihilated, the rings of Saturn, the moons of our earth and of Jupiter, would crumble to pieces and fall inward upon the bodies they now attend, a mass of ruins . . . So it is throughout our world. Look where we may, we see local centres of attraction towards which men gravitate, some exercising less influence, and others more. London and Paris may be regarded as the rival suns of our system, each exercising a strong attractive force, and were it not for the existence of the counter-attraction of local centres like Vienna and Berlin, Florence and Naples, . . . Europe would present to view one great centralized system, the population of which was always tending towards those two cities . . .' (p. 43).

Here we have the outlines of Carey's astro-sociology or socio-astronomy. We see how deeply it has penetrated Carey's mind when we consider what he says about the family. He muses about the possible—nay, certain!—consequences of an attempt artificially to centralise America under a strong capital city. 'The effect would be the same as would be produced in the astronomical world by a similar course of operation. The local governments would fall to pieces, and all the atoms of which they had been composed, would tend at once towards the new centre of gravity that had been thus produced . . . Further, with the growth of centralization, there would be seen a diminution in the counteracting force by which families are held together, despite the attractions of the capital. Whatever tends to the establishment of decentralization, and to the production of local employment for time and talent, tends . . . to enable parents and children to remain in closer connection with each other . . . Whatever tends, on the contrary, to the dimunition of local employment, tends to . . . the breaking up of families' (pp. 43–45). If these sentences still sound sane, the following will perhaps show that they are not: 'The stronger the ties that bind together the members of the various families of which the community is composed, the more perfect will be their revolution on their own axes . . .' (p. 45). Carey's meaning is not very clear; presumably he means: the more self-contained will the families be (though even this interpretation makes the statement tautological). But whatever he means, his mode of expression alone is highly objectionable. To express social facts through astronomical language can lead only to darkness, never to light.

Still, it is not the language so much that one must condemn, obfuscating though it be; it is the thought in, or rather behind, it. If Carey were right, if in society, as in space, 'gravitation' were in inverse ratio to the distance, then a town would have to be more attractive to those near to it than to those far from it —London, for instance, more attractive to the people of Kent than to those of Westmorland. This is complete nonsense. Carey bases himself on one axiomatic conviction, namely that if a proposition is true in astronomy, it must be true in sociology also. The word 'must' is badly misused here. There is no such must. Carey is about as rational as an architect would be, if he tried to build a skyscraper on a piece of cardboard.

However, Carey uses the concept of distance not only in a physical, but also in a human sense. We are justified in saying that a farmer is (socially) distant from a lawyer, as we are in saying that London is (spatially) distant from New York, and Carey is not unaware of the fact that the former type of 'distance' is more interesting for the sociologist than the latter. The greater the human differences, the wider also the possibilities of social intercourse, 'which is but the act of exchanging ideas and services' (p. 198). In chapter VIII, 'On the Formation of Society', where this is discussed, the scientific jargon is almost innocuous: 'In the inorganic world [we find] the power of combination growing with the increase of differences . . . Place a thousand atoms of oxygen in a receiver, and they will remain motionless; but introduce a single atom of carbon, and excite their affinities for each other, and at once motion will be produced . . . Such being the case in regard to all other matter, it must be so in regard to those combinations in which man is concerned, indicated by the term society . . . So, in fact, it is—association increasing with the increase of differences, and diminishing with any diminution therein . . . Among purely agricultural communities, association scarcely exists; whereas it is found in a high degree where the farmer, the lawyer, the merchant, the carpenter, the blacksmith, the mason, the miller . . . and the maker of engines are constituting portions of the community' (p. 199).

Carey is here in sight of a sound and solid sociological insight, namely, that social coherence is different in societies with undeveloped and with developed division of labour—both quantitatively and qualitatively different. The neighbours in a primitive agricultural village live side by side, but have otherwise little to do with each other; each is turned in his work towards nature rather than towards his fellow-men. The inhabitants of a modern industrial and commercial country on the other hand have regular recourse to the market and must do so; each is turned towards his fellow-men as much or more as he is towards nature. Durkheim suggested that social integration in the former case might be called mechanical, in the latter organic, and that the drift of history was from the one to the other. Carey understood both this distinction and this drift. Indeed, in discussing development, he appears for a moment to abandon that addiction to astronomy, physics and chemistry which is otherwise so characteristic of his approach.

'Combination in the inorganic world takes place in accordance with fixed and immutable laws', he says. 'There, however, the bodies that combine have always, and in all places, the same power of combination—the atom of oxygen of the day of the Pharaohs having been precisely the same in composition as that of those of Lavoisier and Davy. With man, the case is different. Capable of progress, his faculties become developed . . . as his mind is stimulated into action by the habit of association with his fellow-man. With him, therefore, the power of combination is a growing one . . .' (pp. 199, 200). A hopeful development, this, in Carey's mind. But, alas! Hopes are no sooner raised than dashed.

A few more lines, and Carey is back in his strait-jacket. 'In the inorganic world, every act of combination is an act of motion . . . So it is in the social one . . . If it is true that there is but one system of laws for the government of all matter, then those which govern the movements of the various inorganic bodies should be the same with those by which is regulated the motion of society; and that such is the case can readily be shown' (p. 200). Now, 'to have motion, there must be heat, and the greater the latter, the more rapid will be the former'. In the physical universe, heat is engendered by friction. Consequently, the case must be the same in the social world. The 'particles' must rub together here, as they do there. The rubbing together of the human molecules, which produces warmth, light and forward movement, is the interchange of goods, services and ideas. The brisker this interchange, the greater the caloric and kinetic effects. 'In the material world, motion among the atoms of matter is a consequence of physical heat . . . In the moral world, motion is a consequence of social heat—motion . . . consisting in "an exchange of relations" resulting from the existence of those differences that develop social life. Motion is greatest in those communities in which agriculture, manufactures and commerce are happily combined . . . That such is the fact will be obvious to all who see how rapid is the spread of ideas in those countries in which agriculture, manufactures, and commerce are combined, compared with that observed in those which are purely agricultural . . . In the one there is great heat and corresponding motion, and the more motion, the greater is the force. In the other there is little heat, but little motion, and very little force' (pp. 90, 91 and 61).

This theory of progress is a natural and necessary implication of the whole astronomical and mechanistic approach to social life. Its essential submission is the assertion that development is due, not to human effort, but to the automatic effect of certain external circumstances or events. It comes about in the manner in which a flame is produced when a match is struck against the side of the box. Surely, there are few who would accept this theory of culture-growth as realistic. But then the whole idea of 'social heat' is no more than a downright absurdity.

Carey, as even his friends will have to admit, was a comparatively simple mind: only a simple mind could produce so naive a theory. The man whom we have to consider now was anything but simple: Georg Simmel. As we shall see in later chapters, Simmel was one of those who led sociology out of the impasse into which the age-old, never resolved, and never-to-be resolved, conflict between realism and nominalism had manoeuvred it. His insistence that society is neither a quasi-thing (like a body) nor yet a quasi-nothing (like a purely mental summing-up), but a system of *relations*, provided a sound starting-point for a better sociology. But there was another facet to Simmel's social theory: his formalism.[1] It was his considered opinion that sociology is concerned, not with social life in all its colour and variety, but only with its form: not with the picture as a whole, so to speak, but only with the outlines. This narrowing down of the science led Simmel into the rank of the nominalists—a by no means necessary development. There is a curious parallel and contrast between Simmel and Durkheim: both belonged to the centre party, the party which did not forget the unity of society in the diversity of its members, nor the diversity of its members in the unity of society. But both deviated from this middle line, Durkheim to the right, towards sociological realism, Simmel to the left, towards sociological nominalism. It is with the individualistic, nominalistic Simmel that we have to deal here.

Already on the first page of his *Soziologie* (1908) Simmel makes it sufficiently clear that he is, to say the least, an anti-organicist. Whence comes the curious tendency to regard societies as substantial wholes, he asks—as something which they obviously are not? And he answers: this false theory is essentially a 'continuation and reflection of the practical power which the masses have gained,

---

[1] On one of the roots of this formalistic theory, that in academic politics, cf. Stark, *The Sociology of Knowledge*, 1958, pp. 22, 23.

in the nineteenth century, *vis-à-vis* the interests of the individual'. Sociological realism is therefore a by-product of the class struggle, an ideology and not the truth. Contemptuously he calls the realistic definition of society a 'hypostatisation of a mere abstraction' (p. 11).

If this were no more than a criticism of, say, Spencer, it would be unexceptionable and welcome. But Simmel seems as little able to keep within the bounds of common sense as Spencer himself. Not satisfied with saying that a body social is not a unitary formation, he asserts that a body physical is not a unitary formation either. He tries to carry the war into the enemy's camp, but in doing so he badly overestimates his strength and gets beaten for his pains. Microscopy, he claims, has revealed that 'life in the proper sense of the word, fundamental life,' consists in 'innumerable processes which ply between the smallest elements of which the macroscopic ones [such as organs] are merely summations'[1] (p. 20). 'Only when the individual processes inside organisms, whose sum or texture constitutes life, were investigated, only when it was recognised that life consists merely in these special happenings in and between organs and cells, did the science of life gain firm ground under its feet' (p. 12). Does Simmel really try to tell us that physiologists nowadays do not, and need not, study wholes like liver and heart?

We have seen above (cf. p. 89) that, for a typical organicist like Radcliffe-Brown, the individual consists of two realities: his physical organism and his social role. For a typical nominalist like Simmel, there is yet a third reality: the personality. The matter becomes clearest in the context of a discussion of the relationship between the sexes. Powerful forces push man and woman towards each other, and their contrast, being a case of complementarity, helps rather than hinders their union. But even here no real unity is achieved: duality proves irreducible. 'It remains impossible for the ego truly and absolutely to apprehend the non-ego' (p. 86). The hard core of the self will not dissolve. No wonder that Simmel describes man in one passage as 'the immediate concrete *locus* of all historical reality' (p. 6), and in another as 'the atom of society', and speaks of 'elements which incessantly gain, lose and shift their equilibrium' (pp. 19,20).

But it is not in the direction of mechanics that Simmel is

[1] '*Zusammenfassungen*'.

pushing, it is in the direction of geometry. There is no doubt that he was to some extent—to a large extent—activated by the same sentiment as Pareto: the hatred of history. To get rid of variation and variability, he made sociology the study of social forms. Forms do not change, only contents do, and if content is disregarded, then there remains a subject for sociology (one can hardly say, a subject-matter) which admits of statements of quasi-mathematical validity. Now, the divorce of form and content is most radically carried out by geometry: geometry studies the triangle in the abstract, not concrete triangles of wood or iron, red or blue colour, thick or thin material. In the same way, Simmel thought, sociology should study the abstract group of three, the triad, not concrete ternary groups of husband, wife and child, or plaintiff, defendant and judge. What can we say about the group of three *in general*, that was the question which Simmel tried to answer. If Carey fancied himself as the Newton of sociology, Simmel, in so far as he was a formalist, wanted to be its Euclid.

There are many passages which allow us to see that Simmel is in fact modelling his sociology on geometry. Perhaps the clearest occurs on page 12. Only by abstracting from content and concentrating on form, we are told there, 'can we grasp, what in society is really "society", just as only geometry determines what in spatial things is really their spatiality. Sociology as the study of the social existence of humanity . . . is related to the other specialized sciences in the same way as geometry is to the physical and chemical sciences of matter: it investigates form, through which alone matter is made into observable bodies—form which, taken by itself, exists only in the abstract, just like the forms of sociation'. It is true that Simmel protests on the same page that he is not inclined to drive the analogy between sociology and geometry beyond the bounds of reason. But this protest loses much of its convincingness when we learn that he sees the main difference merely in geometry's smaller and sociology's greater measure of complication. For, as we have remarked once before, in our chapter on Pareto, to say that there is a distinction in degree between two sciences, is saying in effect that there is none in essence.

Where does all this formalism lead Simmel? It leads him to the conviction that the quality of a society depends upon—nay is, technically speaking, a function of—its quantity. He looks at several aspects of this assumed relationship, but one is particularly important. As we are self-centred and socialised beings at the same time, we do not bring our whole selves into the social nexus. How much of it do we, in fact, bring into it? This, Simmel tells us, depends on the numerical size of the society concerned: much, if the society is small, little, if it is large. He asserts 'that the wide circle favours individual freedom, and the narrower cuts it down'; 'that the larger group has fewer demands on us and cares less about the individual, and therefore hinders the full development even of perverted tendencies less, than the smaller' (pp. 725, 727). It is all a matter of numbers. It is not difficult to see that it is impossible even to discuss this suggestion without abandoning formalism. Who would say that a group of two business partners is ever as closely knit as a dyad of husband and wife? To give Simmel's supposed statistical correlation some semblance of truth, it is necessary to restrict it to the inclusive society. The medieval town of, say, 5000 souls was certainly more closely integrated than the modern town of some 500,000 or 5,000,000 inhabitants. To that extent there is something to Simmel's law. Yet it is utterly untrue that number is the only determinant involved here. One of Simmel's own examples proves him wrong. The Renaissance, he tells us, brought a strong upsurge of individualism and at the same time a widening of frontiers, a cosmopolitanism such as that expressed in Dante's phrase that the world is his fatherland as the sea is of fishes (pp. 731, 732). In fact, however, the upsurge of individualism in the Renaissance is correlated with a closing of social circles. Is it not the heyday of the city state?—the city state which had broken out of the totality of Christendom, not the city state embedded in it as the town of the thirteenth century had been. Florence meant more to Machiavelli (who died in 1527) than it had meant even to Savonarola (who had been executed in 1498). Dante, born in 1265, was, as Simmel ought to have remembered, a type of medievalism, not one of incipient modernity. His dream of the universal empire alone bears witness to this fact, if nothing else—a dream which Machiavelli, the aider and abetter of the power-hungry petty princeling, did not share. Thus the contraction of the social framework of life may, if the circumstances are favourable, lead to a rampant individualism. Since Simmel's day, the opposite has also happened: mass societies have, against his assertions, brought a dwindling of individual freedom. The Germans of 1936 had assuredly less privacy than their forefathers of 1786. Yet the population of Germany was far, far larger in the latter year than in the former. Nor is this merely an effect of totalitarianism which might be written off as an exception to the rule. Even in democratic countries we observe similar tendencies: radio, television, advertising, propaganda, and all the other forms of mass communication, have led to a formerly unheard-of lack of individuality in the average man which goes hand in hand with a rapidly increasing population. Simmel's belief that number is the cause and culture the effect is simply erroneous, a clear proof that his whole approach, his whole geometrical model, is inappropriate.

We have, in the foregoing pages, occasionally used the term 'atomism' and meant thereby a conception of society which sees it as essentially a multiplicity, i.e. a collection of man-atoms or animated monads. In this sense its import coincides to all intents and purposes with that of the more colloquial word 'individualism'. But there is another, more restricted and technical usage of the term with which historians of philosophy have often operated. In their mouths, the term 'atomism' describes a philosophical effort to penetrate to the ultimate building-stones of reality and to see reality as a whole in terms of these ultimate building stones, elements or atoms. A good deal of recent philosophical speculation has been of this kind. Casting about for some absolute bedrock of certainty, the members of an influential school have found it in our sense-perceptions, the reality of which we cannot possibly doubt. If I see a thing, I see it. What more can I want? As for more complex phenomena, these can conveniently be conceived as configurations of sense-perceptions. No objective reality need be ascribed to them: they can be defined as verbal summings-up of simple (and indubitably real) elements. Thus we have on the one hand the absolute reliability of the simple sense-perceptions, and on the other the mere conventionality of the words which describe more than simple sense-perceptions. There is, or rather there appears to be, no point at which uncertainty can enter the picture and begin to plague us: the spectre of metaphysics is exorcised for ever. It is not surprising that this philosophy has had a very wide appeal, in spite of the fact that it does not solve the enigmas of life, but merely defines them away: and it is not surprising that it should have found ardent disciples among sociologists. Perhaps the two most remarkable are George Lundberg, with his *Foundations of Sociology* (1939), and Stuart Dodd, with his *Dimensions of Society* (1942).

It cannot be our task here to discuss their system (in many respects a rather refined one) *in toto*. What we have to do is merely to show that it is a new—and higher—form of sociological nominalism—'higher' because it atomises not only society, but even man, in other words, because even man is not allowed to be an ultimate at which social analysis can be permitted to stop. This shows the whole radicalism of this nominalistic philosophy. 'Degrees, calories, ergs', writes Lundberg, 'are words *symbolizing sensory responses*.[1] "Man" is just another such word. . . . The *unit* "man" is *likewise* an "*effect produced*"—upon the sense organs of the perceiver. It is only when there is relative stability and uniformity in the sensory responses of numerous competent observers that we can postulate either his existence or his unitary nature with reference to the attendant situation to which we also respond' (p. 70).

If Lundberg is thus doubtful about the propriety of ascribing unitary character to man (whom, after all, we can see and touch), it is not surprising, indeed, it is only logical, that he should be more than doubtful about the propriety of ascribing unitary character to a group of 'plurel' (which we can neither see nor touch). 'Society' is to him, not an entity which nature or history have established, but only a portmanteau word which the observing mind has formed for purposes of speedy locution, a definitional trick, an artefact, a classificatory device. 'Group designations, like other classifications, are not to be regarded as inherent divisions given in nature', he writes. '*All* definition and classification is a way of responding to phenomena according to some criteria of similarity or difference or other aspect and . . . therefore . . . no classification has any intrinsically greater reality or existence than any other.' And he quotes with approval the statement of his comrade-in-arms, E. E. Eubank: 'Between the objects themselves there need not be, and frequently is not, the slightest degree of contact or even proximity. The basis of their being clustered in thought is that some point of similarity, real or supposed, leads the mind to include them in a common context' (pp. 340, 341).

[1] Lundberg's italics.

This means, if it means anything, that the concept 'the Italian people' has no more ground in life than the concept 'all those who have hare lips'. But it is easy to see that such an attitude makes a sound sociology from the very first moment utterly impossible. 'All those who have hare lips' appear as a group only in the records of the medical statistician, and of their case it can truly be said that 'the nature of the units is determined by the inventor of the measuring instrument' (p. 234). But the Italian people are one, not only because they share certain assignable characteristics on the basis of which the statistician can count them, but also because they co-operate with each other, exchange goods and services, elect a common parliament to rule them, fight shoulder to shoulder in a war, etc. etc. Thus it is not only the observing mind that connects them, but also continuing, and very real, life-processes, and as these life-processes lie in the centre of the sociologist's field of interest, Lundberg's approach is apt to blind him to what really matters. In other words, his nominalism is excessive and ought to be resisted and rejected.

While this philosophical tendency, and especially its un-restrained radicalism, gives Lundberg a personal and peculiar characteristic, a good deal of his book is simply a modernised version of that rather mechanical imitation of contemporary physics which we have already observed in Carey and Pareto. The following quotations show this with all desirable clarity: 'At the present time physicists find it convenient to explain physical phenomena mostly in terms of the hypothetical elements *electrons* and *protons*. The properties ascribed to these units are attraction and repulsion of their own kind. That is, electrons move towards protons and away from other electrons; protons move toward electrons and away from other protons. The magnitude of the attraction or the repulsion is some inverse function of the distances between the particles. The arrangement of the electrons and protons into various types of groups of different symmetrical relations to each other constitutes *matter*. . . . The social sciences are concerned with the behaviors of those electron-proton configurations called societal groups. . . . It is sometimes con-venient to use different words to designate behavior mechanisms of different systems or levels of electron-proton configuration. But certain basic concepts of motion, energy, and force are equally applicable to all behavior. . . . From the point of view we have adopted, any situation in which we choose to observe association or dissociation is regarded as a field of force. . . . Societal activities are fundamentally forms of energy transformation . . . ' (pp. 203, 204, 263, 231). When we read these sentences carefully, we soon see that the link which Lundberg has established between the science which he has really made his own, physics, and the science which he professes to serve, sociology, is the weakest of all possible links—a purely verbal one. We can, if we like, say both of electrons and protons *and* of human beings that they 'behave'. But the word 'behaviour' merely masks an abyss, or rather pretends to mask it, for it is all too obvious. Lundberg himself admits that the interaction of physical particles and the interaction of human beings are different in kind. 'Interaction among human beings', he frankly concedes, 'is recognized as being in at least one respect highly unique. It is unique in that it takes place by means of the mechanism of communication through symbolic behavior' (pp. 252/3; cf. also 177/8). This is tantamount to saying that electron-proton and human 'behavior' have as much in common as eels and heels when the latter word is pronounced, Cockney-fashion, without the initial h.

There are many other aspects of Lundberg's thought which show his enslavement to mechanistic modes of thought, for instance his comparison of society with a machine where he discusses the problems of social reform (cf. pp. 206, 207), but we cannot possibly scrutinize them all. The upshot is always the same. On reading his book and observing his intellectual alertness and acuteness, one cannot help regretting that he has taken sociology as his chosen field, and not physics or engineering where men of his mental type are much more at home.

XI

MECHANICISM
Extreme Forms

WHEN THE social historian looks back over the nineteenth century, he finds that few developments have made a deeper impression on the human mind than the discovery, study and large-scale utilisation of electricity. Not only did it, almost magically, transform everyday life, but it also seemed to promise new and more profound insights into the mysterious workings of the material universe. Was the energy which made the light-bulb glow not a revelation of all energy, vital as well as physical, and—daring thought!—mental as well as vital? True scientists did not, of course, go quite so far, but even they began to speculate with more vigour than ever before about the unity of nature. Michael Faraday, for instance, surmised that light, warmth and electricity were merely different forms of one and the same natural force, and, more boldly still, suggested that electricity and gravity were somehow connected, even though we are as yet unable to perceive the link. Experiments designed to identify that link misfired, yet Faraday retained the conviction that it existed, that there was unity in nature, or at least in the energy system of nature, its power economy. In view of these preoccupations of the scientists—Maxwell followed later on in his master's footsteps—it is not surprising that some 'sociologists' (one *must* use the word here in inverted commas) should have renewed the effort to squeeze social phenomena into the framework of physics and in particular to show that even they were best to be understood as manifestations of the force of which electricity was the archetype. Henry Charles Carey was once again in the forefront. Thirteen years after the completion of his *Principles of Social Science* —i.e. in 1872—he presented the world with another book which bore the highly characteristic title: *The Unity of Law; as exhibited in the Relations of Physical, Social, Mental and Moral Science.* Capping his own absurdity, he followed his astro-sociology by what one can only describe as an attempted electro-sociology.

There is no evidence that Carey abandoned any of his fundamental convictions between writing the *Principles of Social Science* and writing *The Unity of Law*; indeed, chapter III of the later book ('Of Man—the Subject of Social Science') is for several pages a literal repetition of the corresponding sections of the earlier work. But his approach has become more taut and technically 'scientific'. From being a comparatively moderate mechanicist, advancing age had made him an extreme and reckless one.

As befits a would-be nineteenth-century physicist, Carey takes the law of the conservation of energy as his point of departure as well as his point of constant return. What others only surmised and thought possible, he regards as proven, namely that this law is the key to all phenomena encountered in reality, be they physical or mental, vital or social: 'But recently discovered, it seems now to have become the crown of the edifice of that great system of law by means of which harmony is secured throughout the whole range of matter, from coral insects which build up islands destined to form the nuclei of continents, to the innumerable suns with their attendant planets, of which the universe is composed.' Man, situated half-way between the smallest insects and the vastest suns, must obey, in all he is and in all he does, the same principles as they do: for what else is he but matter vitalised and become conscious? There cannot be two sciences; there can only be one: 'the idea of an unity of law' is 'the necessary complement . . . of that great idea . . . so universally accepted, that of unity of force' (pp. 122 and V).

The sociologist, like the physicist, must therefore ask himself: what is force? And the sociologist, along with the physicist, must recognise that it is, in whatever form we encounter it, a primal energy of which electricity is the archetype. 'Heat, light, . . . magnetism, and chemical affinity . . . the new philosophy resolves all these subtle agencies into modes of motion, asserting that they are all capable of mutual conversion,' indeed, 'that they are one and the same force'. The consequences of this fact for sociology are tremendous. If it is to remain abreast of scientific developments, it must cease to think in terms of gravitation and learn to think in terms of electricity: 'The identity and convertibility of these subtlest of forces have abundantly justified the analogies which had thus far been assumed between the heat and motion of matter and the forces of societary life, but the choice of electricity as the preferable analogue would give us now a greatly larger and happier application of the correspondence' (pp. 116, 117).

What is it that happens when man meets man, when Robinson Crusoe meets, for the first time, Friday? 'Let him have a companion', Carey answers, 'and at once ... the opposing electric states of consumers and producers, givers and receivers, teachers and learners, having been induced, as air awakens the quiescent lungs, and as light kindles and informs the eye, the real man [is] then coming into existence' (p. 126). The real man is social man; but sociality is electricity; and so it is that humanity, even in its highest and finest manifestations, springs from the basic force of all that exists, the very mainspring of reality.

Once again, Carey compares the rubbing along of men in society to the rubbing together of hard objects, but this time it is all interpreted in the vein of electro-mechanics. 'Rubbing and rubbed bodies require opposite electricities, the contact and interaction requiring the sort of co-relation which subsists between an acid and an alkali. That contact is combination, not mere aggregation—distinctive individuality being here, as in every department of societary life, the condition of perfect association. Substances assume vitreous or resinous electricity in adjustment to the conditions or capacities acting or acted upon. Woollen cloth is strongly vitreous with zinc, but with gold or iron it is resinous. Such mutations occur in all electric bodies, varying in their intensities, also, under the influence of diversely related substances. Here again do we find a beautiful correspondence with the law of societary association—an infinitely varying adaptation to, and influence upon, the infinitely varied individualities required for giving rapidity to the societary circulation' (pp. 118, 119).

From this interpretation of association between individual and individual, Carey advances with giant's steps to an equally electro-technical interpretation of the social system as a whole: 'The production of electricity, or its excitation for use, requires order and

relations that are full of suggestiveness to those who desire fully
to understand the conditions upon which alone there can be a
prosperous and permanent societary life. Zinc and copper plates
promiscuously piled are mere rubbish, powerless as the fragments
of any other waste. Let them, however, be connected in orderly
alternation, and the range may continue indefinitely with increase
of latent force, ready upon the instant when the circuit shall be
completed to gather together at one extremity the whole accumulated negative, and at the other the whole accumulated positive,
and thus present an active force sufficient to bind and unbind the
elements of matter . . . This force of immeasurable and resistless
energy flows silently, gently, imperceptibly, through perfect con-
ductors, supplying its currents of vitality to the whole organic
world. Disturbed, resisted, or misdirected, it blasts and crushes,
on the contrary, every obstacle encountered in its course; and
here, again, do we find a perfect correspondence to the social
force. The actual relation of each and every member of a community, as giver and receiver, teacher and learner, producer and
consumer, is positive and negative by turns and relatively to every
difference of function and force in his associates, the whole mass
constituting a great electric battery to which each individual con-
tributes his pair of plates. Perfect circulation being established as
a consequence of perfect development of all the various individualities, the economic force flows smoothly through every
member of the body politic, general happiness and prosperity,
improved mental and moral action, following in its train. When,
however, by reason of failure on the part of those charged with
exercise of the co-ordinating power of the State, the circulation
is obstructed, . . . the gentle vital force is converted into thunder-
bolts whose existence is made manifest by the presence of con-
suming fires. The broken balance rushes by a pathway of ruin to
regain its equilibrium, the war of elements thus presented being
the correspondent of the strife engendered by resistance to the
laws of human life.'

These sentences are the heart of Carey's new sociology. Its gist
can be summed up by saying that the social order is identical
with 'that orderly arrangement which we see to be required in a
galvanic battery' (pp. 120, 119, 126). Remember here, gentle reader,
Johann Kaspar Bluntschli and his comparison of the church to
a bashful maiden with swelling breasts! Is Carey's description of

Turkey and Ireland as 'communities in which the human plates are promiscuously piled' (p. 120) better poetry or worse? The only answer can, surely, be that both are about as absurd as can well be imagined. We all must admire modern science; we all must investigate to what extent physical and social reality can be said to stand under the same laws; indeed, we all must try to extend the area for which common laws can be formulated, for there is no merit in multiplying the areas of, and magnifying the differences in, reality. But when we find supposed social scientists rushing forward as blindly as Bluntschli and Carey did, we must all blush with shame and wince as under the stroke of a lash.

There is really no need to delve deeper into this sea of absurdity; but in view of the fact that mechanicism is, on the whole, inclined to be a-historical or even anti-historical, it may just be permissible to say a few words about Carey's attempt to make his special brand of mechanistic sociology available for an elucidation of the processes of history. Generally speaking, he is a progressivist, even though the law of the conservation of energy would seem to point, or to push, towards a static, rather than towards a dynamic, view of life.

Perhaps Carey's understanding of history is most clearly expressed in the following passage: 'At each and every step of progress the societary positives and negatives become more intimately connected; mind acquires new power over matter; mere brute force tends to yield place to law; the power and the habit of association become more and more confirmed; exchanges become more rapid; values [i.e. costs of production] decline as utilities become developed; production increases as consumption follows more instantly on its path; [and] each societary atom more and more readily finds the place for which it had been fitted—that in which it can best promote its own true interests and those of the community of which it is a part' (pp. 174, 175). This constant, if gradual, reshaping of society until its image comes to coincide with the lay-out of a galvanic battery, will not only improve the workings of the social mechanism, but also the morals of associated men: 'As . . . societary positives and negatives are brought more and more nearly together, kindly feelings become stimulated into action; the husband clings more closely to the wife; the parent feels more and more responsibility for proper care of the little beings by whom he is surrounded; the master becomes more careful of his servant; he himself, meantime, more and more acquiring that feeling of self-respect which, while forbidding that he should truckle to the strong, prompts him to hold out a helping hand to others who, being poor and weak, stand in need of aid from those who influence the movements of the community of which they are component parts . . . The tendency toward equality is thus in the direct ratio of the growth of power in mind to control mere brute matter; that itself growing as the societary positives and negatives are more and more brought into orderly arrangement, and as the interdependence of the various parts becomes more and more complete. The more that tendency [asserts itself], the more rapid is the development of that self-respect—or moral feeling—which forbids our doing to others that which, under similar circumstances, we should *not* desire them to do by us' (pp. 297–299). Even this last sentiment, innocent or infantile as it may appear, is in the end an outcrop of the supposed scientific spirit: the 'compliance with the divine decree' of brotherly love is not to be expected of ethical effort; it is to be the mechanical effect of a quasi-electrical cause, the bringing together of the 'societary positives and negatives' (pp. 375, 374).

One of the weaknesses of Carey (if, indeed, it is a weakness in a sociologist!) was his comparatively slight acquaintance with physics, an acquaintance not beyond the measure ordinarily achieved by the educated layman. He even managed to mis-spell the name of the man who classically formulated the law of the conservation of energy.[1] Now, the same can certainly not be said of the next author whom we propose to study, Sp. C. Haret, whose *Mécanique Sociale* appeared in 1910. Haret was not only a science graduate, but also a professor in the School of Road- and Bridge-Building (and in the University) of Bucharest. The whole appearance and apparatus of his work shows that we meet in him an expert and not an amateur, and a technician, not a *littérateur*.

Let us first, as a kind of curtain-raiser, consider an example of the style of reasoning in which Haret indulges. Spencer's great formula of evolution had been that it leads from incoherent homogeneity to coherent heterogeneity. If this view is correct, then, logically, the starting point of development must have been a state of homogeneity, in other words, a kind of equilibrium, for

[1] Robert Mayer is mentioned only once, on p. 117, and appears there, and in the index, as Meyer.

homogeneous particles can as much be assumed to counterbalance each other as equal men. Why should this condition ever have broken up? In order to answer this question, Spencer asserted that homogeneous masses are inherently unstable—a flagrant piece of special pleading which did not deceive the scientists of the day. Brunhes, for instance, in his *La Dégradation de l'Energie* (1908, p. 346), had no difficulty in demonstrating that the break-up of the supposed initial equilibrium was (in the technical sense of the word) infinitely improbable. Haret, too, tries to prove Spencer wrong, and he does it by the following arguments which show what manner of man he was.

'Let us consider', he writes, 'a society composed of an indefinite number of perfectly identical individuals, between whom a mutual attraction exists which is inversely proportional to a whole and positive magnitude of their distance, and which is the same for equal distances, whoever the individuals between whom it exists. Let us place these individuals at equal distances from each other, so that each of them finds himself at the highest point of a regular tetrahedron whose three other summits are occupied by other individuals. In this way, an indefinite series of equal regular tetrahedrons is formed which are joined by one of their surfaces. It is evident that a system thus laid out will be in equilibrium, for each individual will be equally attracted by all those who surround him, and that in directions which are, pairwise, directly opposed to each other. But if a single person A of these individuals is shifted, however slightly, from his equilibrium position so that he approaches, for example, his neighbours on the right, the attraction which these latter exert on him will become stronger than that of the neighbours on the left. The individual concerned will then follow the stronger attraction and join up with his neighbours on the right. This will give rise to a grouping of two or more individuals, whose increased power of attraction will assert itself all around and will destroy the equilibrium which [before] existed for the neighbouring individuals. Each of them will then yield to the attraction of the group which will be the strongest and come to unite himself with it, [a development] which will create an even stronger centre of attraction. In this way, this centre of attraction will become ever stronger and stronger and continue to attract to itself . . . all the individuals who compose the mass under consideration. Now this mass was, in its original form, homogeneous and in a state of equilibrium. What we have just said proves that this equilibrium was unstable. But if, instead of a force of attraction, we should have assumed that the force which is at work between the individuals was one of repulsion inversely proportional to the whole and positive measure of the distance, and if we had made the individual A approach his neighbours on the right, however slightly, the repulsion which these latter exerted on him would have increased, whereas that of the neighbours on the left would have diminished. The effect would have been that A, yielding to the stronger action, would, instead of removing further to the right, as in the first case, have returned towards the left and tended to re-occupy the position which he had left. The equilibrium would therefore have been stable. This example . . . will suffice to prove that Herbert Spencer's proposition concerning the instability of the homogeneous, which may be correct in certain cases, may also be incapable of verification in certain others' (pp. 76, 78–80).

All this is, strictly speaking, true. But what are we to say of the whole deduction in view of the fact that it is supposed to be a discussion of social history?! What possible bearing can it have on the problems of evolution? If . . . if . . . if! Anything and everything can be proved and disproved in this way. Surely, the social scientist is entitled to a little realism!

Unfortunately, Haret's whole book is conceived in this style. Even where he expressly undertakes to discuss a concrete social phenomenon, he chooses a phenomenon which is not really social. In his second chapter he sets out to prove that sociological problems can just as much be subjected to mathematical analysis as mechanical problems, and he picks as his example the mortality rate. This rate depends, as he tells us, above all on six factors: age; the native vigour of the population; climatic conditions; hygienic conditions; soil fertility; and accidental causes, such as epidemics. Who does not see that all these determinants are physical rather than social? A small social or human trace appears in determinant number 4, hygienic conditions, as this depends to some extent on social arrangements and public instruction, but the other five are simply natural, i.e. sub-cultural and sub-social, data. Death is something that happens to men, not something that they do: and for this reason it is anything but a characteristic social fact, for social facts, in the proper sense of the word, are the configurations and consequences of human conduct. In view of this, the marriage-rate would have been a far better *objectum demonstrationis* than the death-rate, for people marry if and when they want to. Now, it is true that even the marriage-rate (or rather its external aspects) can be analysed by similar statistical techniques as the death-rate, but any honest attempt at thorough understanding will lead to the recognition that its basis, its basic reality, is not the same. Such fixity as the marriage-rate shows is due to the persistence of certain human habits, for instance, the habit of marrying around 22—not to the persistence of certain non-human data such as climate and soil fertility. For this reason a true social science must concern itself basically with the problems of custom and convention, and not with those of nature, of rocks and rains and sun and soot. The physical sciences can never be its proper model.

There is another context in Haret's book where his inability, and the inability of all extreme mechanicists, to deal with social facts becomes even more manifest, and we propose to quote the passage concerned in full. It will amply repay close scrutiny. Under the heading 'Axioms of Social Dynamics', the author discusses the principle of inertia and expresses himself as follows: 'Let us consider an individual in a state of social rest. This is tantamount to saying that his social position does not change . . . [and], in consequence, that he is not subject to any social force, however small; for, by definition, a social force is a cause which produces social movement; and as such movement is, by the hypothesis, non-existent, the force does not exist either. Hence the individual, being already at rest, and not being subject to any force, will remain at rest indefinitely; for if he were to move, he would necessarily have to take some determinate direction; and there is no reason why he should take any specific direction rather than any other. This conclusion', Haret admits, indicating the crucial issue, 'seems contrary to the reality of things. In fact, if we can accept it in rational dynamics, it is only because matter as such is inert and can move from a state of rest only in response to an impetus which comes from *outside*.[1] But man is not in the same case. The cold which forces him to seek for shelter and the means of covering himself, and the need to live in society which imposes on him a certain morality, are indeed social forces which come

---

[1] Our italics.

from outside the individual. But hunger, which induces him to lay aside surplus food in view of [future] days of famine, and his intelligence are the prime factors of his economic and intellectual progress [and these are *interior* to him]. Thus it is that an individual left alone on a desert island, will, thanks to his energy and to his intelligence, know how to make use of his resources, which means that he is capable, by his own effort, of bringing about a variation in his social position' (pp. 85, 86).

What Haret faces, in these lines, is the double fact which makes it utterly impossible to build up a meaningful social mechanics: the fact that man is endowed with life, and the fact that man is endowed with intelligence and will. Already the former fact, physical-physiological though it is, makes it impossible to squeeze human reality into the strait-jacket of rational mechanics, for in rational mechanics effect is always equivalent to cause, whereas in the realm of vitality response is often far in excess of— is certainly not necessarily in numerical proportion to—stimulus. If Haret had thought about the implications of the contrast which he himself draws, he would have torn up his manuscript and returned to his road-and-bridge-building. But he is unwilling to give up his toy, and he helps himself out of his quandary by the cheapest of all possible tricks—by assuming it away. 'The difficulty', he writes brazenly, 'can be easily removed, if one considers intelligence as a simple social force which acts on the individual in precisely the same manner as any other social force. Under this supposition, the individual properly so called is merely an inert element put into social movement by social forces among which we must also count his own intelligence and his own will. In this way, the above conclusion is no longer untrue; for the social rest of the individual will continue so long as no social force will intervene, be it his intelligence or his will or any other' (pp. 86, 87).

This is essentially a piece of prestidigitation. The disturbing fact is conjured away. But the trick is too poor to deceive anybody. What is it that Haret expects us to assume? He expects us to assume that the intelligence and the will which are *in* us, are forces which are *outside* us and push us *from behind*. Brutally expressed, he expects us to assume that we are not men at all but puppets who do the bidding of the puppet master. If there were any sense in substituting a Punch-and-Judy-Show for social reality as the subject matter and model of the social sciences, we could move ahead in the direction of a social mechanics and expect a reward for our pains. But there is no sense whatever in this. Social science, like any other science, must deal with the facts as they are, and not with fictions, however convenient. Otherwise it loses its savour and sense and *raison d'être* and sinks down to an empty pastime like billiards or draughts.

In the lines which we have quoted, the operative clause is clearly the words—'under this supposition, the individual properly so called is merely an inert element'. One could describe this as the de-animation of the human world. This formula is suggested here because it contrasts most instructively with the animation of the material world with which Aristotle is often (and rightly) reproached. The stars are for him, not balls of clay, but little souls that rush across the night sky; stones, children of the earth who, when they fall, run home to their mother. Modern man is inclined to ridicule these conceptions and deride them as childish, but, like the hypocrite of the Gospel, he sees only the mote in his brother's eye and not the beam in his own. What Haret does is the same, in a negative way. Aristotle adds life and consciousness where they are not, Haret subtracts them where in fact they are. What is there to pick and choose between these two equally artificial points of view? Choosing between them would be like choosing between 'too hot' and 'too cold' or 'too little' and 'too much'. Neither alternative can be called 'just right'.

For Haret, of course, the de-animation of the human world means the removal—the forcible removal—of the roadblock in his way. He can now carry on and construct a *mécanique sociale* on the pattern of rational mechanics or mechanics proper. Actually his effort is characterised by a certain mental laziness. He simply takes the physicists' textbook propositions and slightly adjusts them to his purpose. On p. 64, for instance, we read: 'If a material system is subject to a system of forces and a number of constraints, and if these forces are in equilibrium, the total virtual work done by these forces is zero for any virtual displacements consistent with the constraints'. This is followed on p. 65 by this statement: 'If a social body of any kind is subject to certain social forces and to certain constraints, and if these forces are in equilibrium, the total virtual work done by these social forces is zero for any virtual displacements of the social body consistent with the constraints'. In mechanics, this proposition is both meaningful and important; in sociology it is neither. Indeed, in sociology it is doubtful what possible sense it can have at all. What Haret makes of it, and all that he makes of it, becomes clear from the next lines: 'In rational mechanics, the constraints imposed on a material system are generally expressed by equations between the ordinates of the material points which compose it; sometimes they are also expressed by inequalities. In the latter case, the formulation of the principle undergoes a modification in the sense that the sum of virtual velocities becomes zero or negative for all the virtual displacements which are possible in one single direction considered as positive. It is the same,' Haret asserts, 'in social mechanics. The conditions imposed on a social body can sometimes be expressed by equations. For a military man, for a monk, the severe discipline to which they are subjected, imposes on their social movement such limits that they cannot turn aside from the line which is traced out for them and known in advance; it will be possible to describe this line by means of equations. Under the caste system, the social development of the individual is restricted in some directions, sometimes in all directions. . . . Under this régime, the individual can be considered as free to move inside a certain surface to which he cannot rise superior. This state of affairs will be expressed by means of inequalities, by writing that, for the given direction, the ordinates of the individual are inferior, or at most equal, to those of the surface point which lies in that direction' (pp. 65, 66). Statements of this kind consist of two elements: a grandiloquent shell and a miserable kernel. When the shell of scientific jargon is peeled off and discarded and the kernel of positive insight exposed, it is seen that there is a ridiculous contrast between the pretentiousness of the former and the value, or rather lack of value, of the latter. One is reminded of those miserable hotels in which a sardine for supper is served on a silver platter. All Haret tells us is that army men, monks and Mahars or Mangs are not free. We know that without the help of the concepts of virtual momentum and virtual velocity, without equations and all the rest. *Tant de bruit pour une omelette*, as the Frenchman says!

Sometimes, of course, the translation of a proposition or concept of mechanics into sociological terms is not as easy as in the example which we have given. This applies above all to the notion of space. We all know what physical space is; but what can one possibly mean by social space? Yet Haret needs a concept of social space because, without it, all comparison between sociology and mechanics would be impossible, and, above all, the apparatus of the latter science could not be utilised for the former. So there *must* be a social analogue to physical space, and this is how Haret provides it: 'We call society or body social a collection of individuals subject, on the one hand, to their reciprocal actions, and on the other to external influences. The individual is the constituent element of the body social for he is indivisible. He plays, in the body social, the same part as the atom does in a material body. A society is essentially variable . . . One might form an idea of these variations, if one had at one's disposal certain fixed terms of comparison. But in order to find terms of this kind, one must first distinguish the variables on which the state of a society, at a given moment, depends. These variables are in very great number. . . . However, on examining these causes, one sees that they can be ranged into three groups which are: causes of an economic nature; causes of an intellectual nature; causes of a moral nature. . . . Given any two individuals, it is clear that we can draw a comparison between their economic conditions, even if we mean by this word not only their wealth or poverty, but the totality of the factors which determine the physical and material well-being of each of them. We can then conceive', Haret asserts, 'as a determined magnitude what one might call the economic status (*l'avoir économique*) of the individual. The same applies to his intellectual and moral status'.

This alone is utterly absurd, for what is to give us the required figure? What is moral status (*état moral*) anyway? And how can it be quantified? However, let us hear Haret out. We are not concerned here with minor points, but with the major of all major points, the sociological analogue of the concept of physical space. 'Let us call', Haret continues, 'social status or social situation of an individual the state defined by the *ensemble* of the three magnitudes which represent his economic, his intellectual and his moral status. . . . Let us agree, once for all, to represent by x, y and z the magnitudes which represent the economic, the intellectual and the moral status of an individual. Let us take three rectangular axes, OX, OY, and OZ, and construct the point M whose ordinates are the values x, y, z relative to a given individual and to a given moment. . . . If the position of this point in relation to the axes OX, OY, and OZ is known, we shall automatically know the social situation of the individual, for we know [do we?] the values x, y, z which determine that position. The three axes OX, OY, OZ define a space which we may call *social space*' (pp. 42, 43, 49, 50).

It is not difficult to see that the word 'space' is used here in an altogether fictitious, nay fantastic, sense. Not only is the social space here spoken of no proper space, but it does not even resemble one in any way. Space has three dimensions: length, width and height; social 'space' *à la* Haret has also three 'dimensions'— economics, intelligence, and morality. Is economics a kind of length? Is intelligence a kind of width? Is morality a kind of height? Science must, of course, sometimes use concepts and constructs which appear strange at first sight, but they must not, and among true scientists do not, on rational analysis, turn out to be altogether unrealistic, as the use of the word 'space' is here.

We can, as it happens, leave the last word in this discussion to Haret himself. 'A mathematical formula', he writes, 'expresses only a relationship between the quantities which were under consideration, and were, so to speak, set in motion, when that formula was established. If one widens the range of its application, and if one lets it speak in cases for which it was not made, it is apt to become a cause of error' (p. 125). How very true! The formulæ of mechanics were decidedly not made and meant for society; hence they should never have been transferred to sociology; and if they were or are so transferred, then, as Haret himself says, they only become a cause of error, at times, indeed, even more: a nuisance. But still more pungent, and still more justly applicable to himself, is another word of his: 'Human societies have not been called into being in order to satisfy abstract formulæ' (p. 217). It is impossible not to agree with the sentiment expressed in this sentence. What a pity that Haret honoured it in the breach, and not in the observance! His whole book is a continued outrage of its spirit and wisdom.[1]

[1] Dr. I. S. Grant, of the Department of Physics of Manchester University, has been kind enough to read the above discussion of Haret. It was both interesting and encouraging for me to see that the reactions of a modern physicist to Haret's *mécanique sociale* were substantially the same as my own.

XII

EXCURSUS
Classical Economics

ANYONE WHO has read through the last chapter and seen the severe handling that we have meted out to Carey and Haret, will be surprised to hear that a great and, in spite of some addiction to abstract model-building, realistic science has been dominated throughout its history by the mechanistic conception of the social system—the science of economics. But the situation is no different here from that found in the organismic camp: just as some philosophical realism is permissible and has led to fruitful results in the hands of the leading anthropologists, just so some philosophical nominalism is defensible and has helped rather than hindered the leading economists in elucidating the workings of the sector with which they are concerned. What is so repulsive about the extreme mechanicists is not their mechanism so much as their extremism. In the context of our analysis, a study of economics will help us to recognise and to appreciate the truth-content of sociological nominalism as a whole. With this aspect we shall have to deal in the next chapter. Here we shall have to show that modern economics in its entirety is indeed an incarnation of the nominalistic principle of social philosophy.

Our task is relatively easy, for there is far-reaching, not to say universal, agreement on this point. Orthodox economics and mechanistic sociology coincide, and are seen to coincide. Those economists who have embraced sociological realism—and there are only very few, such as Adam Müller and Othmar Spann—

have remained outside the mainstream of economic thinking, disregarded, derided and despised. It can happen that basically mechanistic authors may show here and there some little influence of organismic conceptions; this is true, above all, of Alfred Marshall. But the holistic passages in their works are like tiny boats on a vast ocean. Both classical economics and neo-classical economics—the group Adam Smith–Malthus–Ricardo and the group Walras–Menger–Jevons—show no such influence at all. Indeed, there is, in these leading theoreticians, some evidence of militant anti-organicism.

The only exception to the rule (which, as we shall see, is apparent rather than real) is the Physiocratic School, the school of François Quesnay. Quesnay fits his economic analysis into an organismic frame. There are three classes who, between them, constitute the economic system: the primary producers, the land-owning aristocracy, and the tradesmen and traders. The first are like the stomach of the human body which produces the nutritive juices that feed the whole organism, the second are like the heart which pumps them through the far-flung system, and the last are like the lungs which help the heart to pump, but neither provide nourishment nor yet spread it to, and through, all parts. The economic process is a process of circulation like the circulation of the blood, and there is, according to Quesnay, a physiology and a pathology of the body social, just as there is a physiology and a pathology of the body physical. This sounds very much like consistent organicism, but a close look reveals a somewhat different picture. The years 1758 to 1775, which delimit the period of physiocratic predominance in France, were years of an all-pervading, all-controlling general mechanicism, a mechanicism so supreme that it imposed itself even on the sciences of life. The reader must remember here Lamettrie's characteristic book, *L'Homme Machine*, published in 1748, which Quesnay (who was a doctor) must have known inside out. If the model at the basis of contemporary physiology was in this way entirely mechanistic, it is clear *a fortiori* that the model at the basis of contemporary economics must have been mechanistic also. And this we see, in fact, to have been largely the case. Quesnay finds it impossible to remain within his organismic frame, even so far as language is concerned: after having spoken of economic life as a kind of circulation, comparable to that of the blood stream, he changes over to mechanistic metaphors and talks of wheels and pumps which push the mass of commodities from stage to stage. His concept of economic health is, properly speaking, a concept of equilibrium, his concept of economic disease one of disequilibrium. In a word, organismic nomenclature here masks mechanistic thought.[1] The use of this nomenclature has its importance, just as the appearance of some organicism in Alfred Marshall, and we shall have to revert to the point. Here we wish to emphasise that the superficial verbal organicism of Quesnay and his school is no disproof of the fact that economics is all along the way profoundly and substantially mechanistic.

The theory of Adam Smith is not complicated and clouded by any such inept language. Its features are easy to recognise, and it reminds one from the first moment onward of the contemporary doctrine of Jean-Jacques Rousseau. Rousseau, as we have seen, reduced the social element in man to a bare minimum, and Smith does exactly the same; indeed, in *The Wealth of Nations* (though not in the earlier *Theory of Moral Sentiments*) he goes even a little further. What is it that brings men together in society, in a great system of divided and integrated labour? 'This division of labour', Smith tells us, ' . . . is the necessary, though very slow and gradual, consequence of a certain propensity in human nature . . . the propensity to truck, barter, and exchange one thing for another' (ed. Cannan, p. 15). This 'trucking disposition' (p. 17) is in no way a social instinct: it predisposes men to do business with each other, but its basis is in selfishness and not in sociality. 'Man has almost constant occasion for the help of his brethren', Smith writes in an often-quoted passage, 'and it is in vain for him to expect it from their benevolence only. He will be more likely to prevail if he can interest their self-love in his favour, and shew them that it is for their own advantage to do for him what he requires of them. Whoever offers to another a bargain of any kind, proposes to do this. Give me that which I want, and you shall have this which you want, is the meaning of every such offer . . . It is not from the benevolence of the butcher, the brewer, or the baker, that we expect our dinner, but from their regard to their own interest. We address ourselves, not to their humanity but to their

---

[1] This becomes particularly clear in an *opusculum* of Du Pont de Nemours, published in 1955 by Prof. H. W. Spiegel under the title *On Economic Curves*. Cf. my review in *Kyklos*, 1956, pp. 254, 255.

self-love, and never talk to them of our own necessities but of their advantages' (p. 16).

It is clear already from these words that Smith, like Rousseau, thinks of society in terms of *contrat social*. But the point is put even more clearly by Smith himself. Contrasting man and the lower creation, he says of the trucking propensity that it is 'to be found in no other race of animals, which seem to know neither this nor any other species of contracts'. And a little later he writes: 'It is by treaty, by barter, and by purchase, that we obtain from one another the greater part of those mutual good offices which we stand in need of' (pp. 15 and 17). The difference from Rousseau is here merely that Rousseau speaks of political and Smith of economic contract-making: and in view of the different subjects which the two authors set out to tackle, this is no difference at all.

But the parallel goes much further. Like Rousseau, Smith is an egalitarian: nature has not divided class from class, only human arrangements are responsible for such socio-cultural contrasts as we find. 'The difference of natural talents in different men is, in reality, much less than we are aware of; and the very different genius which appears to distinguish men of different professions, when grown up to maturity, is not upon many occasions so much the cause, as the effect of the division of labour. The difference between the most dissimilar characters, between a philosopher and a common street porter, for example, seems to arise not so much from nature, as from habit, custom and education. When they came into the world, and for the first six or eight years of their existence, they were, perhaps,[1] very much alike . . . About that age, or soon after, they come to be employed in very different occupations. The difference of talents comes then to be taken notice of, and widens by degrees, till at last the vanity of the philosopher is willing to acknowledge scarce any resemblance' (pp. 17, 18). Rousseau habitually expresses such sentiments in far sterner language, but the fundamental attitude is the same. Smith also emphasises that the burden and the pain of laborious effort is the same for all men: 'Equal quantities of labour, at all times and places, may be said to be of equal value to the labourer. In his ordinary state of health, strength and spirits . . . he must always lay down the same portion of his ease, his liberty, and his happiness' (p. 35). In a word, a man is a man and neither less nor more.

---

[1] This 'perhaps' is omitted in some editions.

In view of this double starting-point—a tendency on the part of men to exchange goods and services on the one hand, and a basic selfishness and equality of strength on the other—it is almost unavoidable that Smith should end up with an equilibrium theory, or rather a string of equilibrium theories, for many phenomena are explained in this vein: prices, wages, the population figure &c. Here we can only look at one sample, and we have chosen for presentation the case of price-formation. How is it that millions of producers, working independently of each other, one not knowing what even his next-door neighbour does, fall into a pattern; how is it that this initial chaos gives birth to a final cosmos, the cosmos of want-satisfaction? How is it, in other words, that individual independence leads to social co-operation? The miracle of ordering is performed by the price, and the price forms, as a kind of resultant (in the sense of rational mechanics) between contradictory tendencies (the suppliers' and demanders' interests), on a market which functions like a mechanism. 'When the quantity of any commodity which is brought to market falls short of the effectual demand, all those who are willing to pay the whole value of the rent, wages, and profit, which must be paid in order to bring it thither, cannot be supplied with the quantity which they want. Rather than wanting altogether, some of them will be willing to give more. A competition will immediately begin among them, and the market price will rise ... When the quantity brought to market exceeds the effectual demand, it cannot be all sold to those who are willing to pay the whole value of the rent, wages, and profit, which must be paid in order to bring it thither. Some part must be sold to those who are willing to pay less, and the low price which they give for it must reduce the price of the whole. The market price will sink ... When the quantity brought to market is just sufficient to supply the effectual demand and no more, the market price naturally comes to be either exactly, or as nearly as can be judged of, the same with the natural price. The whole quantity upon hand can be disposed of for this price, and cannot be disposed of for more. The competition of the different dealers obliges them all to accept of this price, but does not oblige them to accept of less' (pp. 58, 59).

All this is manifestly mechanistically explained. What Smith calls the 'natural price' is in substance an equilibrium price. It is the price at which momentary supply and effectual demand (i.e.

demand of sufficient price-willingness to cover the costs of production) meet, or rather form an equation. It is—to bring in the appropriate metaphor—the price at which the two sides of the market scales exactly counterbalance each other, at which the cross-beam is in a horizontal position. If there is less in the scale which is labelled supply, it will go up, and the other scale which is labelled demand will go down. If there is more in the scale labelled supply, it will go down, and the other scale which is labelled demand will go up. In either case the cross-beam will not be horizontal, but inclined, to the right or to the left, according to circumstances. But, as on a good balance, there will always be a tendency for the equilibrium position to be reached. If there is, at the moment, undersupply and the price goes up, i.e. if the demanders make a better offer, the supply will increase and the scale labelled supply will be filled more and come down. If, on the other hand, there is, at the moment, oversupply and the price goes down, i.e. if the demanders offer less, the supply will decrease and the scale labelled supply will soon be less full and come up. For 'the quantity of every commodity brought to market naturally suits itself to the effectual demand . . . The natural price, therefore, is, as it were, the central price, to which the prices of all commodities are continually gravitating. Different accidents may sometimes keep them suspended a good deal above it, and sometimes force them down even somewhat below it. But whatever may be the obstacles which hinder them from settling in this center of repose and continuance, they are constantly tending towards it' (pp. 59, 60). In other words, the economy is a spontaneously self-equilibrating, automatically self-adjusting mechanism.

In so far as the economy functions in this way, Smith's mechanicism is a positive, not a normative one. But a normative element is by no means missing. For the economy *will* only function in this way, *if* it is free—if the sides of the scales can swing freely and find their own level. 'The market price of any particular commodity', Smith explains, 'can seldom continue long below its natural price . . . Its market price [if for some reason too low] would soon rise to the natural price.' But he adds the important proviso: 'This at least would be the case where there was perfect liberty' (p. 64; cf. also pp. 58 and 101). Here again we are reminded of Rousseau, and, indeed, of the disciples of Rousseau who shouted in the streets of Paris: *liberté, liberté* . . .

However, the shout was not only: *liberté, liberté*. It was *liberté, égalité, fraternité*, and the question is whether the normative aspect of the Smithian doctrine contained the egalitarian as well as the libertarian ideal. The answer is in the affirmative—very much in the affirmative. Smith's whole analysis of value is based on a distinction between the original (and good) state of society and the present (not so good) state of society—the state of natural equality and the state of factitious inequality, with the positive value-accent on the former and the negative on the latter.

'In that early and rude state of society which preceeds both the accumulation of stock and the appropriation of land,' Smith writes; in other words: when there were as yet no capitalists and landlords, and all were equal, 'the proportion between the quantities of labour necessary for acquiring different objects seems to be the only circumstance which can afford any rule for exchanging them for one another . . . It is natural that what is usually the produce of two days' or two hours' labour, should be worth double of what is usually the produce of one day's or one hour's labour . . . In this state of things, the whole produce of labour belongs to the labourer.' There is no exploitation. 'But this original state of things, in which the labourer enjoyed the whole produce of his own labours,' Smith ruefully continues, 'could not last beyond the first introduction of the appropriation of land and the accumulation of stock . . . As soon as stock has accumulated in the hands of particular persons . . . the whole produce of labour does not always belong to the labourer. He must in most cases share it with the owner of the stock which employs him . . . As soon as the land of any country has all become private property, the landlords, like all other men, love to reap where they never sowed, and demand a rent even for its natural produce . . . The labourer must then . . . give up to the landlord a portion of what his labour either collects or produces' (pp. 49–51 and 67). Exploitation has come into the world. This is, once again, pure Rousseauian sentiment, his nostalgia for simple, classless society, in a new guise. This is, once again, a theory of the fall. And, once again, a falsification of the social equilibrium is the cause of all the misery: 'What are the common wages of labour, depends every where upon the contract usually made between those two parties [masters and men], whose interests are by no means the same . . . It is not . . . difficult to foresee which of the two parties must, upon all ordinary occasions, have the advantage in the dispute, and force the other into a compliance with their terms' (p. 68). The scales are no longer even, and paradise is lost.[1]

Smith was no sentimentalist like Rousseau; he was a solid and even stolid Scot. But precisely this gives the common doctrine more punch in his hands than it ever had in those of Jean-Jacques.

There is, unfortunately, no room in this book for a discussion of the mechanistic element in the successors of Adam Smith; we can look neither at the pessimistic (or English) school of Malthus, Ricardo and the Mills, nor at the optimistic (or Continental and American) school of Bastiat, Dühring and Ferrara. One member of the latter group we have studied already—Henry Charles Carey. Suffice it to say that both were consistently mechanistic in outlook. In this respect they were much closer to each other, and to their master Adam Smith, than in any other.

A fresh high-water mark of mechanicism was reached in the eighth decade of the nineteenth century, when Carl Menger published his *Grundsätze der Volkswirthschaftslehre* (1871) and Léon Walras his *Eléments d'Economie Politique Pure* (first part 1874). Their teachings constituted the neo-classical doctrine which has become a new and abiding orthodoxy. A mechanistic economics clearly demands two ingredients: a study of the individual atoms who enter into the equilibrium system which we call the national economy; and a study of the relationships between these atoms, a definition of the equilibrium system itself. Menger and his Viennese School elaborated the former; Walras and his Lausanne School the latter. Between them, they provided a mechanistic description and interpretation of socio-economic life which could hardly be more characteristic.

Twelve years after his great work, Menger got involved in a polemic with an economic historian called Schmoller who insisted that induction and description was the proper method of the socio-economic sciences, and not deduction, on which Menger had heavily relied. Underneath this methodological debate, there lurked all the time the irreconcilable contrast between philosophical realism to which Schmoller inclined, and philosophical nominalism upheld by Menger. In his aggressive book, *Untersuchungen über die Methode der Socialwissenschaften* (1883), Menger

[1] For the fact that this picture of the past masks, in Smith just as in Rousseau, a programme for the future, cf. my book, *The Sociology of Knowledge*, 1958, pp. 61 *et seq.*

uncompromisingly defended the individualistic starting-point. Without it, he claimed, no economic science is possible at all, if the word science is to have any meaning in the context. The chapter headings alone speak a very clear language. The third book, for instance, begins with a discussion of 'The Analogy between Social Phenomena and Natural Organisms and its Limitations', a statement with a sharp sting to its tail. But the core of Menger's argument is to be found in the last chapter of the first book: 'On the Reproach of Atomism in Theoretical Economics'. 'The phenomena of the "national" economy', Menger says here in a crucial passage, 'are by no means immediate vital manifestations of a nation as such . . . but the *resultant* of all the innumerable private economic strivings in the nation' (p. 87). The salient word 'resultant', taken from mechanics, is italicised by Menger himself, and he confesses to upholding the thesis 'that the phenomena of the national economy must, in [economic] theory, be reduced, in the last analysis, to individual economic efforts, that is to say, to its simplest constitutive elements, and explained in this way' (p. 83).

This, indeed, is the method which Menger pursues all along. His central theory, i.e. his theory of value, has rightly been described as economic subjectivism, for it is the subject, economic man, from whose individual psychology he derives even the social phenomena of economic life. 'In order to begin with the simplest case,' he writes in the *Grundsätze*, 'let us imagine a subject carrying on an isolated economy, living on a rocky island in the sea where there is only one single source of water' (p. 100). This 'Robinson Crusoe', this 'isolated man' (pp. 102, 103), is for Menger the key to everything. He will value different quantities of water differently. One measure he needs for drink; 19 measures for his domestic animals; 40 measures for cleansing and similar purposes, and 40 measures for comparative luxuries such as his garden and his pets. It is clear that he will value the first bucket-full, on which his survival depends, more highly than the last, which is not vital to him. This is the famous law of decreasing marginal utility (as Menger's son-in-law Wieser called it). It interests us here because it demonstrates Menger's radical individualism, atomism and nominalism. The theory of the social economy is for him no more than an extension of the theory of the economic subject in isolation.

We see how true this is when we consider Menger's analysis

of barter or exchange which, after all, is a social phenomenon (cf. pp. 162 *et seq.*). He takes us from the rocky island to the depth of the primeval forest where there are two individuals in log-cabins, A and B. Both need five horses for purposes of production, and both need five cows for purposes of consumption. Menger now assumes that A has six horses but only one cow, whereas B has six cows but only one horse. Their schedules of valuation will then, in view of the decreasing marginal utility of the animals, the fact that the first is more important than the second, the second more important than the third, and so on, look as follows:

		A		B	
		Horses	Cows	Horses	Cows
1	. .	50	50	50	50
2	. .	40			40
3	. .	30			30
4	. .	20			20
5	. .	10			10
6	. .	0			0

In ordinary language this means that the last horse is useless to A, who simply does not need it, just as the last cow is useless to B. If they arrange a swap, namely the last of A's horses for the last of B's cows, they both will clearly be better off. Each gives away what, to him, has no value, and acquires what has a value of 40. In the given circumstances, a further swap will likewise be indicated. If A surrenders his fifth horse and receives B's fifth cow, and vice versa, A gives away what, to him, has the value 10, and receives what has the value 30, and the same is true of B. The situation will now be as follows:

		A		B	
		Horses	Cows	Horses	Cows
1	. .	50	50	50	50
2	. .	40	40	40	40
3	. .	30	30	30	30
4	. .	20			20

It is obvious immediately that a further swap would be senseless. There would be nothing in it for the parties. All exchanging would therefore come to an end.

We have reproduced, in a shortened form, this whole deduction because it allows us to demonstrate that Menger was not only an individualist and an atomist, but also a mechanicist. For what is it that has happened after the second swap? An equilibrium position has been reached. Or, less mechanically, more mathematically expressed, marginal utilities have been equalised—which comes to the same. All economic life is, for Menger, characterised and explained by this simplified example. Its essence is a continued tendency towards the equalisation of marginal values and utilities, towards equilibrium.

Roughly speaking, Walras can be said to have started where Menger left off. He fixes his attention on the market as a whole. Let us imagine, he says, that all intending buyers and all intending sellers crowd into a vast hall, eager to do business. How will they come together? Somebody, a kind of auctioneer, will call out a price. This *prix crié* will be no more than a shot in the dark; and yet it will be the beginning of order, that is to say, equilibration. Assume that the price tentatively suggested is too high. Then some of the intending sellers will have to fear that they will not get rid of their wares. It will be necessary for them to press forward and to offer whatever they have to sell at a lower price. The price-level will come down. Or assume that the price tentatively suggested is too low. Then some of the intending buyers will have to fear that they will not be able to cater for their needs. It will be necessary for them to press forward and to concede a higher price for whatever they wish to acquire. The price-level will go up. Thus the second price will be more realistic than the first. But whatever happens, the game will go on until the right price-level has been found, the price, that is, at which the market will get into an equilibrium position—more simply expressed, at which offer and demand come into line and the price is exactly right. Walras speaks of a series of *tâtonnements*—freely translated, of oscillations—which lead to this desirable and desired result. The image this term calls up is once again that of a pair of scales. These scales swing up and down for a while until they find their balance, until the cross-beam is in a horizontal position. Once again, we are confronted with pure mechanicism.

Every commodity must, and will, in the course of time, find its equilibrium. This equilibrium will be expressible in an equation. A slight complication arises from the fact that equations must be expressed in some numerical index, and that one commodity must be set aside as *numéraire*, in other words, as money.

In Walras' day this commodity was gold. Now, if we exclude gold (or whatever is used as currency), we are left with n — 1 equations. But there are also n — 1 unknowns, namely the n — 1 prices at which the market, and with it the whole economy, settles down into an abiding pattern of order. Nor have we to worry over the last price, the price of gold. As *it* expresses the equilibrium price of all other goods, all other goods express the equilibrium price of *it*. It is just as correct to say that a certain quantity of gold is worth a loaf of bread or a bottle of beer, as it is to say that a loaf of bread or a bottle of beer is worth a certain quantity of gold. All this means that the market is, after sufficient oscillations, in a determined equilibrium. For every system of equations is univocally determined, if the number of equations and the number of unknowns coincide.

Both Walras' theory and Menger's have made a tremendous impression on the economists—and both have tremendous difficulties, whether the economists like it or not. What Menger does is to assume that our preference scales are numerical, that if we prefer an apple to a pear it is because an apple gives us more pleasure, pleasure with a higher numerical index (say 5), than the pear (which, say, gives us only 4). But this whole formulation is possible only *ex post facto*. Before we choose, there is no saying what gives us more pleasure. And, indeed, the whole concept of a pleasure unit is profoundly problematical. Is the index-figure for the apple 5 or 50 or 500—or any other number? Some economists have introduced hedonic units (have spoken of 1 ut, or utility unit, and 1 wantab, or desirability unit), but such concepts are pure fictions, and they have long ago died a well-deserved death. Under the leadership of Henri Bergson, psychologists have come to recognise that the act of preferring may not be quantifiable. Walras' analysis avoids all such difficulties for it does not descend into the murky depths of the economic man's soul, but remains in the open market and studies his conduct there, a conduct in the clear light of day which everybody can watch for himself. But his doctrine has its own cross. It works well enough in so far as the determination of the price system is concerned. But a full economics is not only concerned with states, such as the state of markets, but also with flows, such as the flow of production, and that is where the weakness of Walrasian mechanicism lies.

In order to widen the application of this mechanicism and

make it, if possible, all-inclusive, the members of the school try to show that most economically relevant actions are, or can be construed as, acts of exchange. Sometimes this endeavour led to notable results. It was shown, for instance, that taxation can be interpreted in this vein. The taxpayer is a buyer who, against an appropriate payment, acquires a valuable commodity, namely security, from the government which is there to provide and to sell it. Such a construct is fairly far from reality, for in reality many extra-economic factors enter into tax policy and tax legislation, and the tax rate is by no means determined, market-fashion, by the demand for, and offer of, the commodity security. Yet the theory is not absurd either. *If* taxes were based on economic considerations alone, they *would have* to be fixed *as if* they were formed on a free market. And as it is arguable that extra-economic motives *ought not* to enter into the process of taxation, we have here a piece of normative mechanicism which is no worse than any other. Yet when it comes to the interpretation of production as an exchange, the difficulties of this mode of explication become insuperable.

What the theory suggests is that production is, properly understood, nothing else than the exchange of certain quantities of the factors of production (land, labour and capital) for the finished article which is manufactured from them. If this is so, then the sum of the costs of production (i.e. of the prices of the factors of production involved) must be equal to the price of the finished and marketable end product; and this is indeed what the theory not only assumed, but even proved. Equilibrium implies this equivalence between the two sides of an exchange equation. So far, so good. But a system in equilibrium is a system of inter-dependence; it must not only be possible to derive the price of the produce from the prices of the factors, but, inversely, the prices of the factors from the price of the product; after all, any and every proper equation can be read from both sides. But this derivation of the factor prices from the final prices—this proof that the former are, as they logically must be, functions of the latter, as the latter are of the former—has never succeeded, in spite of the fact that a good deal of ingenuity has been spent over it. This is the so-called 'problem of imputation', and its presence and intractable nature indicates only too clearly that there is something wrong with the Walrasian system.

Nor is it very difficult to find out what exactly is wrong. Equilibria are states and not processes, but production is a process, not a state. That is to say, it involves time, and as time cannot be accommodated in the framework of static formulæ, there results an artificiality of which the problem of imputation is merely the symptom. To express it differently: the Walrasian equations, being the description of a momentary interdependency, assume that the factor prices are given alongside the prices of the final products, but this is an artificial, nay impossible assumption, because the final products do not, and cannot, co-exist with the (as yet unprocessed) factors which are their raw materials. To put it in yet another way: production cannot be interpreted as a simple exchange, for a gap of time yawns between the two sides of this 'bargain' or 'barter'—a gap of time which would demand a far more complicated mathematical (a dynamical and not a static) apparatus for its description than can be provided on the basis, and in the form, of simultaneous equations. When simultaneity is abandoned, however, the mechanistic model goes by the board.[1]

These difficulties are not spotlighted here in order to criticise the mathematical school of modern economics, which is today firmly in the saddle, or to diminish its prestige. They are in their very nature marginal and not central problems, and leave a good deal of the essential contents of economics as it developed from the Walrasian inspiration untouched. They are brought up here in order to characterise, and not in order to criticise, modern economic theory. Characterisation, however, is helped as much by the discovery of weak as by the discovery of strong points. All that we wanted to reveal was that the *mécanique sociale* of Léon Walras and his disciples showed and shared the limitations as well as the value of its model, that it was mechanistic for better and for worse.

We have spoken only of Walras' *Eléments d'Economie Politique Pure* and not of his *Théorie Générale de la Société* (1867), but this book would also have yielded many materials for our analysis, if we had chosen to put it on the dissecting table. Most significant is perhaps its plea for nationalisation of the land. Unlike capital

[1] For a more detailed discussion of these difficult problems, cf. my two contributions to *Kyklos*: 'Diminishing Utility Re-considered' (1947, pp. 321–344) and 'Stable Equilibrium Re-Examined' (1950, pp. 218–232).

and labour, the land (which is immovable in more senses than one) does not have a market that would function automatically. Therefore, Walras (and his kindred contemporary Gossen) suggested that it should be made more marketable, so as to fit better into a general exchange economy. What was recommended was in substance the replacement of the commodity land by the commodity land-use. If the soil were nationalised and the government sold land-use (or documents entitling their purchasers to land-use) on a free market, i.e. to the highest bidder, then the economy as a whole would work even more like a perfect mechanism than it does now. As can be seen, this programme of reform is as much inspired by an underlying and all-pervading philosophical mechanicism as all the rest.

XIII

The Truth-Content of Mechanicism

WHEN TWO business men come together in order to discuss a deal, their minds are dominated by one purpose, and one purpose only: to have the best of the bargain. However sophisticated they may be, in the last resort they feel very much like the intending buyer in an Eastern bazaar: he has said 14 piastres; he means 12; he would like to have 10; the thing is worth 8; I should like to get it for 6; I might offer 4; well, I'll try 2; a consideration which, with the appropriate adjustments, is characteristic of the intending seller also. What happens, then, in any such discussion, is that one party will try to pull the price down, while the other will try to push it up: it is all a matter of pushing and pulling, in other words, a mechanical contest between two independent and contrary forces, a tug of war. And it is only when the pushing and pulling is at an end, when the two opposing wills have fought each other to a standstill, that the deal will really be concluded. Here, in this simple act, we have at once the deepest root and the highest justification of the mechanistic conception of social life. All the elements of the theory are present: there is, to begin with, no association whatsoever; there are only the individuals concerned; these individuals are entirely selfish; the conditions of co-operation are not pre-existent but consequent to their encounter; they emerge only from their contest after an equilibrium position has been reached; and, ultimately, the balance of forces which has emerged leads to, and, as it were, materialises itself in, a contract. Generalise this pattern, and you have something like Rousseau's theory of the social bond.

As can be seen, there appears to be a substantial coincidence between the realities of the market and the assumptions of the theory. But the similarity goes in fact much further than might be assumed at first sight. What determines the outcome of a price struggle, is not, as a rule, accident, not, for instance, the glibness of the contenders' tongues, though, within limits, even negotiating skill may play a part: no, basically it is what market researchers call the statistical position of the commodity concerned, which decides the outcome. It all depends on the quantities involved: on the one hand, the quantity of the offer; on the other hand, the quantity of the demand. If the offer exceeds the demand, the seller is the weaker partner and the struggle goes against him; if the demand exceeds the offer, the seller is the stronger partner and the struggle goes against the buyer. If we exclude accidental factors, the emerging equilibrium position will indicate, and the ultimately-concluded contract will incorporate, a price which will be the true resultant of the contending forces. Everything happens quasi-mechanically; and everything that happens is expressible in perfectly determinate equations. The momentary supply is clearly a quantity, a simple figure; and the demand, although in the last analysis coming from the dark recesses of the consumer's mind, must at least quantify itself when it begins to operate on the market—quantify itself in a certain determinate price-willingness which will be no less a simple figure than the available supply. Hence everything here invites mechanistic construction and mathematical description; and we cannot but conclude that, on their home pitch, the economists are fully within their rights when they turn to physics for their formulæ and for their tools.

The realism of this mechanistic and mathematical market-analysis has been arraigned by saying that it is not economic quantity but power politics which is really decisive on many markets, such as, for instance, the labour market: that the market mechanism is never allowed to work. But an investigation of what goes on shows soon enough that the observation which is meant to controvert the theory is apt to confirm it. Power, of course, plays its part, but it is power which asserts itself through the market mechanism, not against it. The trade unions, it is said, falsify the play of the economic forces. Lujo Brentano's theory of trade unionism[1] has shown that this is not so. Why have trade

---

[1] Cf. esp. *'Gewerkvereine'* in *Handwörterbuch der Staatswissenschaften*, ed. 1892, vol. IV, pp. 1 *et seq.*

unions arisen in the first place? Because, Brentano answers, the labour market of early capitalism was a market in permanent disequilibrium. When an individual capitalist who controls the means of production (a full money bag) meets an individual workman who has nothing to sell but his labour power (an empty stomach), no fair bargain can be struck: the offer of labour will be so urgent as to preclude any successful bargaining. In order to make up for this inherent weakness on the part of the seller, Brentano tells us—and he is right—trade unionism was invented. Labour united is not so weak, not so much under a crippling handicap, as labour dispersed. Call a trade union a monopoly, if you like: it is a monopoly formed in reply to another monopoly: it is essentially a move to ensure that the scales are even. Mechanicism is, if anything, strengthened by the phenomenon of trade union organisation.

Such power struggle as there is on the labour market, or indeed on any other market, is normally carried on through attempts to influence the statistical position of the commodity in question. This was shown by Friedrich von Wieser in his sociological writings.[1] Indeed, even when industrial peace breaks down, the situation is not radically transformed. For what is it that happens when the workers come out on strike? Soberly considered, what happens is that the offer of labour is, for the time being, reduced to nil. And what is it that happens when the employers enforce a lock-out? What happens is that the demand for labour is, for the time being, reduced to nil. The contest is greatly intensified, but not essentially changed, and the market equations must be re-formulated, but they need not be abandoned. Mechanicism remains realistic: it can accommodate even the abnormal conditions of industrial war.

It appears, from what has gone before, that the mechanistic conception of human relationships has its firm ground in life, just as the organistic conception has, as we have shown in chapter VII. But once again we see that its truth-content is not, as the more enthusiastic supporters of it claim, universal, but merely partial, indeed, strictly limited. Economists are inclined to assume that a market is always a market, and that what goes on on it, is at all times and places the same. But this is not so. Under modern (capitalistic) conditions, there is in fact the tug of war between

[1] Cf. esp. *Das Gesetz der Macht*, 1926.

buyer and seller which allows us to liken the formation of the price to the establishment of a mechanical equilibrium; but in societies of the community type everything is different. The price is not an *emergent* point of order there, but a *pre-existent* one, indeed, part and parcel of an abiding pattern which individual action can hardly modify, let alone create. This precisely made it possible for the medieval thinkers to speak about the just price: the price was thought to be—and in fact was!—given when the contracting parties appeared on the market; it was not a mere starting point of negotiations, but had authority, even binding power, and the parties were expected, nay constrained, to accept it and to accommodate themselves to it. Ontologically, it was prior to the bargain, not posterior to it, as it is in modern conditions. It had 'reality' in the sense of philosophical realism, just as the social order as a whole had; it was not a fleeting compromise left to the contractants, but part and parcel of objective customary law. Hence the mechanistic theory ought to be restricted to individualistic-atomistic societies, just as the organistic theory ought to be confined to closely-knit communities, the clan, the tribe, the village, the medieval town. The former fits modernity, the latter antiquity, and this is the reason why the former has appealed to the economists, the latter to anthropological research.[1]

We have not, however, said enough when we have pointed out that the mechanistic model is applicable only to some societies and not to all, for it is not applicable to the *whole* of *any* society, ancient *or* modern. It is realistic and hence admissible for the elucidation of only some aspects even of the capitalist order. It is certainly sound with regard to the market, but the market is after all no more than a partial phenomenon inside the total phenomenon which we call society. A brief consideration will show that this is so, and why. The encounter of the two sides to a prospective bargain will only lead to a positive and pacific arrangement, if they keep in their dealings with each other within the bounds of ordinance. Should discussion lead to recrimination, recrimination to annoyance, and annoyance to blows, what would emerge would not be a focus of order, but a hotbed of disorder, and this is even more true of collective than of individual bargaining. In other words, to use current sociological jargon, the parties must keep to the definition

---

[1] The matter is more closely examined in my Aquinas Lecture of 1956, published under the title *The Contained Economy* in the same year.

of the situation. But who defines the situation for them? Who establishes the bounds of ordinance, the framework of order, within which alone contract-making can come from a contest of contrary interests? It is society, the wider society, within which the economy is merely a restricted area, a contained sector. This wider social order must in fact pre-exist, and must of necessity be thought to pre-exist, the economic order or equilibrium system. Hence the equilibrium theory, however much it may do for us when it comes to the analysis of economic life, cannot provide us with an inclusive sociology, a sociology of the inclusive society.

And here we see indeed the prime weakness—the far-reaching lack of realism—of sociological mechanicism which has been pointed out by practically all its critics. The concept of contract is a concept of law; there must be a framework of legality before contract-making in the proper sense of the word can start, for what should induce the parties to honour their engagements before the emergence of a spirit of law-abidingness? Rousseauism pre-supposes that which it sets out to explain. It is defeated, not only by observation, but even by simple logic. It is, if anything, inferior to organicism.

It is, however, but fair to emphasise that quasi-mechanical patterns exist, not only in the economic, but even in the legal sector of society, inside that very system of social control which is an absolutely indispensable precondition of constructive-co-operative contract-making. When a man has committed a crime and is brought before the judge, the truth about the matter is elicited, not by direct investigation, but in an indirect way, by pitting accusation and defence against each other. It is regarded as perfectly in order that the guilty man should plead 'not guilty'; indeed, prosecutor and defence are allowed many liberties, the liberty to use subterfuges, equivocations and even tricks: in a word, techniques reminiscent of war, or at the very least of that preparation and continuation of war which we are wont to call diplomacy. We have a battle of wits in which the parties are again expected to fight each other to a standstill, and which—we assume—will make it possible for him who holds the scales to decide on which side there is the heavier weight. This is yet another feature of life to which sociological mechanicism can point for its support. But though we admit that its existence and importance should not be overlooked, it does not oblige us to take back the stricture on the equilibrium concept which we formulated at the end of the foregoing paragraph. For, once again, the situation within which the parties act is socially defined, in fact severely so. Without the concept of 'contempt of court' and the stern measures enforced to avoid and avenge it, an orderly process of law would be as little possible as an orderly functioning of the market without general pacification and policing. Nor is there, at this point, much contrast between modern and earlier societies. Nowadays the authority of the courts is so well established that some of the cumbersome formalism of primitive times has become unnecessary, for instance the obligatory use of set and solemn language, with a few tongue-twisters thrown in, which, on a cruder level, helped to keep the temper of the parties down. But this is, after all, a purely technical difference between the modern and the ancient procedural practice, and there can be no due process of law without efficient safeguards against the outbreak of violence before the face of the law personified, the judge.

We should say, then, that sociological mechanicism can draw more support from the study of facts *in* society than from that of the facts *of* society. But though we can hardly imagine that a society as a whole should have arisen from the clash and equilibration of individual forces, there were times when these forces tended to become free, and when society was, in consequence, on the way towards a state in which it was, comparatively speaking, individualistic and atomistic, i.e. more built on the pattern of a mechanical equilibrium than on that of an integrated organism. At such junctures, mechanistic theories tended to appear, and that for the very good reason that they were, again comparatively speaking, realistic. Of course, though comparatively realistic, they were also, as a rule, largely ideological, that is to say, they not only reflected the fact that society *was*, at the time, more a loose collection of individuals than a tautly coherent body, but also the desire *to make* society into a loose collection of individuals, to end an earlier taut coherence. In theory, we can cleanly divide truth and ideology; in practice, they all too often appear intermixed in the manner of milk and tea.

An early period at which, as some would say, the fibres of the body social relaxed, or, as others would put it, the individual secured a good measure of his due personal independence, is marked by the appearance of the philosopher Epicurus, who was born in 341 and died at Athens around 270 B.C. Already in the days of Plato (427–347) the old, closely integrated social constitution of the city began to show signs of severe strain, indeed, of incipient dissolution. At once a philosophical movement sprang up to reflect, and to promote, this shift in the social situation. Still echoing the judgement of the guardians of order and tradition, we are wont to call them, by a pejorative name, the Sophists. For a very good reason, which will emerge presently, we can also describe them as the Greek Enlightenment. Epicurus, their main disciple, taught that the end of human society was the promotion of individual interests; that it was created by the consent of each of its members; and that it was, in essence, a pattern of reciprocity, not a body endowed with an ontological reality of its own. 'Justice is not something that has a value of its own,' Epicurus is reported by Diogenes Laertius to have taught. 'It exists exclusively in mutual contracts and comes into being wherever there is a reciprocal engagement not to inflict injury, and not to receive it'.[1] This is sociological nominalism; and it is a nominalism in contact, if not with the state of contemporary society, then at least with a tendency in it. Nor is the mechanistic prop to the theory missing. In his philosophy of nature, Epicurus strongly upheld the atomistic position, and whatever prestige he managed to give it, radiated outward from it and suffused his sociology and politics.

But the great, the, so to speak, classical period of mechanicism was the long drawn-out age which began with such writers as Marsilius of Padua (ca. 1270–1343) and ended with such writers as Immanuel Kant (1724–1804)—or, to speak of what matters more in the present context, where we are concerned with the relative truth-content of this kind of doctrine, the age which stretched from the establishment of the embryonic form of bourgeois society in the medieval city to its momentary realisation, on a national scale, in the great French Revolution. In discussing this factual development and its intellectual concomitants, it is necessary to make a distinction between bourgeois society and capitalism. At best we could speak, as some have done, of classical capitalism, meaning thereby its form before the onset of that tendency towards closer integration, which we can observe, above

---

[1] *Lives of the Philosophers*, X, 150, *cit*. M. Guyau, *La Morale d'Epicure* 1878, p. 148.

all, since ca. 1875. By bourgeois society or classical capitalism we mean a pattern under which the carrier of social, and especially economic, life, is the man often called a master manufacturer, the craftsman or, at most, small scale entrepreneur in industry, a figure whose parallel in agriculture is the peasant or, in certain countries, the farmer. These types were independent producers with no bosses above and few, if any, minions below them, secure in their independence by virtue of the control of their means of production, tools in the one case, land in the other, and housing in both. Not that society ever consisted only of peasants and artisans, only of free and equal men, but the approach of social development to that pattern was increasingly close, and it not only engendered an individualistic, atomistic, mechanistic and contractual social philosophy, with its climax in the ideas and ideologies of Enlightenment, but also provided, within certain limits, a transitory justification for it.

The medieval city, embedded as it was in a wider world of which hierarchy was the key-note, can hardly be described as an abode of human equality. A goldsmith was a better man than a silversmith, who in turn was a better man than a coppersmith. Yet these invidious distinctions were washed in over the town walls from the outside rather than native to the town itself. Certain basic rights were common to all citizens; and where class contrasts developed, such as those between patriciate and proletariat, they soon evoked class struggles which, in the end, secured substantial democratisation. Both the advent of the mendicant orders and the outbreak of the Reformation with its idea of a universal, and not a privileged, priesthood, were part and parcel of a continuing effort towards an applanation of the social structure. Clearly, the townsmen could see, in the not too distant future, a society of equals among equals which would not, like the declining feudal order beyond the walls, be a hierarchy with emperor, pope or king as head, knights as arms and serfs as feet, but an assemblage of neighbours, one as strong or as weak as the next, whose forces would counterbalance each other—a society reminiscent of a circle, with all points equidistant from the centre, rather than of a pyramid, with the apex far removed from—and high above—the base.

When the town walls were torn down and the nation became the inclusive framework of social life, this image of the future of society became, if anything, even clearer. True, the burghers and peasants were now only the third estate, over whom there lay, incubus-like, the privileged strata of nobility and clergy, but just for this reason the conclusion seemed inescapable that all that was needed in order to make society an association of free and equal men was the removal of these minority groups. Wealth was not thought to present a major problem. There were, of course, wealthy people, just as there were large-scale factories, but both appeared, not unnaturally, as outgrowths and appendages of the *ancien régime* and would disappear with it. Why were some people rich, for instance the share-holders of the Hudson Bay Company? Because the king had given them an exclusive privilege. Why were some factories large, for instance the Carron Iron Works? Because they manufactured cannons for the king. The abolition of legal prerogatives and the abandonment of war, the 'sport of kings', would, it was felt, do away with all that prevented the social mechanism from working properly and from producing that equilibrium of individual forces which was 'natural' and would for ever establish harmony among men and a happiness undreamt of before.

It was to the implementation of this anticipated pattern of social life that the men of the French Revolution devoted themselves, and in so far as they succeeded, they not only realised a social dream, but at the same time also validated a social theory, that mechanicism which had had its most impressive spokesman in Jean-Jacques Rousseau. The detail does not belong to this place, but it will be useful to look, however briefly, at one revolutionary enactment which illustrates our point in the most convincing manner—the so-called Loi Le Chapelier of June 14–17, 1791. What this act did, especially in its salient article 4, was to forbid the formation of both employers' and working men's associations. 'If, against the principles of liberty and of the Constitution, the citizens belonging to the same occupations, arts and crafts should take counsel with each other and enter into agreements with the aim of collectively refusing, or of not granting otherwise than for a certain price, the services of their industry or of their labour, the aforesaid deliberations and conventions, whether or not confirmed by oaths, shall be regarded as unconstitutional, attacks on liberty and the Declaration of the Rights of Man, and null and void.' This ban was meant, as we had better repeat, not only to inhibit the development of what we now call trade unions, but also to nip in the bud all possible conventicles and conspirations on the part of factory owners. That this was so is shown by a decree of Germinal 26–29, year II: 'Financial companies are and remain suppressed. All bankers, traders and other persons are forbidden to form establishments of this kind, whatever their pretended purpose, and whatever their description.'[1] It is hardly possible to be more peremptory than that.

Our concern here is not so much with the enactment as such, or its content, as with the rationale of it, its ulterior purpose. An expert has summed up in the following words the 'key thought of the Constituent Assembly' in passing this law: 'As the Constitution has recognised all rights as equal, the freedom of contracts between workman and employer has become a reality. A monopoly does not exist; the two parties are on the same level so far as the free discussion of the conditions of employment is concerned. Having need of each other . . . they have every interest to come to a soundly based agreement. Competition affects the employer as much as it does the workman, and the equilibrium could be broken only by an alliance of one of the contracting parties with those like him'—which it was precisely the purpose of the law to prevent. Hence, the whole piece of law-making we are studying here was an attempt to make certain that society was, and would remain, an assemblage of disconnected individuals striving to pit their strength against each other and to balance their forces. 'This is further confirmed', we are told a little later, 'by the parliamentary reports of the time, and the intervention of one deputy, Roederer, is noteworthy. He denounces corporate organisations, not only as a political danger which would divide the citizens and set them against each other, but above all as a factor making for economic disequilibrium . . .'[2]

Of course, things did not work out as the Rousseauians inside

---

[1] *Cit.* J.–M.–J. Biaugeaud, *La Liberté du Travail Ouvrier sous l'Assemblée Constituante*, 1939, pp. 51, 52, 55.—The example offered in the text is taken from French history, but English history, too, would have yielded a good illustration: the deep-rooted dislike, noticeable all through the eighteenth century, of political parties, and the settled belief that only independent Members of Parliament would always vote in support of the general interest. (I am grateful to Dr. J. R. Western for discussing this matter with me and providing me with some interesting material which I could not, however, include in this chapter without making it unduly long.)

[2] *Loc. cit.*, p. 50.

and outside the Constituent Assembly thought they would. 'The concentration of capital is not hampered in any way by this law', writes our historian, 'but . . . the coalition of workers is forbidden, and for this reason the disequilibrium which the Constituent Assembly wished to avoid, made its appearance.'[1] True enough: but this is no more than the wisdom of hindsight. Nor did the challenge of the concentration of capital remain unanswered by the sons of the Revolution when it raised its head: the free divisibility of inheritances, prescribed by the Code Napoléon, was meant to dissolve, at a man's death, the masses of property which he had built up during his life. In any case, whether later generations saw the equilibrium theory confirmed or disproved by subsequent developments, the fact remains that around the year 1789 French society approached very closely to a state of affairs under which it was, to say the least, not absurd to see it as essentially an association of free and equal men, a system of individual forces which mutuality held together much in the way in which the stars of the high heavens are kept in harmony—in spite of all their independence—by the attractions and repulsions of which they are the source.

In France, this condition—essentially the moment of transition between the inequalities of the feudal system and those of full capitalism—did not last very long; indeed, one could almost speak of a kind of historical razor's edge. But there was another political formation that showed the same characteristics a good deal more clearly and for a longer time: those thirteen New England colonies which we know as the kernel of the United States of America. The social contrasts of feudalism were largely unknown in Massachusetts and Connecticut; nor did the social contrasts of capitalism unfold quite so rapidly there as in Europe. There was a special reason for this: the open frontier to the west, the availability of free land. Locke had already emphasised the importance of this factor.[2] Whoever was dependent could gain independence by moving inland and becoming a settler: no pool of hopelessness could collect in the cities by the Atlantic shore. Furthermore, the men who made Massachusetts and Connecticut were Puritans, and the Puritans sought rather than fled solitude. Hence a kind of society developed which fitted in well enough with the

[1] *Ib.*, pp. 54, 55.
[2] Cf. my book, *The Ideal Foundations of Economic Thought*, 1943, pp. 19, 20.

Rousseauian ideal: dispersed homesteads, not hovels on top of each other; few common concerns, and those arranged, as they arose, by amicable agreement among the neighbours; everybody as rich or as poor as his industry made him; he who dug more ground, reaping a richer harvest. The contractual pattern, too, was associated with the American social and political constitution, for if ever a commonwealth was founded by a covenant, it was that which sprang from the covenant of the Pilgrim Fathers on board the Mayflower. It is difficult to believe that Rousseau, scion of Calvinist Geneva, did not know of, and think of, the Calvinists of the New World, when he wrote *Du Contrat Social*.[1]

Of course, here, too, the reign of liberty and equality did not last very long. John Taylor's *Inquiry into the Principles and Policy of the Government of the United States*, published in 1814, was its obituary. But what is so interesting is that social thought anticipated, rather than followed, the coming demise of the social order in equilibrium. We have said that the use of organismic language by the Physiocrats has its significance, and we begin to see that significance here. Even while the liberation of man was still in prospect and progress, the feeling gained ground that a society of full freedom would not be possible, that the social order needed a firmer cement than the equilibration of individual forces, if it was to last. Rousseau is even more of a straw in the wind here than Quesnay. In *De l'Economie Politique* and *Du Contrat Social* he uses the body metaphor freely, even though he calls it at once 'a common and in many ways little-exact comparison' (cf. I, p. 389, and II, pp. 229, 230). And in *La Nouvelle Héloise* he expresses himself as follows: 'It is a great error, both in the domestic economy and in the civil, to wish to combat one vice with the help of another, or to form a kind of equilibrium between them: as if that which undermines the foundations of order could ever serve to establish them.' This does not prevent him from writing later on in the same book: 'One can triumph over the passions only by pitting them against each other' (cf. IV, pp. 256, 257 and 310). The latter is really the stronger sentiment in Rousseau; he was and remained essentially a mechanicist. But the occasional appearance of passages of organismic import heralds that mighty return of organicism which we can observe after 1815.

---

[1] On all this cf. my book, *America: Ideal and Reality. The United States of 1776 in Contemporary European Philosophy*, 1947.

As we have seen in chapter VII, there is, around the middle of the century, a renewal of confidence in the capitalist order, and with it, in individualism and liberalism. This, in turn, leads to a reversal of intellectual trends: mechanicism had been in the shadows for a while, now it emerges again into the light. The ripest fruit of this recovery of its prestige is the works of the great economists which appeared right at the end of this new nominalistic period which, as has been pointed out, breaks off with the onset of the Great Depression. It is as if the convictions and cogitations of thirty or forty years tried to incarnate themselves in truly classical statements worthy of their importance. But the new mechanicism is not quite like the old: it is above all much narrower. In view of the vast class contrast and conflict that had sprung up between the owning and non-owning strata, there could now be no question of a total social equilibrium such as Adam Smith and Rousseau had envisaged. There could only be talk of an equilibrium of economic forces—which meant that society was regarded as a mechanism for the maximisation of material production rather than for the maximisation of human harmony. Yet, within these closer confines, the theory was realistic enough. When Menger and Walras laid down their pens, in 1871 and 1874 respectively, the economy had reached its nearest, never-to-be-beaten approach to quasi-automatic functioning. From then onward, the forces of conscious control were again on the attack, though they did not gain much ground until the great wars of the present century. In the 'seventies there were as yet no high tariff walls; the gold standard had made all countries into one currency area; trade unionism was largely restricted to the skilled workers; the so-called 'new unionism' which was to organise the far more important unskilled, was only just appearing over the horizon. In a word, there was, if no longer equality, at any rate comparative liberty; and this it was which gave strength to an economic, and, by implication, social theory which insisted that social facts and institutions are merely resultants of independent forces, not aspects of a pre-existing integrated pattern.[1]

If the total interpretation of the history of social thought which is upheld in this book is correct, we must expect that the second

[1] Cf. the more detailed discussion in the Woodward Lecture which I gave at Yale University on April 1, 1958, published under the title 'The "Classical Situation" in Political Economy' in *Kyklos*, 1959, pp. 57–65.

generation of neo-classical economists (who lived and worked during the Great Depression) should show some inclination at any rate towards organismic conceptions. And this is indeed the case. We have already referred to this side of Alfred Marshall, and with his name we must couple here that of John Bates Clark, another significant figure.[1] The shift from more mechanistic to more biological conceptions was easily accomplished, for Walras had put the idea of functional interdependence into the centre of economic theory, and this idea can be interpreted both in a mechanistic-mathematical and in a biotic-physiological sense. A careful analysis of some finesse would be needed in order to show how (and to what extent) the term changed its meaning, or at least its undertones and overtones. It cannot be undertaken here. But there are passages in which the matter becomes altogether manifest. One occurs at the beginning of book V of Marshall's *Principles of Economics* (ed. 1952, p. 269). Giving a preview of his argument, Marshall writes: 'As we reach the higher stages of our work, we shall need ever more and more to think of economic forces as resembling those which make a young man grow in strength, till he reaches his prime; after which he gradually becomes stiff and inactive, till at last he sinks to make room for other and more vigorous life. But to prepare the way for this advanced study we want first to look at a simpler balancing of forces which corresponds rather to the mechanical equilibrium of a stone hanging by an elastic string, or of a number of balls resting against one another in a basin.'[2] What the great economist implies is that the mechanistic model is only a first and crude approximation to the facts, whereas the organistic model comes much closer to them and makes a far fuller and finer understanding of them possible.

After the turn of the century—i.e. after the spasm of the Great Depression had passed and the economic mechanism was again working smoothly—the pendulum swings once again towards a predominance of pure mechanism, both inside economics and outside it, in the social sciences at large. The age of Vilfredo Pareto arrives. Vainly would one look in his *Manuale di Economia*

---

[1] Cf. Roll's account of him in his *History of Economic Thought*, ed. 1950, pp. 426 *et seq.*

[2] Cf. also p. 635: 'Biology . . . teaches us that the vertebrate organisms are the most highly developed. The modern economic organism is vertebrate. . . .''

Politica (1906) for those echoes of organicism which are not infrequently found in Marshall's *Principles of Economics*; what his *Trattato di Sociologia Generale* is like, we have seen. Pareto outdoes even Menger and Walras; Menger because he ejects from his system the psychological elements whose measurability must be doubtful, Walras because he discards the traces of normative thinking which still abound in the works of the master. From the death of Marshall (in 1924) onward, economics becomes mathematical out-and-out; and the Pareto spirit spills over into sociology as well and fills such influential thinkers as Lundberg. The economic crisis of the 'thirties and the growing concern with planning brought neither a turning-away from mechanicism nor a turning towards more holistic modes of thought, although both movements might have been expected, and the question arises why the model of physics has remained so firmly in command, in spite of the radical change in the objective situation.

The answer is not difficult to give. The twentieth century is pre-eminently the period of theoretical and applied physics which has gone from strength to strength, outdistancing in prestige all the other sciences without exception. Pareto and his disciples, great and small, liked the mantle of the physicist, as Spencer, in his day, had, for the very same reason, fancied himself in that of the biologist. Once again we see that the parallel holds. But not entirely, for the lure of physics is far more potent than that of biology ever was, or ever can be. Bergson has told us why.[1] Man, physically very ill-equipped for the struggle of survival, is forced, from the first moment onward, to live by his wits: his intellect is well-nigh his only effective weapon. Therefore his mind is directed outwards, towards that objective world within which the human race has to maintain and assert itself, and in the process it acquires a certain bent which it is difficult to get rid of later on. Our mentality is such that we feel most at home in what is measurable or at least quantifiable, and we have a tendency to range the branches of learning in accordance with this criterion. The most mathematical are the best, the least mathematical the worst. The man in the street admires machine-building because all is calculation there; he feels sorry for medicine because so much in it depends on guess-work. For the philosophic mind, this primitive

[1] Cf. my books, *The Sociology of Knowledge*, 1958, pp. 314 *et seq.*, and *Social Theory and Christian Thought*, 1959, pp. 180 *et seq.*

evaluation of the comparative status of the sciences is, of course, utterly unacceptable; but how many sociologists or economists are philosophically minded? Let us face it: most of them would rather have a quasi-mathematical doctrine than a true one. This, of course, is treason—treason, if not to the letter, then at least to the spirit of science, for the true scientific spirit demands that the complexity of the factual world be boldly confronted, and not conjured away by substituting for it a simplified and fictitious model. But it is with the service of Science as it is with the labourers in the Lord's vineyard: many are called, but few are chosen.

PART THREE
Society as a Process

XIV

The Conquest of the Traditional Dichotomy

EVERY SOCIETY is, as we have pointed out, both a unity and a multiplicity, and for that reason every sound social theory must be both holistic and atomistic, however contradictory this may sound: holistic, in so far as the society studied is integrated, atomistic, in so far as it is not. This book—and, indeed, the whole history of the social sciences—proves that it is almost impossible to maintain the necessary balance. Ages with a well-knit social system, or with a longing for it, have tended to exaggerate the unity of society and have thrown themselves headlong into the arms of organicism; ages with a loosened social texture, or with a desire for individual freedom, have, on the other hand, tended to exaggerate the element of multiplicity and have thrown themselves with as little discretion into the arms of mechanicism. Not surprisingly, periods of transition have shown themselves less biased and thus nearer to the truth than settled ones—which is almost another paradox, but none the less a fact. A look at Edmund Burke will show that this is indeed so.

Burke, born in the year 1729, was still brought up in the best liberal-mechanicist tradition. But the experience of the French Revolution developed in him a strong sense of the dangers of unbridled individualism and a corresponding desire for firmer social discipline. A famous passage in his *Reflections on the Revolution in France* (1790) shows him intellectually between two worlds, the world of holism on the one hand, the world of atomism on the other. 'Society is indeed a contract,' he writes, 'but the state ought not to be considered as nothing better than a partnership agreement in a trade of pepper and coffee, calico or tobacco, or some other such low concern, to be taken up for a little temporary interest, and to be dissolved by the fancy of the parties . . . It is a partnership in all science; a partnership in all art; a partnership in every virtue, and in all perfection. As the ends of such a partnership cannot be obtained in many generations, it becomes a partnership not only between those who are living, but between those who are living, those who are dead, and those who are to be born. Each contract of each particular state is but a clause in the great primaeval contract of eternal society, linking the lower with the higher natures, connecting the visible and invisible world, according to a fixed compact sanctioned by the inviolable oath which holds all physical and all moral natures, each in their appointed place' (*Works*, ed. Rivington, 1826 *seq.*, V, pp. 183, 184). The very bombast of this passage is characteristic, for it is meant to hide an unsettled mind—a mind whose unsettlement it merely helps to reveal. What is it that Burke is telling us? That society 'is indeed a contract', but is certainly not one; that it is indeed a human artefact, but belongs essentially to the order of nature.

A comparison of other pages brings the brokenness of Burke's thought even more clearly into prominence. Speaking with the voice of the eighteenth century, he writes: 'The rights of men and governments are their advantages; and these are often in balances of good; in compromises sometimes between good and evil, and sometimes between evil and evil. Political reason is a computing principle . . . '. But in another context he hotly condemns what he has just asserted, maintaining 'that in politics the most fallacious of all things [is] geometrical demonstration' (pp. 126 and 313).

There is, then, confusion—but it is not the useless and dangerous confusion of the barren mind; it is much rather the fertile and promising confusion of the open intellect, the confusion which precedes creation. Unable to see society either in mechanistic or in organistic terms, Burke slowly comes to realise that it is in essence cultural, that is to say, not the product of natural forces, be they inanimate or animate, but an achievement of human effort—something which man has added on to the lower realities. 'Political arrangement, as it is a work for social ends, is to be only wrought by social means', he says. 'There mind must conspire with mind. Time is required to produce that union of minds which alone can produce all the good we aim at' (p. 305). These words are much more significant than they might seem at first sight. For what they indicate is that Burke takes the phenomenon of sociality out of the natural setting in which both mechanicists and organicists had set and seen it, and transfers it to the realm of history, a truly human matrix. It is in this new spirit that Burke, in *An Appeal from the New to the Old Whigs*, defines society as 'the ancient order into which we are born' (VI, p. 207).

But Burke came to his insights in an entirely unconscious way, almost, one might say, by groping in the dark. The traditional dichotomy in social philosophy could hardly be resolved in this way; what was needed was a conscious effort to overcome it, and for that the world had to wait the better part of another hundred years. A book now nearly forgotten—Alfred Fouillée's *La Science Sociale Contemporaine*, first published in 1880—gave a mighty impetus in this direction. Sociologists ought to remember it with more affection than they do.

Being a child of his age, Fouillée was influenced by, and went a long way with, such leading organicists as Spencer and Espinas. He can even say: 'We have the right to include societies in what the naturalists call the organic realm, in contradistinction to the inorganic realm.' But on the very same page on which this passage appears, there is a footnote which tells another story: 'M. Espinas, in his very remarkable book on *Sociétés Animales*, has asserted too complete a coincidence between society and the animal properly so called. This has led him to imagine [the existence of] a "social consciousness" more or less analogous to the individual awareness which the animal has of its organism ... Such a social consciousness would be incompatible with the particular consciousness which each member of society has of himself. It is precisely the diffusion of individual consciousness among all the parts [of society]—united, as we may add, to the idea of, and to the desire for, social integration—which, according to me, characterises societies and makes them a realm of its own' (pp. 158, 159). Fouillée, as we can see, goes with Espinas, but only part of the way; he stops where he ought to stop, where reason becomes unreason.

It is admirable how clearly Fouillée focussed the problem before him. 'Two fundamental conceptions of society,' he says, 'divide, to this day, the spirits between them. These two conceptions ...

are [the theory of] social organism and [the theory of] social contract. Although they appear at first contradictory, a detailed analysis of them both shows that they are equally true and consequently reconcilable. The one seems to derive all in society from the fatal laws of [objective] life and nature, the other from the free play of thought and men's [subjective] life; the one speaks above all of slow development in subordination to the fixities of tradition, the other seems to hope for the creation of a new world through freedom. The one places its trust in the almost unconscious conduct of which the body social is the scene; the other puts it in the strength of ideas and of the will.' The two points of view are commonly presented as contradictory, and we are invariably invited to embrace the one and reject the other. But, Fouillée says, in our opinion rightly, 'in their positive foundations, the two theories are both correct; the one is [in itself] as true as the other. Their errors arise [merely] from false deductions and false interpretations; and consequently the full truth is the scientific synthesis of these two theories' (pp. 392, 393). This merging of the streams is what Fouillée hopes to bring about, and the sentences which we have quoted indicate already how he proposes to achieve his aim. Organicism, he explains, thinks in terms of a subconscious urge to associate, contractualism in terms of association through fully conscious action; but it is in both cases *man* who acts, and in man the subconscious and the conscious are not two worlds apart; on the contrary, they form a continuum. The conscious will is fed from a subconscious root, and the subconscious root-stock tends, spontaneously, to express and perfect itself in conscious conduct. Bluntschli would find the origin of the state in a natural sociability, Rousseau in artificial contracting, but 'they do not see', either of them, 'that sociability, being the tendency to associate, resolves itself into a tendency to conclude contracts' (p. 8).

If there is any society at all which is prefigured and preformed by nature, and which would consequently confirm the submissions of organicism, it is surely that of male and female, husband and wife. But, Fouillée asks, is the marriage partnership not at the same time also the archetype of a conscious union, a society which comes into being through a contract? And is it not the same with the children? Originally, they remain with the parents because they must, because nature bids them so, but after a while they remain out of their own free will, because it suits them, and there is no assignable moment when the one condition gives way to the other: organic and contractual arrangement shade into each other like the colours of the spectrum. There is certainly transition, indeed, radical change, but no radical break. Or, to speak even more correctly, transition and change occur only in our conceptual interpretation of the family, not in the family itself. In life, the marriage contract matures into organic union, and the organic union of parents and children weakens into a utilitarian association by entirely imperceptible steps: there is continuity, and not that discontinuity which the clamour of the philosophical parties and partisans with their warring definitions would suggest.

Developing his theme, Fouillée tries to establish two correlated points: firstly, that an organism, though essentially a unity, is also a multiplicity; and secondly, that a contractual whole, though essentially a multiplicity, is also a unity, and not necessarily a precarious one. 'What is, according to all the physiologists, the first and the most essential feature of a living body? It is the *co-operation* of dissimilar parts for the preservation of the whole.' This co-operation, if it is successful, can be called, in the style of philosophical realism, harmony, or, if we so prefer it, in the style of philosophical nominalism, equilibrium of forces: in life this comes very much to the same thing. It would be wrong to forget the independence of the cells over their interdependence in the organism: 'Nothing is so egoistical at the outset as the *animalcula* of which an animal is composed; each one draws everything to himself, and it is the equilibrium of these egoisms which constitutes life. On seeing the marvel of the end result, one would [be inclined to] say, no doubt, that each cell has worked for the others, yet it has worked only for itself; one would [be inclined to] say that it has set before itself as its end the welfare of the whole, and yet it has had no other end but its own preservation which [simply] happens to be mechanically tied in with that of the other cells.' 'We do not know what life as such is,' Fouillée writes, 'we know only that, in the form in which we encounter it, it is made up of *several lives leading in the end to a state of equilibrium*' (pp. 78, 89, 87[1]).

While an organism is in this way—against the popular idea of it—a composite thing, a contract creates—again in contradiction

[1] The italics are Fouillée's own.

to common conceptions—a unitary formation. It is absurd to think of a nation as an association one can contract out of, or which one needs to contract into; but that does not mean that a nation cannot be interpreted as a network of tacit agreements and arrangements. 'He who says contract,' Fouillée writes in a lapidary sentence, 'says solidarity'. 'The [concept of] *contrat social*', he also writes, 'does not logically imply . . . the break-up of the state: the French nation is constituted by all the Frenchmen *together with the totality of the general and particular contracts which bind them together*. And this bond is the most solid and the most durable of all because it does not depend on any single individual will, but on forty millions of wills which have obligations towards each other and even towards the generations whose inheritance they accept . . . Society is, consequently, under this system, not a simple nominal *collection* of individuals . . . It is, on the contrary, an *organism* [of a kind] . . . Contracting has precisely the aim of making that organism more perfect and more solid' (pp. 16, 14, 15, 29). What Fouillée does in these passages can perhaps be summed up by saying that he virtually abandons the old conceptions and replaces them by the new key-concept of *solidarity* which can be regarded as expressive both of the essence of organic and of that of contractual integration.

But though this is the upshot of his analysis, he chooses to use the old conceptions, or at any rate the old terms, for the formulation of his new definition of sociality. He calls society '*a contractual organism*' (p. 111 and often). This is a very clever throw. On the surface, we have in this phrase a contradiction in terms; but, more profoundly considered, we have in it an altogether realistic description of the basic social fact. Society *is* both a multiplicity *and* a unity, and so 'contractual organism' is entirely apt. Fouillée also calls it 'an organism which exists because it has been mentally conceived and willed' (p. 115)—conceived and willed like a contract, and constituted as a unity like an organism. Fouillée comes close here to a lawyer's concept which has great sociological significance, the concept of the legal personality. The state is in law a personality: it can act as such, sue and be sued, and so on. But it is not a personality outside the law: legal fiction apart, it is a will of wills, not a will of its own—and in this way it both is, and is not, an independent entity.

Fouillée claims that his conscious and considered contradiction in terms closes for ever the protracted war of the philosophical schools: 'From the point of view of contractual organism, nominalism and realism coincide: human society is something man designs, and it is also an objective reality . . . Political striving, in a society of beings endowed with reason and volition, has to be a work of art in order to be a work of nature, and the contractual organism is precisely the reconciliation of these two things' (pp. 121, 122). With the spurious contrast between nominalism and realism, there also disappears the old conflict between causalism and finalism, so far at any rate as the social sciences are concerned. Men strive to realise a vision of society which they have set before themselves: in so far as they strive to realise it, it is their end (in the sense of finalism); in so far as they set it before themselves, they are its cause (in the sense of causalism); for, and here Fouillée opens up an avenue along which cultural sociology has ever to advance, in the sphere of humanity, we must operate with the concept, nay, the reality, of a conscious cause.

It was one of Fouillée's convictions that society is becoming more and more contractual (though this means for him that it is also becoming more and more coherent, i.e. organical), and this idea links him with the thinker whom we have to consider next —Ferdinand Tönnies, whose famous *Gemeinschaft und Gesellschaft* first appeared seven years after Fouillée's book, in 1887. Tönnies is nearer to the central position of a specifically cultural sociology than even Fouillée had been, because he sees the basis of all social life in a *will* to associate, that is to say, not in a natural fact or law, but in an exclusively human attribute. The very first words of his book bear witness to this belief: 'Human wills stand in manifold relations to one another.' It is this fact which matters to the sociologist: it is this fact which must provide the key to the understanding of all social phenomena.

When we speak of willing, we do not, however, always mean the same thing. If a man who is in the throes of thirst sees a glass of water, he wants it, and we say that his will is directed towards it; if a man who is engaged in trade sees the chance of a profit, he also wants it, and we say again that his will is directed towards it. But the first kind of will is essentially different from the second. The first is entirely natural. It is in the last analysis the inborn craving to survive, and therefore we can also speak of an existential will here. The second is not so much natural as rational.

There is no dark urge at the bottom of it, but rather a cool and clear calculation, a cunning balancing of chances. Perhaps we can best throw the contrast between the two types into high relief, if we raise the question: *why* does the man concerned display this appetition, why does he will what he wills? In the case of the thirsty man and the glass of water, it is not possible to give a satisfactory answer, unless it is an answer to say that there is an elementary striving to be, and that this desire for drink is a manifestation of it. We are immediately up against mystery: the mystery of life, the mystery of existence. But when we consider the business man and his prospective profit, when we ask him why he buys, at this time, the shares or the wares he is buying, we shall get very full reasons: there is no mystery at all; on the contrary, there is nothing but rationality. The motive is as assignable as it is unassignable in the other case.

From these two forms of willing, Tönnies tells us, spring two forms of society: *Gemeinschaft* and *Gesellschaft*, community and association.[1] When a man marries, he follows as a rule what we fondly call the voice of the heart: love, as an experience, is in the last analysis inexplicable, and so is sympathy. If calculation is brought in, if the man wants the dowry rather than the girl, we feel that something is wrong here, that the relationship is spoilt. Community repels and recoils from the monetary motive, and the marriage bond is, or rather ought to be, a communal bond, not merely an associational bond. But when a man looks for a business partner, he would be quite wrong if he allowed himself to be guided by sympathy and sentiment. He must be able to trust the other fellow, trust his judgment, not just like him: what would happen if he joined up with a likeable scoundrel or a lovable half-wit? The relationship would lead to loss and ultimately to ruin. Association demands and thrives under the monetary motive, and a business firm is an associational bond, not a communal one. The contrast between the two social formations is manifest. Yet let us remark straight away that it must not be exaggerated. No hurt arises for the community of husband and wife if the wife does bring a dowry, just as no harm comes to the association of partners in commerce if they feel friendship for each other. The community can be strengthened through an admixture of the

---

[1] Though *Gesellschaft* means literally society, we prefer to keep this word for more general use.

associational element, the association through a dash of communal feeling. Community and association are not mutually exclusive; the question is merely, what predominates.

Marriage bond and business firm are forms *in* society rather than forms *of* society, but Tönnies' dichotomy applies to forms of society as well. An example that springs to mind at once is that of town and country. The village has more communal traits than associational ones, whereas the situation is the other way round in a typical town. And this fact reflects not only a spatial, but also a historical contrast. Older societies were communal rather than associational, newer societies are associational rather than communal (a truth which Tönnies elaborates without nostalgia or sentimentality). We need only compare a primitive clan with a capitalist society. The clansmen thought of themselves as incarnations of the same life; buyers and sellers, or employers and employees, assuredly do not.

Tönnies pursues this basic dichotomy into many of its ramifications. Take, for instance, a loan. Lending a helping hand is one thing in a community, and quite another thing in an associational setting. In a community it comes under the heading of neighbourliness, in an association under that of business. Charging interest is unbecoming in the one context and a matter of course in the other: hence the prohibition of usury in precapitalist societies and its regular presence (though under a less pejorative name) in modern capitalist societies. Or take the relationship of superior and inferior, master and man. How different is the mutual attitude between a farmer or peasant and his helpers from that of a factory owner and his hands! It is not, as Tönnies explains it, a difference in value, as if the one set of relations were good and the other bad. It is, rather, a difference in kind. In a community superior and inferior may like or loathe each other, and dipping the bread into the same bowl may as easily lead to more loathing as to greater liking: but whatever the tone or timbre of the relationship, it is one of psychological involvement, and this is characteristic of community, as its absence is characteristic of association. The shareholder who, in a modern concern, is the employer of his plant's employees is not a real person at all to those whose labour he buys, nor, for that matter, is the manager who does the actual managing. The factory director is at best a name to the workers, and so is the worker to the factory directors.

In the context of the present investigation, the great importance of Tönnies' discussion and distinction consists in this: that (as he himself clearly realised) the two types of social ordering which he sets against each other demand for their description different images. Community is a unity rather than a diversity, and so calls up the image of unitary substances, e.g. that of the body physical. Association is a diversity rather than a unity, and so it calls up the contrary image of distinct, if related, forces, e.g. those that pull the sides of a pair of scales down or push them up. This recognition, too, is to be found right at the beginning of Tönnies' text. 'Human wills stand in manifold relations to one another . . . The relationship itself . . . is [according to its degree of integration] conceived of either as real and organic life—this is the essential characteristic of *Gemeinschaft*, or as imaginary and mechanical structure—this is the concept of *Gesellschaft*. *Gemeinschaft*. . . . is the lasting and genuine form of living together. In contrast to *Gemeinschaft*, *Gesellschaft* is transitory and superficial. Accordingly, *Gemeinschaft* should be understood as a living organism, *Gesellschaft* as a mechanical aggregate and artifact.'[1]

As can be seen, Tönnies appears to justify both traditional forms of sociology, realism as well as nominalism. But this means in effect that he justifies neither—indeed, that he invalidates both. For, as we have already emphasised, community and association are not, in life, separate phenomena; they are separate only in thought, by virtue of definition. To quote once more from the first lines: 'Every [social] relationship represents unity in plurality or plurality in unity.' Every social relationship is therefore bound to exhibit organism-like and mechanism-like features, though, of course, in accordance with its character, in different proportions. Tönnies underlines this with all due emphasis. He divides only in order to unite. No relationship could possibly come nearer to the symbiotic, organismic pattern than that of mother and child; for a while they are literally one body. Yet hardly has the separation taken place, when associational elements appear. Even breast-feeding rests on selfish urges, hunger on the one side, relief from glandular pressure on the other. No relationship, on the other hand, could possibly come nearer to the mechanistic-contractual pattern than that of exchange; while they yet higgle and haggle,

[1] In the English translation, published under the title *Community and Association*, the above quotations are found on pp. 37 and 39.

the negotiators are literally pulling against each other. But hardly has agreement been reached, when communal elements appear. Both partners are benefited by the business deal they have arranged. And as it is the tendency for children to leave their mothers when they grow up, so it is the tendency for buyers and sellers to renew their contacts and contracts and to make permanent what was, to begin with, but momentary and transitory. To speak realistically of society, means therefore to speak of organism and mechanism at the same time—in other words, it means constantly to mix one's metaphors. But this would be a bad, an unbearable thing. Where metaphors have to be mixed, it is far better to discard them. This, it would appear, is the logical consequence of Tönnies' whole investigation. He makes it understandable that some societies (those of the community type) have conceptualised themselves in organismic language, others (those of the associational type) in mechanistic terms. But he forces us at the same time to conclude that both have in this way overlooked part of their reality: communities their associational, associations their communal side, and for this reason their social theories have not been, what they ought to have been, truth in its entirety.

It was the pioneering effort of men like Tönnies and Fouillée which created an intellectual climate in which the third sociology, the cultural school, could unfold and mature. We shall try to elucidate its essence in the next chapter; here we should like to wind up by a look at the thinker who, perhaps more ably than any other, drew the necessary conclusions from the fact, increasingly recognised by all free from prejudice, that both philosophical realism and philosophical nominalism are inappropriate in sociological theory: Georg Simmel. We have seen that Simmel did not manage to preserve the necessary balance, that, in the end, he came down on the side of nominalism after all. But this regrettable lapse does not destroy the value of those parts of his work which are untainted by it.

'There is an old conflict over the nature of society', Simmel said in his address to the first meeting of the German Sociological Society in 1910. 'One side mystically exaggerates its significance, contending that only through society is human life endowed with reality. The other regards it as a mere abstract concept by means of which the observer draws the realities, which are individual human beings, into a whole, as one calls trees and brooks, houses and meadows, a "landscape". However one decides this conflict, he must allow society to be a reality in a double sense. On the one hand are the individuals in their directly perceptible existence, the bearers of the processes of association, who are united by these processes into the higher unity which one calls "society"; on the other hand, the interests which, living in the individuals, motivate such union: economic and ideal interests, warlike and erotic, religious and charitable. To satisfy such urges and to attain such purposes, arise the innumerable forms of social life, all the with-one-another, for-one-another, in-one-another, against-one-another, and through-one-another, in state and commune, in church and economic associations, in family and clubs.'[1] These words show, to some extent, Simmel's bias towards individualism and formalism, but they also show the distinctive nature of his doctrine and the wisdom contained in it. Society is for him neither a fact of the objective world nor a fiction of human discourse: it is a *tertium quid*. Simmel has risen superior to the limitations of the man in the street and those kindred ones characteristic of the earlier sociologists. Equally dominated by materialism, the only alternative they ever saw was that between some*thing* and no*thing*. Simmel understood that society is certainly no thing, but also that it is not, for that reason, nothing. It consists of those invisible and intangible, but nevertheless decidedly real threads which go from man to man and weave a network between them and around them. It is, properly understood, an *interhuman* reality.

One of the most significant passages in Simmel's *Soziologie* are the pages in which he discusses solitude. Solitude must not be contrasted with sociality, for sociality remains in and through solitude, and this proves that the social element is not secondary in man (though it does not have the undivided primacy either). 'The concept of solitude', Simmel writes, 'by no means signifies merely the absence of all society, but precisely its somehow imagined and only subsequently negated presence. Solitude receives its unambiguously positive meaning as a distant effect of society—either as an echo of past, or as an anticipation of future, relationships, either as longing or as conscious rejection . . . The whole bliss and the whole bitterness of solitude are surely only

---

[1] 'Soziologie der Geselligkeit', translated as 'The Sociology of Sociability' and published in *The American Journal of Sociology*, vol. LV, 1949/50, pp. 254–261. We have quoted the opening lines.

different reactions to influences received in society; solitude is a form of interaction from which the one side has been *realiter* withdrawn . . . and continues to live and act only *idealiter* in the mind of the other subject' (*Soziologie*, p. 77). When man is alone, then precisely do we see that he is neither a mere individual, nor yet a mere collective creature (p. 719).

If the social element is in this way co-constitutive even of man in isolation, any extreme nominalism would be erroneous, though any extreme realism would be no less so. Simmel reminds his readers that, according to Kant, nature is a unity nowhere but in the observer's mind. This, he insists, cannot be said of society. 'Society is an objective unity which does not require [for the establishment of its unitary character] an observer uncontained in it . . . The things of nature . . . are further from each other than [human] souls; the union of one man with another which lies in understanding, in love, in common effort—there is no analogue to it in the spatial world, in which every entity occupies its own place which cannot be shared with any other' (p. 29). 'In this book', Simmel also writes, 'I describe the living functional interaction of elements as their unity. It is more than their mere summation and stands sociologically in contrast to it' (p. 66).

Simmel is at his best, and particularly profound, where he tries to make it clear that some of man's most deep-rooted mental habits militate against a proper comprehension of the phenomenon of sociality. The very words by means of which we must do our thinking incline and induce us to contrast 'individual' and 'society', but this whole distinction is altogether spurious and nefarious. 'The individual is in a double position: he is comprised in society and at the same time stands over against it; he is a member of the social organism and at the same time himself a closed organic whole; he is a life unto himself and a life for society. The essential point . . . is that "inside" and "outside" . . . are not two determinations which stand side by side—even though they may, on occasions, develop into mutual hostility—but describe the altogether unitary position of man living in society. His existence is not only, when its contents are divided up, partially social and partially individual: it stands under the fundamental, reality-determining, not further reducible category of a unity which we cannot express otherwise than by saying that it is a synthesis or co-terminousness of the two logically contradictory qualities of being member and being independent, being created by, and contained in, society, and living out of one's own vital centre and for the sake of it. Society does not consist of individuals who are partially non-social, but of beings who experience themselves on the one hand as fully social existences and on the other—preserving the same substance—as fully personal ones. These are not two points of view which would lie side by side without relation ... but they form between them a unit which we call a social creature, a synthetic category' (pp. 40, 41). All this may sound unduly complex, but the complexity lies more in our language than in life. In life—in social life—unity and diversity are simply one, and they are one because interrelation, the very essence of sociality, fuses them together.

From this vantage-point Simmel discovered a whole new world of social phenomena which the sociological realists and the sociological nominalists had both failed to notice. The simple act of self-adornment—putting on lipstick or choosing a bright necktie—has, for Simmel, sociological importance, for it is meant to have its effect in social commerce, in inter-human relationships. The discussion of artificial scent and its use (pp. 659 *et seq.*) is an example of this widening of the sociological interest. The organicists, with their tendency to play up the social factor, had always seen more than the mechanicists; but even they had been half blind, for they had investigated only those phenomena of human interaction which had become solidified, and never those which were, so to speak, still in solution. They had spoken about marriage, not about coquetry, about law-courts, not about lying, about war, not about hate. What is so great about Simmel is the wide sweep of his net. He could truly say with Terence: *Homo sum; humani nihil a me alienum puto*—I am a man; nothing that pertains to man is for me a matter of unconcern. His was a *human* science of human society, and this most radically distinguishes him from those who aped the sciences of the subhuman spheres.

What we must above all retain out of Simmel's far-flung investigations is, of course, his definition of society. This, as we have seen already, is simple enough. 'Society exists where several individuals enter into interaction' (p. 5). 'A plurality of elements becomes a unity' (p. 21). Nothing could be more elementary and nothing more true—yet those who are caught in the false alternative: thing or nothing, have always resisted Simmel's intermediate concept of sociality. It is said that the wild Irish could not understand, or would not believe, the doctrine of the Trinity which St. Patrick was preaching to them, and that the Saint, in his near-despair, thought of the clover-leaf (which is one and three at the same time) as an impressive symbol which would break down their stubborn resistance. Simmel tried an equally suggestive image: the image of the human hand. 'The fingers enjoy relative independence of each other and possess a movability of their own, but yet they are indissolubly tied together and find their true meaning only in cooperation. It is for this reason that they offer a most striking simile to the social union of individual men' (p. 127). Needless to say, Simmel's metaphor can as little resolve and exhaust the mystery of sociality as St. Patrick's that of divinity, but it ought to be pondered again and again by all who want to know what a society really is.

XV

The Essence of Cultural Sociology

BEFORE THE days of Fouillée and Tönnies, sociology was like a healthy man trying to walk on two crutches, the one labelled physics, the other physiology—crutches which hindered rather than helped his progress. The growing realisation that society is always and everywhere both a unity and a multiplicity knocked these sham supports away, for if, in order to secure realism, both the organistic and the mechanistic models had to be applied at the same time, neither of them could possibly be useful any longer: they simply cancel each other out. Sociology had now to stand on its own feet, and it found the experience neither testing nor trying. On the contrary, the self-condemned weakling rejoiced, and rightly, in his real, at long last realised strength.

The coming of a cultural school in social philosophy can therefore be described as an act of liberation—liberation from the erstwhile voluntary bondage to the natural sciences. Society, it was seen now, is neither a creation of the laws of mechanics nor a reflection of the laws of biology: it is man's own work, sprung from his will, sustained by his will, perfectible through his will. When sociology secured its own autonomy, it also opened the eyes of all to the autonomy of man. But care must be taken lest the new theory fall into the errors of the old: to disregard dividing-lines, to exaggerate, to regard as absolute what is only relative. The natural and the social sciences can never part company, for reality is one, and if reality is one, man's picture of it must be unitary too. Perhaps we can compare the old and the new relationship between mechanics and biology on the one hand, sociology on the other, with the help of a spatial simile. Realism and nominalism both laid claim to universal rule: pan-organicism (what Dilthey calls 'objective idealism') regarded everything as animate, pan-mechanicism (what Dilthey calls 'naturalism') as basically inanimate. There was in either case a unified empire under one strong hand. The third philosophy (the 'idealism of freedom')—in sociology: the cultural approach—however, is dualistic. It allows that the laws of nature are imperative, but it also insists that they leave room for an area of indeterminacy. It is as if we had a country with concentric circles: an outer belt under the sway of mechanical forces, an intermediate ring under the sway of vital forces, and an inner core where cultural forces reign supreme. Or, slightly to change our metaphor: the laws of mechanics are, according to this manner of thinking, such that they limit—but at the same time also permit—the phenomenon of life; the laws of mechanics and biology between them are such that they limit —but at the same time also permit—the phenomenon of culture. What the cultural school of sociology suggests is that society, being subsumable neither under mechanics nor under biology, being, on the contrary, an essentially human reality, must be thought of as belonging to that heart-land which is indeed surrounded by the dominion of impersonal forces, but is in itself, in its proper sphere, the abode of freedom.

The crusade for the autonomy of the social sciences must today be directed against excessive materialism—not against the sciences of material reality of course, for these are their helpful and peace-loving neighbours, but against those who would make the sciences of material reality into sciences of human, cultural reality also, who would push them beyond their rightful borderlines in order to invade and engulf the neighbouring territory. It will, however, be appropriate, at this point, to remind ourselves that the front was not always facing the same way. There was a time when the threat came from the right rather than from the left—from theology rather than from physics or biology. In men's speculations about the Godhead, two ideas have been particularly important: the idea of God as the Creator (the unmoved mover) and the idea of God as the Co-ordinator (he who brings cosmos out of chaos); in other words, the idea of the God who worked on the first day, and the idea of the God who worketh still. The former conception holds no necessary threat to the autonomy of sociology, but the latter does, and this threat was rebutted by one of the greatest sociologists of all time, Giambattista Vico. Without polemics, yet with a firm purpose, he developed, in his *Principi di una Scienza Nuova* (1725), an interpretation of society which makes it man's own work, and in doing so he brought out many of the features which must characterise any and every cultural sociology.[1]

Being himself truly and profoundly religious, Vico does not deny the divine origin of man, but he insists that God gave man everything that he needed to build his own society, in order to socialise and thereby to humanise himself. Our first forefathers were indeed semi-bestial, but already they were potentially sociable and kind, and what happens in history is that this potential sociability and humanity becomes actualised (or, what is also possible in view of men's freedom, that this actualised sociability and humanity degenerates again and there is return to the state of semi-bestiality). It is interesting to see how Vico must fight, as the modern cultural school is forced to do, against both an over-emphasis and an under-emphasis on the determination of the course of development. According to one philosophy of history, which pre-figures organicism, everything is pre-determined: the pattern is there from the very beginning and individual action must fit itself into it. According to another conviction, which pre-figures mechanicism, everything is indeterminate: there is no pattern pre-existent, but only a pattern emergent; individual action is free, and reality, as it shapes, its resultant. Vico rejects both interpretations. The pattern of history is pre-existent *in posse* and emergent *in esse*. Or, to speak more simply, man has it in him to become truly man—the semi-bestial oaf of the beginning has it in him to become the humanitarian personality of the fulness of time—and history is this unfolding to perfection, this realisation of the promise, or, indeed, its loss.

The detail is not important here, and to some extent it is disappointing, for Vico was a man born before his proper time. But two salient principles stand out and are unassailable: human society is a cultural phenomenon, and human society is a process. Human society is, first of all, a cultural phenomenon because sociability is transmitted by tradition, developed in experience, and inculcated through education. This need not mean that it does not perhaps have a natural root, though it is well-nigh impossible to identify such a root. Trying to discover it, is like trying to see

[1] Concerning Pascal, a kindred spirit, cf. my book, *Social Theory and Christian Thought*, 1959, pp. 63–76.

in absolute darkness. What the classical nature-*versus*-nurture controversy showed was above all that nature and nurture can be divided by definition, but not in observation. Yet it hardly matters to social philosophy whether there is such a root, for what is undeniable is that it will come to nothing, that it will not develop, unless cultural influences foster it and tend it. All study of child life, sophisticated as well as naive, scientific as well as purely impressionistic, proves that the infant is completely self-centred, and that the social sentiment, especially in its fuller forms, is of tardy growth. Nor are we restricted, in making up our minds in this important matter, to the observation of that rather abstract quality, sociality in general. It is much easier and more instructive to watch a concrete social endowment, for instance language, in its development. Nature has given men the necessary apparatus for the use of language, a tongue in the physical sense of the word; but it is not she that gives him language itself, a tongue in the linguistic sense of the word, a mother tongue. King James IV of Scotland sent two infants to the island of Inchkeith with a deaf-and-dumb nurse, in order to see whether they would spontaneously learn to speak. He expected that they would reveal to him the original language of mankind; but we can be sure that Sir Walter Scott is right, who, after telling the story, concludes by saying that the children will at best have known how to 'bleat like the goats and sheep on the island'.[1] This prime social medium can be acquired in one way, and one way only: it has to be learnt, and so has sociality in general. It is no accident that Vico was a great educator as well as a great social philosopher.

When we say today that human society is a process, we do not in the first place think of history as a whole. Vico did, but this proves, more than anything else, that he was a forerunner of modern sociology rather than a representative of it, that he was as yet concerned with the philosophy of history rather than with the philosophy of social life. But he was right in insisting that sociality is nothing static, that it is something which is at any time, either on the upgrade, or on the downgrade. As especially the members of the Simmel school have emphasised, human beings are either moving towards each other, from contact to amalgamation, or away from each other, from unity to conflict. Yet there is more to the conception of sociality as a process than even that.

[1] *Tales of a Grandfather*, chapter XXIII, ed. 1892, p. 211.

If society is an *inter*-human reality—if it is, to use Simmel's graphic phrases, all the with-one-another, for-one-another, in-one-another, against-one-another, and through-one-another which we find in the various departments of life—then it is not something that either is or is not, but something that *happens*. It has reality, but not the reality of a thing. It has the reality of an event, or rather chain of events. We see here that cultural sociology is indeed an alternative to both organicism and mechanicism. For organicism, society is a fact; for mechanicism it is a fiction; for the cultural school it is a process.

Process means therefore much more in the context of sociology than any concrete process, be it the process of social experience, be it the process of personal education, be it the process of cultural transmission, or be it the process of universal history. It even means more than all these processes taken together, important though they are both singly and in conjunction. It describes the very essence of social reality. But Vico's treatment of history as the social process *par excellence*, though it constitutes, from our modern point of view, a misplacement of emphasis, does hold a great lesson for us. Though we should be quite wrong to merge sociology in, or to model it on, the study of history, there is yet more in common between historiography and sociology than between sociology and either biology or mechanics. For history is the record of human conduct, and human conduct it is that sociology has to elucidate. There is no greater laboratory of social experimentation than the past, and it is a pity that sociologists, fascinated by other kinds of laboratory, have not learnt more from it. Sociology is a study of man. It is history, and not only the present, that shows us what man is like. Past man is not present man, but he is *man*, and therefore at least a foil to the sociologist's contemporary researches—the best sort of 'control' there can possibly be.

The history of the cultural school in sociology has not yet been written, and no attempt will be made to present it in this book, be it even in outline, for we are concerned with types of thought and not with individual thinkers. Indeed, the whole concept of culturalism is as yet ill-defined, and it is one of the purposes of this investigation to help in making it more concrete, to give it face and sharpen its features. But by way of illustration, we should like to glance at two important men who have contributed greatly to it—Charles Horton Cooley and William Graham Sumner. In the next chapter, we shall then round out the picture by discussing Emile Durkheim and Max Weber, though there we shall also have to report, regretfully, the partial persistence of the old dichotomy in the new setting.

We have seen above, in the quotation given on p.215 /216, how hard Simmel had to strive to demonstrate that unity and multiplicity, far from standing in contrast to each other, are really the same thing in the social phenomenon. The passage we have reproduced is true, but it is laboured, and this proves that he has not quite penetrated to the core, for the core of the matter is simple. Cooley is far superior in this respect: he makes the same point not only more convincingly, but almost without effort, and this shows that he is the more advanced thinker, even though his decisive book, *Human Nature and the Social Order*, appeared six years before Simmel's *Soziologie*, in 1902.

'A separate individual', Cooley writes on his first page, 'is an abstract unknown to experience, and so likewise is society when regarded as something apart from individuals. The real thing is Human Life which may be considered either in an individual aspect or in a social . . . but is always, as a matter of fact, both individual and general. In other words, "society" and "individuals" do not denote separable phenomena, but are simply collective and distributive aspects of the same thing, the relation between them being like that between other expressions one of which denotes a group as a whole and the other the members of the group, such as the army and the soldiers . . . So far as there is any difference between the two, it is rather in our point of view than in the object we are looking at . . . A *complete* view of society would also be a complete view of all the individuals, and *vice versa*; there would be no difference between them. And just as there is no society or group that is not a collective view of persons, so there is no individual who may not be regarded as a particular view of social groups. He has no separate existence . . . In his life a man is bound into the whole of which he is a member, and to consider him apart from it is quite as artificial as to consider society apart from individuals' (pp. 1–3). How simple it all sounds in Cooley's presentation!

Trying to manoeuvre us out of our unhappy mental and linguistic habits, Cooley takes a number of further concepts which are always coupled and contrasted with each other, but which

are, properly considered, not to be divided and divorced. Here
we can look at two samples only: suggestion and choice; love
and self-assertion. When we speak of suggestion—characteristically we usually speak of social suggestion—we imply that society
is supreme, man subject to it; when, on the other hand, we speak of
choice—characteristically we usually speak of individual choice—
we imply that man is free, society unimportant. But the contrast
collapses when the two phenomena are more closely scrutinised.
The apparently freest choice is the application of a scale of values
which we have developed in our intercourse with others; the
apparently most mechanical imitation of others is yet a kind of
selection and we invariably ring personal changes on the communal theme. 'The popular view . . . thinks of will only in the
individual aspect and does not grasp the fact that the act of choice
is cause and effect in a general life; and . . . it commonly over-
looks the importance of involuntary forces, or at least makes them
separate from and antithetical to choice . . . The distinction between suggestion and choice is not [however,] a sharp opposition
between separable or radically different things, but rather a way
of indicating the lower and higher stages of a series . . . We speak
of suggestion as mechanical; but it seems probable that all psychical life is selective, or, in some sense, choosing . . . On the
other hand, our most elaborate and volitional thought and action
is suggested in the sense that it consists not in creation out of
nothing, but in a creative synthesis or reorganisation of old
material' (pp. 18, 15, 16).

The ideas of love and self-assertion are commonly thought to
be even more mutually exclusive than those of suggestion and
choice, but here, too, the facts are different from what they seem.
'We may, perhaps, distinguish two kinds of love,' Cooley tells us,
'one of which is mingled with self-feeling, and the other is not.'
In neither is there the tension between self-surrender and self-
assertion so often alleged. In the one case, the self tends to fade
out and cannot stand in opposition to anything; in the other case,
love itself becomes filled with self-centredness and thus cannot be
said to be distinguishable from it. 'In so far as one feels . . . a dis-
interested, contemplative joy . . . the distinterested love . . . which
has no designs with reference to its object, he has no sense
of "I" at all, but simply exists in something to which he feels no
bounds. Of this sort, for instance, seem to be the delight in natural

beauty . . . . , the joy and rest of art . . . and the admiration of persons regarding whom we have no intentions . . . Love of this sort obliterates that idea of separate personality whose life is always unsure and often painful . . . But love that plans and strives is always in some degree self-love . . . The love of a mother for her child is appropriative, as is apparent from the fact that it is capable of jealousy. Its characteristic is not selflessness, by any means, but the association of self-feeling with the idea of *her* child. It is no more selfless in its nature than the ambitions of a man' (pp. 129–131).

These are interesting analyses, but they are no more than preliminary skirmishing. Cooley's main *coup* is the proof that self and society are not, the one primary, the other secondary, but are, in his unsurpassably felicitous phrase, *twin-born*. Certainly, we must begin (as life does) with self-awareness, but this is a plastic, even empty sentiment, and capable of far-reaching socialisation. What the self will contain, nay, what it will be, depends on the life-experience which it will undergo.

This life-experience, as Cooley (who was not only a great sociologist, but also a great psychologist) describes it, begins with a completely undifferentiated stream of images. Neither is the animate at first distinguished from the inanimate, nor, within the animate, the self and the others. 'Personal feeling [i.e., in Cooley's terminology, feeling connected with persons] is not at first clearly differentiated from pleasures of sight, sound, and touch of other origin, or from animal satisfactions having no obvious cause . . . The general impression left upon one is that the early manifestations of sociability indicate less fellow-feeling than the adult imagination likes to impute, but are expressions of a pleasure which persons excite chiefly because they offer such a variety of stimuli to sight, hearing and touch . . . Indeed, there is nothing about personal feeling which sharply marks it off from other feeling; here as elsewhere we find no fences, but gradual transition, progressive differentiation' (pp. 46, 47).

Later on, the living and the lifeless are increasingly contrasted, if for no other reason, than because the latter (the wall) is always the same, whereas the former (the mother or nurse) shows a thousand interesting, nay kaleidoscopic changes, for instance through the eye which is of particular importance in this context. 'By the time a child is a year old the social feeling that at first is indistinguishable from sensuous pleasure has become much specialized upon persons' (p. 49). But—and this is decisive—I and you, *ego* and *alter*, are as yet on the same level. The child will not say, 'I am hungry', but 'Johnny is hungry'; and when the concept of self does appear, it appears as a rule in connection with the concept of the neighbour, for instance, in the context of contention, of conflict. 'This is mine, not yours.' 'The sentiments of self develop by imperceptible gradations out of the crude appropriative instinct of new-born babes', and appropriation, in a social setting, is logically appropriation against somebody else. It is in this way the 'you' that defines the 'me'—and self and society are twin-born. Or, as Cooley also expresses it, society is the looking-glass which the self needs in order to know itself. Take the looking-glass away and self-knowledge vanishes. Take the 'you' away, and there can hardly remain an 'I'. There may remain a body, but not a true man—not a personality.

The all-important fact that I and you, self and society, are always on a level—ontologically equivalent, so to speak—is further illustrated by one of Cooley's most daring similes. 'Suppose we conceive the mind as a vast wall covered with electric light bulbs, each of which represents a possible thought or impulse whose presence in our consciousness may be indicated by the lighting up of the bulb. Now each of the persons we know is represented in such a scheme, not by a particular area of the wall set apart for him, but by a system of hidden connections among the bulbs which causes certain combinations of them to be lit up when his characteristic symbol is suggested. If something presses the button corresponding to my friend A, a peculiarly shaped figure appears upon the wall; when that is released and B's button pressed, another figure appears, including perhaps many of the same lights, yet unique as a whole though not in its parts; and so on with as many people as you please . . . To introduce the self into this illustration, we might say that the lights near the centre of the wall were of a particular color—say red—which faded, not too abruptly, into white towards the edges. This red would represent self-feeling, and other persons would be more or less colored by it accordingly as they were or were not intimately identified with our cherished activities . . . Thus the same sentiment may belong to the self and to several other persons at the same time' (pp. 97, 98).

The sociological message of this simile is the assertion that human minds are not as separate from each other as human bodies, and this conviction is essential, not only for a sound sociology, but also for a sound common-sensical view of human coexistence, provided it is systematically elaborated. For how is it that man comes to know man, comes to understand man, comes to co-operate with man? Once again there are three possibilities. We can either assume that the apparently divided minds of men are really one, aspects of a collective mind, and then we are in the area of organicism. This idea has played a great part in French thinking, and we find it even outside French social philosophy in such significant literary movements as that of *Unanimisme*. But the one-soul theory is obviously metaphysical. Enemies of metaphysics may therefore be driven back to the opposite position which corresponds to mechanicism. There is not one mind of a nation, for instance, but as many minds as there are people in it. But if these minds are thought to be as unconnected as the corresponding bodies, an insuperable difficulty at once arises. For where is then the mental bridge, the connecting medium, which opens the I to the you, the self to society, and *vice versa*? Cooley's argument merges here with that of a great contemporary of his, Max Scheler, with whom he has surprisingly far-reaching affinities. In *The Nature of Sympathy*,[1] Scheler surveys the theories which have undertaken to explain the knowledge of other minds from a consistently individualistic point of view and shows that they all failed. If it is said, for instance, that we see other people, realise, on the basis of the sense impression which we receive of them, or rather of their bodies, that they are very much like ourselves, and conclude that they also have minds as we do (a wide-spread theory), the knowledge of other selves is not really made credible; for such reasoning by analogy would only lead us to the fiction of a man analogous to us, not to the fact of a man different from us; and a second influential theory which operates, not with logical inference, but with empathy, splits upon the same rock. Those who realise this impasse of radical individualism in the face of the phenomenon of true communication between minds have often felt that they must, once again, change over to the concept of a collective mind, to the interpretation of society as an organism of minds. The Cooley-Scheler doctrine makes this unnecessary and thereby remains realistic. It can best be described as a theory

---

[1] Originally published in 1913; English translation by P. Heath, with an introduction from my pen, in 1954. Cf. esp. pp. XXXVIII *et seq.* and part III of the text.

of *intersubjectivity*, and this makes it the *via media* which in fact it is. The self appears in it as a focus in a universal stream of happening in which the other selves are also foci. We know, and we can effectively communicate with, other minds because behind us all there is the common life which holds us together as a unity in diversity—a true unity in a true diversity. 'The vaguely material notion of personality, which does not confront the social fact at all but assumes it to be the analogue of the physical fact, is a main source of fallacious thinking about . . . social and personal life . . . If the person is thought of primarily as a separate material form, inhabited by thoughts and feelings conceived by analogy to be equally separate, then the only way of getting a society is by adding on a new principle of . . . social faculty . . . or the like. But if you start with the idea that the social person is primarily a fact in the mind, and observe him there, you find at once that he has no existence apart from a mental whole of which all personal ideas [ideas relating to persons] are members, and which is a particular aspect of society . . . To many people it would seem mystical to say that persons, as we know them, are not separable and mutually exclusive, like physical bodies, so that what is part of one cannot be part of another, but that they interpenetrate one another, the same element pertaining to different persons at different times, or even at the same time: yet this is a verifiable and not very abstruse fact' (Cooley, pp. 89. 90).

It is clear from what has gone before, that Cooley is concerned primarily—indeed, almost exclusively—with the mind. The coarser facts of nature do not interest him, and he dismisses even the human body in a short passage, insisting that it is not to be identified with the person who often refers to 'his body' in the same manner in which he refers, for instance, to 'his books'—as part of his equipment, not his self (cf. pp. 144 *et seq.*). This self-restriction makes Cooley's a very partial sociology, and, like all that is partial, it is misleading, if taken by itself, even though it is not misleading if fitted into a wider frame. What the sociologist has to explain is not only the socialisation of the inner man, but also that of his outward action, and this is the task performed by William Graham Sumner in his *Folkways* (1906). Sumner's work should therefore be regarded as the necessary complement and corrective of Cooley's.

Cooley's problematic one-sidedness can best be seen in his

starting-point. He assumes that man's social development begins with self-awareness which is, however, a neutral sentiment that can as easily be penetrated by social as by selfish contents. What he forgets, what he does not, to say the least, sufficiently consider, is the fact that the neutral mind is encased in a not-so-neutral body, a body which is, by its whole nature, inclined to self-preference. Sumner begins with this wider idea of man, man as body and mind, man as mind in body. The body may, by its whole nature, be inclined (to put it mildly) to self-preference, but in a social setting the very selfishness of it becomes a fostering soil of sociality. Feeling pleasure and pain, it craves the one and shuns the other. Once burnt, the child will flee the fire. But suffering does not come to us only from things, it also comes to us from our fellow men if we do anything that annoys them, and so we try to avoid their hostility as we do the hotplate or the stove. In this way our behaviour, plastic and adaptable as all that is human, will be turned away from anti-social and towards social modes of conduct. Experience will show us what to do and what not to do, and it will harden into habits—habits supported by social sanctions which will ever be in the background. These sanctioned habits Sumner calls folkways. They are individual and collective at the same time, 'habits for the individual and customs for the group' (pp. 3, 4). They are an inter-human reality. They are cultural for the young learn them, and have to learn them, in the school of life. And they are in several senses of the word processive. They are formed in a process, that of mutual adjustment; they inhere in a process, that of interaction; and they are handed on in a process, that of tradition. As the reader can see, Sumner's theory is typical of the cultural approach.[1] 'The ability to distinguish between pleasure and pain', Sumner says in introducing his

---

[1] Some books on the history of social thought treat Sumner in the chapter on Social Darwinism. He certainly came from Darwinism and remained in his politics a Darwinian all his life; but in his theoretical work he advanced far beyond the Darwinian position. Incidentally, individualistic Darwinism (in contradistinction to the collectivistic-racialist version of people like Gumplowicz) is a good fostering soil for a cultural conception of social life, strange though this may sound, because it stresses both the importance of the biotic factor, and the independence of, and the competition between, the individuals as such. It thus creates the same dualism out of which there sprang in Spencer the concept of ego-altruistic sentiments which marks his nearest approach to the teachings of the cultural school, and was, in fact, one of the traditions out of which Sumner shaped his system. Cf. my essay on 'Herbert Spencer's Three Sociologies' in *The American Sociological Review*, Aug. 1961, pp. 519–521.

doctrine, 'is the only psychical power which is to be assumed . . . Pleasure and pain, on the one side and the other, were the rude constraints which defined the line on which efforts must proceed . . . Thus ways of doing things were selected, which were expedient . . . Along the course on which efforts were compelled to go, habit, routine and skill were developed . . . The operation by which folkways are produced consists in the frequent repetition of petty acts, often by great numbers acting in concert or at least acting in the same way when face to face with the same need. The immediate motive is interest', the interest to avoid pain in general, and the specific pain of human conflict in particular. 'By habit and custom it exerts a strain on every individual within its range . . . We have to recognize it as one of the chief forces by which a society is made to be what it is' (pp. 2, 3).

With this folkway concept, Sumner provides precisely what Cooley failed to provide: a theory of social control. 'The life of human beings, in all ages and stages of culture, is primarily controlled by a vast mass of folkways handed down from the earliest existence of the race . . . Custom regulates the whole of a man's actions . . . All are forced to conform, and the folkways dominate the societal life' (pp. 4 and 38). It is, so we may, nay must, say, in linking Sumner and Cooley, because the folkways socialise men's outer conduct, that men's inner mentality comes to be socialised.

A superficial reading of Sumner might give the impression that his theory is somewhat weighted on the individualistic side, that society is for him the resultant of individual actions and posterior to them, rather than the antecedent, the prior reality. But this would be an erroneous interpretation. First of all, it is clear that the folkway pattern is there, in tradition, when any individual is born, and that the individual is fitted and forced into it by education in the widest sense of the word. 'The mores come down to us from the past. Each individual is born into them as he is born into the atmosphere . . . Each one is subjected to the influence of the mores, and formed by them before he is capable of reasoning about them' (p. 76). But even if we try to see the problem collectively rather than individually, from the racial rather than from the personal point of view, if we try to ascend to the *first* formation of the folkways, we are by no means forced to assume that they are secondary, that they are conventions and quasi-contracts, though they can today be interpreted in this vein. Sumner rightly

refuses to discuss meta-history. 'All origins are lost in mystery
. . . We never can hope to see the beginning . . .' (pp. 7, 8). But
he admits the possibility, and thereby restores the balance, that a
social mode of conduct may have come down to us from some
sub-human ancestors, that our modern cultural (acquired) sociability may be heir and successor to a prehistoric natural (inborn)
gregariousness. 'It is generally taken for granted that men inherited some guiding instincts from their beast ancestry, and it
may be true, although it has never been proved. If there were such
inheritances, they controlled and aided the first efforts to satisfy
needs' (p. 2). If, indeed, there ever was such an inborn gregariousness, so we may complete Sumner's argument, it must have weak-
ened in the course of the ages and produced in the end the type
of man we know and we are—man social and selfish at the same
time. A cultural coherence must have taken the place of a one-
time natural coherence, and twentieth-century sociology, to be
realistic, must be the study of an interhuman reality, and over-
emphasise neither the independence of the individual nor the
strength of the social bond.

That there is no one-sidedness in Sumner can also be
seen from the fact that he describes society as a system
of 'antagonistic cooperation'. In many parts of nature we find
that living things with clearly contrary interests co-operate for the sake of a greater common concern. One of Sumner's
examples is that of desert animals and desert plants. 'The plants
and animals of the desert are rivals for what water there is, but
they combine as if with an intelligent purpose to attain a maximum
of life under the conditions.' Society is such a kind of combination
and co-operation, too. Men are and remain selfish, even within
the social system, but the social system satisfies many elementary
needs and can thus coexist with, nay draw support from, men's
very selfishness, i.e. lack of sociality. 'Men strive with each other,'
but 'competition and combination are two forms of life association which alternate through the whole organic and superorganic
domains.' In their struggle for survival, which is essentially a war
against a common foe, namely nature, men find that standing
together makes for strength, for advantage to all. 'It is, therefore,
the competition of life . . . which produces societal organisation.'
This co-ordination and part-reconciliation of selfishness and sociality is particularly characteristic of advanced societies, societies

in which self-interest and social interest are both exceptionally strong. 'Antagonistic co-operation is the most productive form of combination in high civilization. It is a high action of the reason to overlook lesser antagonisms in order to work together for greater interests' (pp. 16–18).

The concept of antagonistic co-operation, so contradictory in appearance, and so fully realised, without contradiction, in fact, is to Sumner what the idea of a twin-birth of self and society is to Cooley: the thought-form in which nominalism and realism are securely merged and their age-old discussion finally stilled. But there is yet one more conviction of Sumner's, upheld on almost every page of his book, which proves that he is a member of the cultural school, indeed, a typical representative of it: the insistence that men produce their social order in freedom. Those basic adjustments which we call folkways and which combine into a coherent system (and system of coherence) are in no way predetermined. In the great process of trial and error in which men strive to find some norms and forms of coexistence which will allow them to get along with each other with the minimum of conflict, they hit upon many different solutions to their difficulties and disagreements—compromises, conventions, customs and so on—and therefore every concrete society is found to be unlike every other. Cultural comparisons prove this: 'The two great . . . divisions of the human race are the oriental and the occidental. Each is consistent throughout; each has its own philosophy and spirit; they are separated from top to bottom by different mores, different standpoints, different ways, and different notions of what societal arrangements are advantageous. In their contrast they keep before our minds the possible range of divergence in the solution of the great problems of human life' (p. 6). Later in the book, Sumner discusses the characteristics of, and contrasts between, Japanese and Chinese, Hindu and European society and quotes with approval from Hearn's famous study of Japan: 'The discipline of the race was self-imposed. The people have gradually created their own social conditions' (p. 72). It is not nature, not, for instance, physical inheritance, that makes a nation what it is: it is its own historical effort, its effort in freedom.

Sumner shows that there is a chain of connection between the human adjustments at the basis of a society and the cultural achievements which that society brings forth in the course of its development, and which are its finest flowering and fulfilment: from the folkways spring mores, from the mores institutions, laws and ethics, and from them in turn an inclusive style of existence which is the fostering soil of a specific philosophy and art. 'All that has been said . . . about the folkways . . . leads up to the idea of the group character which the Greeks called the ethos, that is, the totality of characteristic traits by which a group is individualized and differentiated from others' (p. 70). What begins as custom ends as culture. But this is only possible because custom *is* culture. The whole logic of Sumner's thought leads to this conclusion, nay forces it upon us, and for this reason his work is a continuous assertion, as well as a continuous illustration, of the cultural character of our common life.

XVI

The Persistence of the Traditional Dichotomy

THE WORKS of Fouillée and Tönnies, and even more those of Cooley and Sumner, should have proved to all and sundry that the social scientist must avoid one pitfall more than any other: to divide in thought what is undivided in life. Yet the unfortunate tendency to sunder and contrast the self and society has persisted throughout, and created, within the cultural school itself, the same dichotomy which since the beginning has split the materialistic tradition in the social sciences in twain.

How very difficult it is to avoid such a split can be seen from a brief glance at the development of the Simmel school. For Simmel, as we have shown, the forms of human interaction are the subject-matter of sociology. The concept of interaction happily avoids both Scylla and Charybdis, both nominalism and realism, but it is not the same with the concept of form. For the old question again arises: are forms facts or fictions? To put it in another way: are they, in any sense of the word, self-existent, or are they merely aspects of content? If the former view is taken, we are back in realism—forms are then facts of a kind; if the latter, we are back in nominalism—forms are then merely fictions, and real is only what is concrete, the content. Modern man will always, almost instinctively, plump for the latter view: where there is no matter, there cannot be any form either. But Simmel himself was already inclined to move in the opposite direction,[1] and although few of us may find his considerations quite convincing, they are certainly far from absurd.

[1] Cf. e.g. *Soziologie*, p. 583.

According to one of Bernard Shaw's more discerning *bons mots*, an English Lenin, should the country ever get one, would be called Prime Minister and go to kiss the King's hand. Two facts are brought out in this joke: firstly, that forms may persist when contents change; and secondly, that forms may be, on occasions, gone through merely for form's sake. The English have for a long time now lived under a substantially democratic, nay republican, constitution: as it is sometimes somewhat vulgarly expressed, the only thing into which the queen may put her nose is her handkerchief. But the forms of monarchy have survived, knee-breeches and all, thus showing that they are perhaps more than merely aspects of content. In general it might be said to be part of the English genius to realise new contents within old forms. Nor has the kissing of the queen's hand by a great dignitary of state upon entering into his office any material significance: the act is a pure formality, and yet it is invariably gone through when the occasion arises. Such considerations may well lead a man to speak of an independent existence of this or that form.[1] Of course, it must remain doubtful to what extent the content of English life has in fact changed since truly monarchical times. It is possible to assert that England's political constitution is even today to some extent monarchical, that the Crown is still a power as well as a symbol. This is a point on which it is very difficult to make up one's mind. And because this is so, because good arguments can be adduced for as well as against the independence of form from content, we cannot be surprised that both a realistic and a nominalistic tendency have developed from Simmel's own position in which the old contrast was contained in a masked form.

The realistic alternative can best be studied in Alfred Vierkandt who, characteristically, came to sociology from social anthropology. What he was interested in was not so much the historically given and observable forms of interaction, but the (assumed) essences behind these forms, the pure ideas which only incarnate and concretise themselves in tangible appearances. As the reader can see, we have a Platonizing tendency at work here: as Plato taught that we must see behind the changing phenomena lasting noumena to which we may ascribe real, if metaphysical, existence, so Vierkandt wanted to discover and uncover the things-in-themselves of social life, its *a priori* forms. According to this way of

[1] *Loc. cit., Eigenbestand ihrer Form . . .*

thinking, there are not only innumerable acts of submission, but there is also submission as such; there are not only innumerable members of society, there is also society as such. Leopold von Wiese did not believe this; he took the other turning and developed, not a Platonic, but a positivistic doctrine. As characteristically, he was, to begin with, an economist. He strongly insisted that the single human being is, and must ever be, the starting point even of sociological investigation, and there is in him a good deal of predilection for mechanistic metaphors and mathematical formulae. Simmel's sociology was in this manner not a final merging of two branch roads into a broader highway, but merely a crossing point, an intersection: one line leads from Plato to Vierkandt, the other from Epicurus to von Wiese. Both pass through Simmel, but they unite in him only in order to divide again.

The contrast between Vierkandt and von Wiese can be observed on a higher level and on a larger scale in the parallel contrast between Emile Durkheim and Max Weber. Both belonged to the cultural school; both accepted, for instance, the dichotomy elaborated by Tönnies and the proposition that the two dissimilar forms of social organisation are ever coexistent and confused;[1] but whereas Durkheim emphasised, within the framework of a cultural conception of social life, the importance of the collective factor, Weber insisted that collectivities are merely collections of individual men and should never be hypostatised into something else or something more.

The assertion put forward in the foregoing paragraph that Durkheim was a member of the cultural school will not, it is to be feared, be universally accepted. It seems in fact to be a widespread conviction that he was a representative of organicism,

---

[1] Cf. Weber, *Wirtschaft und Gesellschaft*, ed. 1947, pp. 21 *et seq*; Engl. transl. by A. R. Henderson and T. Parsons, *The Theory of Social and Economic Organisation*, 1947, pp. 124 *et seq*. Durkheim, *De la Division du Travail Social*, 1893, pp. 66 *et seq.*, Engl. transl. by G. Simpson, *The Division of Labour in Society*, 1947, 63 *et seq*. We are confronted here with a bothersome confusion of terminology, for Durkheim calls modern society organic in coherence, whereas Tönnies speaks of contractual, and hence mechanistic, ordering. The reason is that Durkheim places the main emphasis on the division of labour which is, of course, far greater in modern than in ancient society. The division of labour makes men as different from each other as the bodily organs are: hence his nomenclature. But where men are really different, each pursuing his own trade, there their co-operation is brought about by contract-making: hence Tönnies's nomenclature. As can be seen, the differences between Durkheim and Weber–Tönnies are verbal, not substantial.

and some, though not, in our opinion, completely convincing, evidence can be summoned to buttress this view. Benoit-Smullyan, in an article entitled 'The Sociologism of Emile Durkheim and his School',[1] has suggested that Durkheim's social theory should be described as agelicism. This new word is derived from the Greek vocable for herd; 'by "agelicism" we mean', Benoit-Smullyan writes, 'the general sociological doctrine which maintains . . . the causal priority of the group *quâ* group . . . [and the assertion] that social states and changes are not produced by, and cannot be directly affected or modified by, the desires and volitions of individuals'. This sounds like pure realism; but another and subtler student of Durkheim, Harry Alpert, has given us a different picture. He insists that we must distinguish a 'substantialist social realism' (e.g. Lilienfeld's) and a 'relationist' realism. By the latter term is meant a conception of the social system which sees it as a network of relations, but emphasises that these relations are facts rather than fictions, that they have reality, though a reality *sui generis*, not a physical, material, thingly reality. Clearly, what Alpert calls relational realism is what we have called the third sociology, cultural sociology, sociology rooted in the idealism of freedom, with some slight bias towards objective idealism, i.e. towards organicism. With this estimate it is impossible to disagree; Alpert has the texts, i.e. the facts, on his side. And he establishes his negative even more completely and convincingly than his positive. 'Substantialist social realism . . . implies that society is an ontological reality, a substantial entity having corporate existence apart from, or, to use the traditional phrase, over and above, the individuals who comprise it. *In this substantialist connotation of social realism, Durkheim is not, never was, and never became a realist.* It is surely misleading, if not erroneous, to classify him as such.'[2]

For reasons into which we shall go in a minute, Durkheim laid great stress on the debt which man, as a cultural being, owes to society, on the fact that *cultured* man, in contradistinction to physical man, is a creature, a creation, of society. There are many passages of this import; but there are also passages which show that all the stress on the social factor does not make Durkheim a one-sided sociological realist. At the outset of his career, for

---

[1] Cf. Barnes, *An Introduction to the History of Sociology*, 1948, p. 499.
[2] *Emile Durkheim and His Sociology*, 1939, p. 151. The italics are Alpert's.

instance, he wrote in a book review: 'Society has nothing meta-physical about it. It is not a more or less transcendental substance . . . Since there are only individuals in society, it is they, and they alone, who are the factors of social life.'[1] And here is a quotation from his last major work, *Les Formes Elémentaires de la Vie Religieuse*: 'The clan, like every other sort of society, can live only in and through the individual consciousnesses that compose it. So if religious force, in so far as it is conceived as incorporated in the totemic emblem, appears to be outside of the individuals and to be endowed with a sort of transcendence over them, it, like the clan of which it is the symbol, can be realized only in and through them; in this sense, it is immanent in them and they necessarily represent it as such . . . Social life, just like the ritual, moves in a circle. On the one hand, the individual gets from society the best part of himself, all that gives him a distinct character and a special place among other beings, his intellectual and moral culture. If we should withdraw from men their language, sciences, arts and moral beliefs, they would drop to the rank of animals. So the characteristic attributes of human nature come from society. But, on the other hand, society exists and lives only in and through individuals. If the idea of society were extinguished in individual minds and the beliefs, traditions and aspirations of the group were no longer felt and shared by the individuals, society would die.'[2] This is the voice of culturalism, not of materialism; self and society appear as correlates, not as one superior to the other.

When we ask where, in Durkheim's system, we see best the reconciliation of nominalism and realism—one of the decisive tests for the attribution of a thinker to the cultural school—the answer is: at the point where his ethics and his sociology meet. For Durkheim, the individual was the highest of all values, a conviction in which he never faltered, and this alone proves that he was no one-sided philosophical realist. But *if* the individual is indeed the highest of all values, this is so because *society* has developed in him those qualities which make him valuable: before society, apart from society, outside society, he is hardly more than a beast. Speaking of 'the characteristic sacredness with which the human being is now invested', he writes: 'This character is not

---

[1] *Cit.* Alpert, *loc. cit.*, p. 153.
[2] Engl. transl. by J. W. Swain, *The Elementary Forms of the Religious Life*, ed. 1926, pp. 221, 347.

inherent. Analyse man as he appears to empirical [purely physiological] analysis and nothing will be found that suggests this sanctity . . . But . . . the human being . . . has acquired an incomparable value. It is society that has consecrated him . . . Thus very far from there being the antagonism between the individual and society which is often claimed, moral individualism, the cult of the individual, is in fact the product of society itself.'[1]

However much the individual may receive from society, the fact remains, and Durkheim is, in spite of his supposed agelicism, not oblivious of it, that he is not merely a recipient: that to Durkheim, as to Sumner, the relation of self and society is one of give and take. 'Because beliefs and social practices . . . come to us from without,' Durkheim writes in *Les Règles de la Méthode Sociologique*, 'it does not follow that we receive them passively or without modification. In reflecting on collective institutions and assimilating them for ourselves, we individualize them and impart to them more or less personal characteristics . . . It is for this reason that each one of us creates, in a measure, his own morality, religion and mode of life. There is no conformity to social convention that does not comprise an entire range of individual shades.' A man who could write these lines, should not be classed with the organicists. True, he never forgets the social factor and its tremendous importance. 'This field of variations', he says in the next sentence, 'is a limited one.'[2] But this is only the sober truth, not the exaggeration so characteristic of organicism. Durkheim uses here the very same image we have used above, the spatial simile. Individual freedom is a 'field of variations' limited by an outer area in which the objective powers predominate and even dominate.

But Durkheim is a member of the cultural school not only in practice. He is so even in principle. Disciple of the philosopher Boutroux, he accepted from his master the postulate that each science must explain the phenomena with whose study it is entrusted in its own terms, and not in terms appropriate to another science and to another sector of reality; and in particular that those phenomena which we traditionally describe as higher must not

---

[1] *Sociologie et Philosophie*, translated by D. F. Pocock as *Sociology and Philosophy*, 1953, pp. 58, 59.

[2] Engl. translation by S. A. Solovay and J. H. Mueller, edited by G. E. Catlin, *The Rules of Sociological Method*, ed. 1950, pp. lvi, lvii.

—because they cannot—be explained in terms of some lower reality. For instance: if somebody undertakes to explain some biological phenomenon purely on the basis of mechanics, he is sure to go wrong because that which is dead cannot elucidate that which is alive. Or, to come nearer to our centre of interest: the phenomena of thought cannot be sufficiently explained on the basis of bodily phenomena, the functioning of our brain cells, for instance. The point is established with particular emphasis in an important essay of 1898, entitled *Représentations Individuelles et Représentations Collectives*. 'Representational [i.e. mental] life is not inherent in the intrinsic nature of nervous matter . . . A representation is not simply an aspect of the condition of a neural element at the particular moment that it takes place . . . It is something quite new which certain characteristics of the cells certainly help to produce but do not suffice to constitute . . . Nothing could be more absurd than to elevate psychic life into a sort of absolute, derived from nothing and unattached to the rest of the universe,' but 'the mental condition does not derive directly from the cell'.[1]

This principle, applied to social reality and the social sciences, is a powerful preservative against what might be called the materialistic pitfall: the attempt to subsume sociology under, and to merge it into, mechanics or biology. But it is at this point that we also see the unbalance in Durkheim's mind, the reason why he has been classed with the sociological realists, and why we have to regard him as, to some extent, marginal rather than central to the cultural school. Surely, the dividing line that needs emphasising is that between human reality and non-human reality, between the sciences of man and the sciences of nature. Sociology cannot be made a kind of physiology, because man is too different from the cell to be identified with it, and it cannot be made into a kind of mechanics, because he is too different from the molecule to be even remotely likened to it. This is how Boutroux's postulate should have been applied; and if it had been so applied, it would have had the full support, never to be despised, of common sense. But it is not so that Durkheim does apply it. The line he draws does not divide the study of man and the sciences of nature, but sociology and psychology, and this is a different, and far more problematical, matter.

'If . . . we begin with the individual,' Durkheim writes in *Les*

[1] *Sociology and Psychology*, pp. 23, 24.

Règles de la Méthode Sociologique, 'we shall be able to understand nothing of what takes place in the group . . . There is between psychology and sociology the same break in continuity as between biology and the physico-chemical sciences. Consequently, every time that a social phenomenon is directly explained by a psychological phenomenon, we may be sure that the explanation is false.'[1] It looks as if these words re-opened the gulf which the extreme realists had interposed between the social whole and its parts, that very gulf which men like Fouillée had striven so hard to close. Georg Catlin, the editor of the English version of the work from which we have just quoted, administers a strong rebuke to Durkheim: 'Cells and the individual consciousness belong to sharply different orders of existence, whereas individual and collective consciousnesses do not,' he writes, and this 'is an objection to which Durkheim gives no attention proportionate to the importance of the role which an emergent collective consciousness plays in his works'.[2] However, we must not misunderstand Durkheim, even though he himself must bear the main responsibility for the misunderstandings which have arisen. He does not suggest that the psychology of the fully socialised and cultured individual is irrelevant to, and could conceivably stand in contrast with, sociology, but only that the psychology of the pre-social individual is so or does so. The matter becomes altogether clear in chapter 4 of *Le Suicide*. Arguing mainly against the nominalist Tarde, he insists that imitation should not be regarded as a possible key to the understanding of social phenomena. 'That imitation is a purely psychological phenomenon appears clearly from its occurrence between individuals connected by no social bond', Durkheim says here. 'The imitative function when exercised has in itself no power to form a bond between them . . . Our method of imitating human beings is the same method we use in reproducing natural sounds, the shapes of things, the movements of non-human beings. Since the latter group of cases contains no social element, there is none in the former case.'[3] What Durkheim says is, in effect, that if there is a tendency to imitate, this belongs to man's psychophysical equipment and has therefore little to do with his learnt sociality and culture. What he really contrasts is not sociology and psychology in the common acceptance of the word, but sociology and a purely

---

[1] Engl. transl., p. 104.   [2] *Loc. cit.*, p. xxiv.
[3] Engl. transl. by J. A. Spaulding and G. Simpson, *Suicide*, 1951, p. 123.

a- or ante-social psychology, and this is entirely legitimate. As can be seen, Durkheim is after all contrasting nature and culture rather than man and society.

Yet, when this is said, the fact remains, and must be emphasised in fairness to those who interpret Durkheim differently from Alpert and myself, that our author expresses himself often as if he *were* an extreme realist. For instance: 'A thought which we find in every individual consciousness, a movement repeated by all individuals, is not thereby a social fact . . . It is [only] the collective aspects of the beliefs, tendencies and practices of a group that characterize truly social phenomena . . . Certain of these social manners of acting and thinking acquire, by reason of their repetition, a certain rigidity which on its own account crystallizes them, so to speak, and isolates them from the particular events which reflect them. They thus acquire a body, a tangible form, and constitute a reality in their own right, quite distinct from the individual facts which produce it.'[1] In such statements, Durkheim does not go far beyond, say, Sumner's folkway concept, but there is a tendency to emphasise the collective component, society, more than the distributive aspect, the individuals, and this does betoken a definite unbalance in his theory which proves the persistence of the traditional dichotomy of nominalism and realism in the cultural school.

The most fruitful question we can raise in this context is *why* Durkheim showed this anti-individualist bias, and the answer is to be found in his political strivings. Durkheim was thirteen years of age when his country was humiliated on the battlefield of Sédan and the slow and painful process of reconstruction began. The new republic was a sickly child, and it looked for a long time as if its feeble light were to be blown out. But Durkheim clung with every fibre of his being to the ideal which the re-born French democracy pursued—the ideal of a liberal, secular, open society in which even a Jew like M. Durkheim could play his full part as an accepted and respected citizen. We can understand that he wished to do what lay in his power in the new republic's struggle for survival, and that this wish became even more intense after the Dreyfus scandal, with its sharp antisemitic side, broke in 1894. 'Durkheim . . . can be understood only as an actor in a human drama the program notes of which read: Place—France; Time—

[1] *The Rules of Sociological Method*, pp. 6 and 7.

The Early Days of the Third Republic', Alpert writes. 'His entire career, in fact, is inextricably interwoven with the trials and tribulations, the struggles and misfortunes, the triumphs and achievements of a nation in the process of its own remaking. A people had determined to rule itself and was faced with the task of firmly establishing itself socially and morally . . . It soon came to realize, however, that democracy demanded a national moral unity on a secular basis' (*loc. cit.*, p. 29; cf. also p. 192). This, however, was woefully missing. Strife rent the nation from end to end, and individualism was rampant, above all among the educated classes and the academics. It was against this individualism that Durkheim fought. The polemical tone of most of his writings shows that his pen was not that of the detached scholar, of the dweller in ivory towers. It was unavoidable (though it is at the same time regrettable) that Durkheim's political preoccupations should also colour his theoretical view of society—weight it, so to speak, on the side of the integrative (i.e. constructive) forces as against the individual forces (which he could not help regarding as destructive, or menacing destruction). This gave his analyses their apparently 'realistic', or at any rate sharply anti-nominalistic, surface; but in the depths Durkheim's social philosophy is—in spite of everything—a cultural one, based on a dualistic philosophy, an idealism of freedom.

Changing over now to a consideration of Max Weber, we see at once that in him we are confronted with a thinker whose place is securely within the cultural tradition. In the first paragraph of *Wirtschaft und Gesellschaft* he defines sociology as 'a science which attempts the interpretive understanding of social action', and action is defined as including 'all human behaviour when and in so far as the acting individual attaches a subjective meaning to it'. 'Action is social in so far as by virtue of the subjective meaning attached to it by the acting individual (or individuals), it takes account of the behaviour of others and is thereby oriented in its course.'[1] This very starting point peremptorily precludes all aping of physiology and physics. Molecules attach no subjective meanings to whatever they do; indeed, they do not do anything; whatever happens with them, happens to them rather than by them. Nor is the case of animals much different. They may have physical urges,

---

[1] Engl. transl. by A. R. Henderson and Talcott Parsons, *The Theory of Social and Economic Organisation*, 1947, p. 80. All references are to this version.

instinctual drives, even more or less clearly conceived ends in view; but it can hardly be said of them that their conduct carries a subjective meaning or flows out of a psychological motivation, if the words meaning and motivation are at all taken in their proper sense.

This distinction in the object of the social and the natural sciences—subjectively meaningful conduct here, objective, unintended happening there—is matched, strengthened and completed by a parallel distinction in the aims of the two groups of disciplines. The sciences of man can and must achieve understanding, whereas the sciences of the subhuman spheres are necessarily restricted to description. An example, not taken from Weber, but entirely in the line of his thought, will make this clear and thereby show that even the study of animal societies is essentially different from, nay largely irrelevant to, the study of human societies. There can be little that is more closely comparable in men and animals than mother-love. Yet human mother-love is fully understandable to us, whereas animal mother-love is at most partially so; indeed, if the word 'understandable' is taken in a full and proper sense, it is not adequately understandable. 'The maternal solicitude of the common earwig is . . . striking', we are told. 'Her care for the eggs is unremitting . . . At intervals she carefully takes them one by one in her mouth, and licks them all over.'[1] This appears at first to be understandable, for do not human mothers, too, fondle and kiss their babies? But take an earwig's egg, wash it and put it back, and see what happens. All mother-love is at an end; the budding new life is unceremoniously rejected and abandoned. In studying the child-care acts of insects, 'investigations by the German entomologist Weyrauch have shown that these activities are governed by an integration of the tactile and olfactory senses'. This is where there lies a difference so decisive that comparison with man is altogether out of the question. We cannot re-live the animal's experience of parenthood: the insect functions through mechanisms which, with us, do not enter into the phenomena concerned—quite apart from the fact that we do not function mechanically at all, while insects do. If the earwig babies' smell changes, they cease to be babies, even to their own mothers. Now, this a human being cannot possibly understand. The proposition that a mother will naturally cease to love her baby after it has had a bath is utterly incomprehensible to humans.

[1] Harold Bastin, *Insect Communities*, 1956, p. 37.

Here we can describe, but not 'understand'; here we can 'know about' the facts, but not comprehendingly penetrate them.

The organicist will perhaps say that earwig behaviour is understandable after all, for we can interpret it in terms of function. But Weber makes it clear that for him the uncovering of functions and the analysis of functioning is not the essence of social study —not proper comprehension—for the best functionalist interpretation is only description *ab extra* and not understanding *ab intra*. 'This functional frame of reference', he says, 'is convenient for purposes of practical illustration and for provisional orientation. In these respects it is not only useful but indispensable. But . . . this is only the beginning of sociological analysis as here understood. In the case of social collectivities, . . . as distinguished from organisms, we are in a position to go beyond merely demonstrating functional relationships and uniformities. We can accomplish something which is never attainable in the natural sciences; namely the subjective understanding of the action of the competent individuals. . . . This additional achievement of explanation by interpretive understanding, as distinguished from external observation, is of course attained only at a price—the more hypothetical and fragmentary character of its results. Nevertheless, subjective understanding is the specific characteristic of sociological knowledge' (pp. 93, 94).

The upshot of Weber's cultural approach can be simply summed up by saying that for him society is human interaction, and the science of society is the understanding of the interacting individuals as human beings. In terms of our simile: for Weber, sociology is the study of that inner circle of reality where autonomous human conduct can be observed and comprehended, and which is bounded by, but not identical with, an outer realm of facts which we can indeed know but not (in his specific sense of the word) understand. Such an attitude excludes, in principle, the distortion of the mental image of society by any spurious influences emanating from the natural sciences, both its distortion by biology in the sense of philosophical realism, and its distortion by mechanics in the sense of philosophical nominalism. And yet we find that Weber was a nominalist.

As it is obviously impossible for us to 'understand', in Weber's specific sense, anything but the action of individuals, this nominalism follows from his definition of sociology as an understanding science, although, as we shall see, he had other, and less scholarly, motives for adopting it as well. In one of his most important essays, he writes as follows: 'The aim of our study: "understanding", is . . . the reason why understanding sociology treats the single individual and his action as the last unity, as its "atom" (if this problematical comparison may be, for once, permitted). . . . The individual . . . is the one and only bearer of meaningful conduct. No . . . mode of expression should be allowed to veil this fact. It lies in the nature, not only of language, but even of our thinking, that the concepts in which we apprehend action make it appear in the form of a continuing existence, of a thing or of a "person-like" formation endowed with a life of its own. . . . Concepts like "state", "co-operative", "feudalism" and the like are for sociology, generally speaking, categories of special kinds of human interaction, and it is its task to reduce them to "understandable" action, and this means, without exception, to the actions of the individual human beings involved.'[1] In this passage, the dissolution of society into its man-atoms appears more as a methodological device than as a statement of ontological convictions; but there are formulations in which we see that nominalism *was* Weber's philosophy, and not only a method. In his *magnum opus, Wirtschaft und Gesellschaft*, he compares jurisprudence with sociology and tells us that the former may consider the state as a quasi-person, but the latter must not: 'For sociological purposes there is no such thing as a collective personality which "acts". When reference is made in a sociological context to a "state", a "nation", a "corporation", a "family" or an "army corps", or to similar collectivities, what is meant is . . . *only* a certain kind of development of actual or possible social actions of individual persons . . . In sociological work these collectivities must be treated as *solely* the resultants and modes of organization of the particular acts of individual persons, since these alone can be treated as agents in a course of subjectively understandable action.' The italics are, characteristically, Weber's own. A little later he writes still more strongly: 'Even in cases of such forms of social organization as a state, church, association, or marriage, the social relationship exists exclusively in the fact that there has existed, exists, or will exist, a probability of [repeated social] action in some definite way . . . It is vital to be continually clear about

[1] Cf. *Gesammelte Aufsätze zur Wissenschaftslehre*, ed. 1951, p. 439.

this in order to avoid the "reification" of these concepts. A "state", for example, ceases to exist in a sociologically relevant sense whenever there is no longer a probability that certain kinds of meaningfully oriented social action will take place.'[1] What Weber felt was that if you take the acting and interacting human beings away, there may remain things like the White House or Buckingham Palace, but not societies like the United States of America or Great Britain, for the realities properly so called are human realities, complexes of subjects, and not objects which are merely the adjuncts, the gears and tools, of societies, but not the societies themselves.

We have hinted that Weber's adherence to a nominalistic philosophy had non-scientific as well as scientific reasons, and we find them soon enough if we consider the man as a whole, the total phenomenon, as it were, known as Max Weber. The case is far more complicated than that of Emile Durkheim, and it is impossible to do full justice to it here. Only a few indications can be given. The German bourgeoisie was, up to 1918, virtually debarred from political decision-making. It had to accept restriction to the private sphere and there—divorced as it was from public life with its sobering give and take—it developed, not only a bent for metaphysics, but also a specifically individualistic philosophy. Goethe expressed its gist in a famous quatrain:

> 'Common folk and world transcender,
> They confess and they agree:
> Highest good life could engender
> Is man's personality.'[2]

This is what Weber, too, fervently believed. His individualism came to him from three sources: his father, a go-ahead business man, impatient of governmental interference in economic affairs; his mother, a woman of deep personal piety, condemning all authoritarianism in religion; and his University, Heidelberg, which was situated in the politically most liberal of all German *Länder*, Baden, which looked askance at Prussian methods of domination and demanded more democracy for her people. No wonder that Weber, under this triple impact, became an individualist.

[1] Engl. transl., pp. 92 and 108.
[2] The poem is contained in *Westöstlicher Divan*.

But Weber's nominalism sprang from, and was fed by, yet another root. The dissatisfied German bourgeoisie was not only individualistic, but also rationalistic. Had not Kant been her best philosopher? All observers agree that Weber was something of an eighteenth-century type born after his proper time. But the rationalist is naturally suspicious of words which may be hollow, which may have nothing in and behind them. Weber was so suspicious, and fought sham rhetoric wherever he found it with almost lion-like passion. Unfortunately, German politics was in his day dominated by the high-sounding phrase. There were, on the one hand, the nationalists who speechified about throne and altar, the crown and the flag and so on; there were, on the other hand, the socialists who filled their followers with utopian hopes of a heaven on earth, 'the last battle that is to come', and so forth. Both nauseated Weber, who thought that a man filled with cant was less than a man, that man only reached his proper status when he was an independent personality with clear ideas of his own, not a camp-follower with cheap stultifying ideologies accepted from others. To say that the German nation was more than the contemporary Germans, the Church more than the individual believers, a University more than lecturers and attendants at lectures, seemed to Weber the style of thought, or rather talk, of the street-corner politician, unworthy of the philosopher committed to the truth. Thus there was born in him a bias which was diametrically opposed to that of Durkheim: an anti-collectivistic bias as deep-seated as the Frenchman's bias against the personality cult.

We find, then, in cultural sociology the very same contrast and conflict as outside it, in sociology at large. The main question is, of course, whether the hostile attitudes can be reconciled so that the deviations from the truth on either side counterbalance each other and finally drop off, leaving behind the sound kernel of all social thought. Happily, this reconciliation is not difficult to achieve. It is, *in nuce*, contained in Weber's and Durkheim's own definitions of sociology. Weber's, as we have seen, runs as follows:—'Sociology is a science which attempts the interpretive understanding of social *action*.' Durkheim, for his part, calls 'sociology . . . the science of *institutions*, of their genesis and of their functioning'.[1] Now, social action and social institutions are not separate phenomena, but part of a continuum. An institution

[1] *The Rules of Sociological Method*, Engl. ed., p. LVI. The italics are added.

arises when individual actions congeal, as it were, into action-patterns, when what is transient, a succession of transient pieces of conduct, becomes organised into an abiding form of life. Both Durkheim and Weber knew this. Durkheim emphasises the lasting whole, but he does not forget the individual component: 'Collective ways of acting or thinking have a reality outside the individuals who, at every moment of time, conform to it. These ways of thinking and acting exist in their own right . . . Of course, the individual plays a role in their genesis.' Weber emphasises the individual component, but he does not forget the abiding whole. Where he begins to speak about usage and custom, he says: 'It is possible in the field of social action to observe certain empirical uniformities. Certain types, that is, of action . . . are found to be wide-spread, being frequently repeated by the same individual or simultaneously performed by many different ones. Sociological investigation is concerned with these typical modes of action.'[1] This passage is half a step in the direction of Durkheim's definition of social institutions, just as our quotation from Durkheim is half a step in the direction of Weber's concept of social action.[2]

But the real—the really secure—bridge between Durkheim and Weber is Sumner's work. In the folkway concept, individual action and collective institution are shown to be one, the latter representing an objectification of the former, the former a starting-point of the latter. A cultural sociology as we envisage it, would have to be based on Sumner's inspired study of the process of social life, completed by Cooley's analysis of the individual and yet socialised mind, and enriched by the deep insights of Emile Durkheim and Max Weber and those who have followed in their wake.

[1] Durkheim, *loc. cit.*; Weber, *The Theory of Social and Economic Organization*, p. 110.
[2] One of the most remarkable attempts in recent years to fuse the Durkheim tradition with that of Max Weber is the system of Talcott Parsons which could well be used as an illustration of what, in the text, has repeatedly been called 'the third sociology'. Its adequate discussion would, however, demand much more space than we could possibly give it within the framework of the present book.

XVII

Conclusion

THE FIRST and foremost task which any social theory has to fulfil is to provide a sound definition of society, for unless there is a reliable general idea of what society is, no valid detailed pronouncements about matters social can possibly be made. In this respect, there is a decisive difference between the cultural school on the one hand, and the two materialistic schools on the other. The cultural school is based on what might be called a direct definition of society: society is human interaction. Society is here regarded as a phenomenon *sui generis*, as in a class of its own. The materialistic schools work with indirect definitions: they take a roundabout route, the one *via* organism, the other *via* mechanism. Society is not in a class of its own, but belongs to a wider class and is merely a special case within it. This is what the medieval philosophers called definition *per genus et differentiam*: giving first a generic description (physical body in the one case, equilibrium system in the other), and adducing then the more specific qualities which differentiate the thing defined from the other members of the group (a body made of conscious, not unconscious, cells; an equilibrium of animate, not inanimate, molecules). Clearly, this procedure makes sense only if the specific differences are smaller than the generic agreements, otherwise the definition splits wide open, so to speak. In the basic concept of mechanicism, as any unprejudiced observer will admit, this is the case. The coincidences between the social order and the ordering of a mechanical system are superficial, the difference between the two profound. How can one compare what is dead with what is alive, what is without mind with what is conscious, what is without will with what is endowed with volition? A man is not a molecule. A realistic idea of what either of them is precludes all subsumption under one concept.

It is not quite the same with organicism. True, man is not a cell either, but the question is whether the difference between man and cell is not smaller than the coincidence in character between the social order and the ordering of the body physical. And here a sector of reality forces itself upon our attention which can be said to constitute a connecting link between human society on the one hand, and organic wholes like the body physical on the other: animal societies, especially the great hymenopterous societies, bee hive and ant hill. It has often been remarked that a swarm of bees moving through the air looks like a unitary beast, a kind of bird, in flight, and this is something more than a mistaken sense-impression. For if we enter into the study of bee hive and ant hill, we soon see that there is an organic division of functions which closely parallels that in an animal. Some bee types and some ant forms concentrate on reproduction; they are the gonads and germ-cells of the quasi-animal called hive or hill; others do the feeding, foraging or fighting; they are the outer limbs, the muscular tracts of that same quasi-animal. Subsumption of body physical and hymenopterous communities under the wider concept 'organically integrated whole' is therefore permissible, is, to say the least, not unreasonable. If it could be shown that human societies and hymenopterous societies are substantially similar, the case for sociological organicism, for philosophical realism in the social sciences, would be powerfully strengthened.

Needless to say, superficial writers have asserted over and over again that human societies and hymenopterous societies are very much alike. But here, for once, the natural sciences can really help us.[1] The question is whether the picture of bee and ant life which entomologists have built up, coincides with, or contrasts with, the picture of human life, in so far as the social aspect is concerned, and the answer clearly must be, as in the case of mechanicism, that the coincidences are superficial and the differences profound. The sociologist who reads A. D. Imms's authoritative book, *Social Behaviour in Insects*, or Harold Bastin's useful summing-up survey,

[1] I am grateful to Dr. E. J. Popham of the Department of Zoology of Manchester University for introducing me to the relevant literature, for reading the above discussion of insect societies, and for assuring me that what I have said is in complete agreement with the findings of recent entomological research.

Insect Communities, will feel like a man moving through a dream landscape: nothing is like the reality to which he is accustomed and which he knows so well; everything is incomprehensible, everything is strange.

The first fact which stands well out is that hymenoptera, by and large, function mechanically. This does not mean that there is not a fringe of intellect, a certain capacity to store up, and to profit from, past experiences, a limited amount of variation and adaptation of behaviour. But compared to man's potentialities, these trace endowments dwindle into nothingness. 'Insects in general are markedly deficient in the faculty that we speak of as intelligence', Bastin writes. 'Some of the more highly specialised kinds, particularly bees and ants, appear to retain past impressions—to remember, as we say—and to profit by experience to a limited extent. But in most of their reactions insects are governed solely by what is called instinct. Without instruction or opportunity for imitation, they perform all manner of intricate operations for their own or their offsprings' benefit. The only possible inference is that . . . each succeeding generation inherits from its parents a self-acting nervous mechanism, comparable on the material plane to an elaborate piece of clockwork, wound up and ready to perform its destined movements as soon as the spring is released' (ed. 1956, pp. 17 and 18). Scientists, it is true, nowadays dislike the term 'instinct' which Bastin uses, but this makes very little difference, for they have merely substituted for 'instinctual behaviour' 'innate behaviour'. Indeed, this new mode of expression only serves to make the contrast between insect sociality and human sociality all the more obvious. Human sociality is learnt, not inherited. There can be no comparison between the two.

But this is only a beginning. Insect societies are exclusively familial: 'insect society', Dr. Imms informs us, 'has developed solely upon a family basis' (ed. 1947, p. 110). Hence if there is to be any comparison at all, it cannot be that between human society at large on the one hand, hive and hill on the other, but merely between the latter and the human family group. The words of Nikolai Gogol which we have written as a motto on the title page of this book—'to become kindred in spirit without being kin in blood: that is what only man can do'—are not only metaphorically, but even literally and scientifically true. It is not necessary to be a contractualist in order to assert that a pattern which excludes contracting is not really comparable with a pattern in which contract making looms very large and is at any rate one of the methods of integration. And can we forget that even the human family, biotic though it is, begins with a contract, the marriage vows?

But perhaps the most important point of dissimilarity is the degree of integration exhibited by insect societies, their unity. It is this unity which makes it possible and permissible to compare hive and hill with organic wholes. In human societies there is nothing like it, and therefore they cannot be so compared. In insect societies, Imms writes, 'each individual member . . . labours with the utmost diligence; its toils last the day long, and even night by no means always brings respite. Individual aspirations, comfort or pleasure find no place in such an economy, yet there is neither dissension nor strife. Individual lives are of little account . . . [and] each is intimately merged into that of the community of which it is a part, and is unhesitatingly sacrificed in its service whenever occasion demands' (p. 111). And Bastin writes even more clearly: 'Although no physical continuity exists between them, they work together harmoniously to promote the prosperity of the association as a whole. In other words, a community of insects functions as a biological individual exactly comparable to a multicellular organism, such as a tree or one of the higher animals' (p. 21). The ant hill or the bee hive may be an ideal for man (though it could be realised only at the price of his dehumanisation), but a state like it has never yet been a reality anywhere.

Almost as important is the next fact: insect societies, unlike human societies, are hard and fast, unchanged and unchangeable patterns. They have no history; they are not even subject to evolution. Imms makes the point very strongly: 'Even before our Simian ancestors had assumed any real semblance of human form, insect societies were as we find them to-day . . . The development and establishment of insectan castes have taken place on an hereditary and instinctive basis, and they seem to have gained only in fixity during the vast interval of time that has since elapsed' (p. 110). The contrast with man, a progressive creature, and the only one in nature which we know, is also underlined by Adolf Portmann in his magisterial work, *Animals as Social Beings*. Animals are preservers of hereditary forms, men searchers for what is new. Can such a tremendous dissimilarity in life be conjured away with the aid of a wide and vague paper definition?

The mention, by Imms, of the caste system brings us to the last point we wish to raise. It alone would suffice to clinch our argument against organicism. We have seen that the subsumption of bee hive and ant hill under the concept 'organically integrated wholes' was justifiable because these types of social organisation are characterised by a division of function between the nutritionally and the reproductively active forms in them which lies parallel to the division of function between the digestive and the sexual tracts in the coherent organism. Human society, too, has a division of labour, and the organicists have made the best of it. But the two phenomena only look alike; they are not in fact alike. When an ant is born, its fate is to all intents and purposes fixed. Some can reproduce, others cannot, and there is an end to it. Not so with man. The baby born in the slums is no different, physiologically, from the baby born in the mansion. What will become of him may be relatively predetermined, but is not absolutely so: his fate is at most socially circumscribed, but by no means physically delimited. We must be careful here not to overstate our case. Some kinds of caste division among insects are due to differential nutrition, and hence to post-natal influences only, and to that extent they are nearer to human class distinctions than others. But the decisive ones appear to be pre-natally—genetically—caused. The observed facts, Imms says, oblige us 'to conclude . . . that polymorphism, of the type found in ants and termites, is predetermined in the germ-plasm . . . The advanced condition of caste differentiation among these insects does not appear to be explicable, except to a limited extent, on the basis of nutrition . . . When we come to the more fundamental characters exhibited by the dimorphic males and females in different ants and the differences separating the winged queens from the apterous workers and soldiers, some other explanation is necessary. The available evidence leads us to conclude that, since the differences involved are so rigid and fixed, they are of an hereditary character' (pp. 100, 101, 65). This hereditary character of ant castes and non-hereditary character of human class divisions is not surprising —assuming we accept the evolutionary hypothesis—if we consider that ant societies (which can be traced back to the Eocene period) have had time for the germ-plasm to become permanently modified, whereas there can be no question of that in human society, a very recent formation in terms of the great world-clock.

But the theory of evolution, if accepted, would show even more convincingly than all these differences together, decisive as they are, that ant community and human association are so sharply contrasting that the assertion of generic sociological similarities between them is utterly unreasonable. We do not need, for our purposes, the argument which is now to follow, and it must be said and emphasised that a good deal of it is speculative, though it is all speculation with a scientific basis to it. According to one theory which has some anatomical evidence to back it up, man and insects can both be traced to a common ancestry, the genus Articulata. If so, we are confronted here with a case of *divergent* evolution. Nature, pushing forward from the common starting-point, tried, so to speak, two experiments in sociality: on the one hand, an experiment in integration, on the other hand, an experiment in freedom—on the one hand, a social order in which the pattern is antecedently given and the individuals involved have to submit to it, on the other hand, one in which the pattern is not antecedently given, but has to be elaborated by the individuals involved. This is Henri Bergson's view of the matter, and a most ingenious one it is. If it is correct (of course, this is a very great 'if'), then insect societies and human societies are not, in their evolved forms, comparable with each other—as little as slavery and freedom are.

We can draw an instructive parallel here with the male and female bodies (another case, if on a different level, of divergent evolution). Each sex has some vestigial traces of the organs essential to the other; men, for instance, have rudiments of mammilary glands; but they are just rudiments and no more, memories as it were of the common starting-point, but utterly unimportant to the fully-grown individual. And so it is with animal societies and human societies. The one is fixed, the other is free. Ants and bees have some adaptability, but it is vestigial only; men's social pattern has something of predetermination about it, but not much; there is about as much intelligence in the hive and hill as there is instinct in human society; there is as much in common between them as between the sex equipment of a normal grown-up human male and a normal grown-up human female. Scientific exactitude demands that the parallels and overlappings be mentioned in a total account, but it demands even more that they be pronounced far too few and marginal to allow of an assimilation, let alone an identification, of the two forms of life. And for this reason human society cannot be called an organism, even though insect communities can. Sociological realism is finally disproved. Let those who believe that human societies are merely enlarged families; that sociality in man is inborn, and that he does not stand in need of social education; that there is neither intelligence nor selfishness at work in social life; that men invariably kill themselves by overstrain in the service of the community to which they belong; that everything in social life, including the class structure, is now as it ever was, and as it ever will be and must be; that there is neither the fact of past evolution nor yet the possibility of future reform—let those who hold these views continue to stick to organicism. The rest of us must be excused, if we prefer a different sociology.

All this can only confirm us in the conviction that sociology should not, in the future, develop along either mechanistic or organistic lines. But all this raises once more, and in an even acuter form, the question why it has developed precisely along these two lines in the past. We have already explained why some centuries have preferred organicism to mechanicism, and some mechanicism to organicism. But we have yet to show why these two materialistic movements have been, for a very long time, jointly or severally preferred to the cultural approach, and why the cultural approach, in spite of its inherent truth, has not, so far, gained the decisive victory over its competitors which it deserves. We shall do this now, and thereby complete the picture.

The best way of deploying our argument is by following a roundabout route—by showing why the natural sciences first made a false start, why it has taken them ages before they found their own true selves, and why they have moved from triumph to triumph since this has happened. The case is historically a closed one, and therefore particularly revealing. What we can learn from it will be—*mutatis mutandis*—applicable to the development of the social sciences also.

A look at the image of the physical world entertained by the primitive races invariably reveals that they find it difficult, not to say impossible, to rid themselves of what Cooley called personal ideas when they approach the impersonal realm. Even the

Romans, for all their sophistication, would not say 'it rains' (*pluit*), but rather 'the Sky-god rains' (*Jupiter pluit*). The personalisation of the impersonal, the humanisation of the subhuman, is thus a thoroughly characteristic trait of the primitive mentality. Radcliffe-Brown's study of the Andaman Islanders shows how consistent this transposition of natural facts into social terms is. 'The Andaman Islanders', he writes, 'personify the phenomena of nature with which they are acquainted, such as the sun and the moon . . . The most usual statement in all the tribes is that the sun is the wife of the moon and the stars are their children . . . In the North Andamans, thunder and lightning are commonly personified. The lightning is Ele or Ali, and the thunder is Korude or Korule. Some of the natives spoke of Mimi Ele (female) and others of Maia Ele (male). He lives in the sky . . . The lightning is due to his shaking his foot . . . Thunder (Korude) also lives in the sky. It is said that he makes the thunder by means of a large round stone . . . The only explanation of the tides . . . was to the effect that they are caused by a fish . . . which drinks up the water and then lets it out again . . . An . . . account of how earthquakes are caused is that when a man dies he goes to the spirit world which is beneath the earth. The spirits hold a ceremony . . . At this ceremony they have a dance . . . As they shake the rainbow in dancing, this causes earthquakes . . . Among the most important of the Andamanese beliefs are those relating to the weather and the seasons. These are under the control of two beings named Biliku, Bilik or Puluga, and Tarai, Teriya or Daria . . . All storms are said to be made by Puluga or Biliku . . . The spirits are believed to be the cause of all sickness and of all deaths resulting from sickness . . . ' (pp. 141, 145, 146, 147, 157, 139). There is a good deal more in this vein, but there is perhaps no need to extend our quotation. It is clear that the Andamanese see nature as a field of personal, or at least quasi-personal, forces, and not as a field of impersonal ones, and that they are altogether consistent in their phantasmagoric interpretation of physical phenomena.

Why, then, should these tribes, whose brains are not much different from ours, conceive of nature in such terms? To be quite brutal about it: why should they be so stupid? Radcliffe-Brown has laid his finger on the correct explanation. What he says is absolutely convincing. We should like to quote him here *in extenso*, for we can learn from him much, not only about the thought of other societies, but also, by implication, about the thought of our own. 'The fundamental interest of the Andaman Islander, as of all men in primitive societies, is his interest in persons and personal relations', he says. 'All the thoughts and feelings of the Andaman Islander centre in the society; for him the world is merely a stage on which the social drama is perpetually enacted. He co-ordinates all his thoughts, emotions, and interests around the society, and in the legends he builds up a picture showing the connection between the society and those phenomena of nature which affect it . . . Natural phenomena affect him immediately by their influence on his own life and on the life of his fellows, and are thereby the source of a number of emotional experiences. In order to express these, he has to make use of that part of his own experience that is already thoroughly organised, namely, that relating to the actions of one person as affecting another or as affecting the society. Only in this way is he able to organise his experiences arising from the processes of nature, to classify and render definite the vague impressions that are aroused in him. He interprets nature in terms of the world with which he is most familiar, the world of persons, being enabled to do so by the presence within him of a regulated and definite body of experience which he has derived from his relations with persons from the time of his first awakening to the consciousness of the external world . . . Primitive man . . . organises and develops his . . . experience by conceiving the whole universe as if it were the interaction of personal forces . . . The personification of natural phenomena is one of the methods by which the Andaman Islander projects into the world of nature the moral forces that he experiences in the society . . . This . . . helps us to understand some of the Andamanese beliefs . . . When any evil befalls the society it is . . . as though some one were angry at some offence. Thus the moon and Biliku are represented as persons who can be offended, and whose anger has unpleasant results [namely, violent storms]. Conversely when all goes well, it is because there is harmony or solidarity between men and the nature beings which affect men's lives.' In a word, what these primitives are doing is 'making the moon and the monsoons a part of the social order', or 'bringing within the circle of the social life those aspects of nature that are of importance to the well-being of the society' (pp. 390, 379–381).

Modern man has for ideas of this kind nothing but contempt: at best, he may be mildly amused by them. What he does not see is that he is inclined to do the very same thing. We have made this point already in our critique of Haret; here we want to repeat and reinforce it, and to raise it to a higher level. Is it not clear, from reading Radcliffe-Brown's analysis, that the last centuries have done to the social sciences exactly what the primitive races and our own earlier centuries did to the natural sciences, blocked their road to free and successful development and turned them into blind alleys out of which there could be no escape into the open, in which alone unimpeded progress is possible? We can formulate the fatal error of the primitive in his approach to nature by saying that he does not see nature as it really is, but as it ought to be, or would have to be, in order to be explicable in terms of his favourite field of experience, namely society; or, alternatively, we can say that he substitutes for reality a fictitious model which personifies what is impersonal and humanises what is not human. Only a few words need be transposed in these statements, the truth of which no sensible person will deny, in order to have the reason why our social sciences have not unfolded recently in the same magnificent manner as the physical sciences. The fatal error in modern man's approach to society has been that he has not seen society as it really is, but as it ought to be, or would have to be, in order to be explicable in terms of his favourite field of experience, namely nature; the fact which explains all is that modern man has all too often substituted for reality a fictitious model which de-personalises what is personal and dehumanises what is human.

The sociology of knowledge can explain without difficulty why the modern history of ideas has taken the course which we can in fact observe. In that great period of crisis which we call the Renaissance, society's value-system was totally transformed, one could almost say, reversed. Up till then, man, seen in his social relations, had been the focus of interest; from then onward, man in his relation to the world of things. The matter cannot be discussed here in all its manifold aspects, but there is hardly any need for such a detailed discussion because this is an area of substantial common consent. Only one point will be picked out in order to show, as by a flash-light, how great the revolution has been. When a thing is stolen and sold to an innocent, unsuspecting stranger, and the original owner finds it and demands it back, our modern codes, born of the spirit of capitalism, protect his right rather than the good faith of the third party; medieval law, born of the spirit of community, ordained otherwise. It let the right of the third party prevail, for what it wished to preserve was good faith, not the control of goods. For the physical sciences this transformation of the value system of society has had the splendid results we all know. For them, the red light changed to green. But for the social sciences, the change was far from helpful or beneficial. It would be an exaggeration to say that the green light changed to red. There had been the excessive prestige of theology before, and there has been no necessity to accept enslavement to the natural sciences since. But if there has been no necessary enslavement to the natural sciences, there has been far-reaching, all too far-reaching, voluntary enslavement to them, and if the present book has proved anything, it is this.

Many who have professed to study society, have in reality done no more than imitate the sciences of nature. They have thereby, in principle, reduced the social sciences to the plight in which nature study was among the Andamanese. When modern man feels superior to the primitive with his child-like ideas of the physical universe, as he invariably does, he ought to be shown his own image in the mirror. This is what we have tried to do in these pages. The caricature of social life which we find in the works of Carey and Haret or Bluntschli and Schäffle, and, indeed, in those of Spencer and Pareto, is merely a pendant to the caricature of the facts of nature which we find in the minds of those naked savages on the distant Andamans. Truly can we say to our materialists, scornful of others: Physician, heal thyself!

Should we conclude, then, that the labours of the organicists and the mechanicists have been all in vain, that the materials they have provided are not usable by a genuine science of society, such as the future might evolve? By no means; these materials are usable, though not in the way their providers fancied. As we have pointed out before, on more than one occasion, there is a certain realism even about the organistic and mechanistic models. It is because of this limited and partial—alas, all too partial!— realism, that organistic and mechanistic schools have developed. Other sciences than physiology and mechanics might have been chosen as patterns on which to build a sociology, but they have had no appeal. Nobody would suggest that the social scientist should imitate metereology, for this discipline does not appear to have got very far. But what about chemistry? What about crystallography? Why should no social chemistry, why no social crystallography, ever have developed? The question is not as vain and as ridiculous as it might seem. A sociology based on chemistry *and* a sociology based on crystallography have in fact been called for, but, significantly, both these calls have found no echo.

It was no less a scientist than Thomas Huxley who suggested that the sociologists should emulate and copy the chemists. Criticizing the fashionable organicism of his day, Huxley expressed himself as follows: 'The essence and foundation of every social organisation, whether simple or complex, is the fact that each member of the society voluntarily renounces his freedom in certain directions, in return for the advantages which he expects from association with the other members of that society . . . It appears to me that this feature constitutes the difference between the social and the physiological organism. Among the higher physiological organisms, there is none which is developed by the conjunction of a number of primitively independent existences into a complex whole. The process of social organisation appears to be comparable, not so much to the process of organic development, as to the synthesis of the chemist, by which the independent elements are gradually built up into complex aggregations—in which each element retains an independent individuality, though held in subordination to the whole. The atoms of carbon and hydrogen, oxygen, nitrogen, which enter into a complex molecule, do not lose the powers originally inherent in them, when they unite to form that molecule, the properties of which express those forces of the whole aggregation which are not neutralised and balanced by one another. Each atom has given up something, in order that the atomic society, or molecule, may subsist. And as soon as any one or more of the atoms thus associated, resumes the freedom which it has renounced, and follows some external attraction, the molecule is broken up, and all the peculiar properties which depended upon its constitution vanish. Every society, great or small, resembles such a complex molecule, in which the atoms are represented by men, possessed of all those multifarious attractions and repulsions which are manifested in their desires and volitions, the unlimited power of satisfying which, we call freedom. The social molecule exists in virtue of the renunciation of more or less of this freedom by every individual . . . And the great problem of that social chemistry we call politics, is to discover what desires of mankind may be gratified, and what must be suppressed, if the highly complex compound, society, is to avoid decomposition.'[1]

It would have been easy to take up this suggestion and develop it further. An intending social chemist would not have found it one whit more difficult to manufacture a sociological parallel to the Boyle-Charles law than Haret did to the Newtonian propositions. But the experiment appears never to have been tried. Why? We shall see before long.

Exactly eighty years after T. H. Huxley, a physicist, Dr. Reinhold Fürth, recommended to the students of society that they should take crystallography for their model. His attacks were directed against the mechanistic fashions of the day, as Huxley's had been against the contemporary vogue of biology. Rejecting the traditional argument *à la* Haret, he points out that it 'rests entirely on the supposed analogy between "forces" in the strict sense of physics and in the loose sense of everyday language. Now, in physics force is a well-defined and measurable quantity which has the mathematical characteristics of a vector, as can be proved by experiment. Hence, by superposition, a number of forces acting on one and the same object, e.g. part of a solid structure, can cancel out, and this is the condition for "equilibrium". But what the sociologist or politician means by "force" . . . can neither be defined mathematically nor measured quantitatively, and there is therefore no justification for the assumption that a superposition of various such "forces" can ever lead to their mutual compensation'.[2]

Casting about for something that can be put into the place of the traditional model, Fürth comes to the conclusion that the new discipline of 'statistical mechanics' holds great possibilities. 'Its principal field of application is the physics of systems consisting of a very large number of particles of the same kind, so-called "assemblies" of particles . . . Now, social communities are also assemblies consisting of individuals who in many ways show

---

[1] Cf. 'Administrative Nihilism', *The Fortnightly Review*, [November] 1871, p. 536.
[2] Cf. 'Physics of Social Equilibrium', in *The Advancement of Science*, vol. VIII, No. 32, March 1952, p. 429.

similar behaviour. It may therefore be expected that the assemblies of statistical mechanics could be used as adequate models of social communities' (pp. 431, 432).

The comparison must, however, be made more concrete. There are assemblies with particles of weak mutual interaction, like gases, and assemblies with strong or very strong mutual interaction, like liquids and solids. Dr. Fürth rejects the former as inapposite and suggests that the latter are apposite. 'Communities of animals and human beings are clearly . . . assemblies in which the interaction between the individual members is very considerable. It would therefore be quite wrong . . . to use a loose assembly of particles as a model for a social community . . . Thus we are almost forced to adopt the model of a "close assembly" and by doing so we must expect to find the features of the co-operative phenomena of statistical mechanics in many social processes' (p. 433).

Some of the conclusions of Dr. Fürth, e.g. about the 'remarkable stability of democratic communities with mixed population, such as Switzerland, the United States and the British Commonwealth of Nations', which 'may at least partly be ascribed to the soundness of their structures on the principles of strength of material bodies' (p. 434), are no more acceptable than the divagations of Carey and Haret. Here we are interested only in the theoretical aspect and this seems to be best summed up in the following passage: 'The question of social stability appears now in a new light. Instead of being comparable to the equilibrium of a rigid mechanical structure or an oscillator, like a pendulum under the action of external forces, it is now seen to be the analogue to the equilibrium of a close assembly of particles like a piece of crystal, under the opposing influences of the interatomic forces and the thermal agitation of the constituent particles' (p. 433).

While he who believes that society is a phenomenon *sui generis* will be convinced neither by Huxley nor by Fürth, it must be pointed out that their comparisons are nearer to social reality than those of Spencer and Pareto. Both Huxley and Fürth criticise contemporary ideas out of a correct understanding of their inadequacy. For what Huxley says is that a society is less coherent than a physical organism, and what Fürth says is that it is more coherent than an equilibrium of independent forces, and in these assertions they are altogether justified. Yet Huxley and Fürth have preached to deaf ears, while Spencer and Pareto have, like the

Pied Piper of Hamelin, drawn crowds of followers after them. Why?

The fact is, first of all, that in the guise of the would-be scientism of organicists and mechanicists there lurk powerful and attractive social ideals: in organicism the ideal of a truly integrated society, a society in which selfishness does not militate against the social bond and the social weal, in mechanicism the ideal of a society in which the individual is not cramped, in which the social forces promote, but do not inhibit, the development of human personality. It is a strange paradox that those who thought themselves least involved in idealistic dreams were in fact most so. But even self-styled scientists have a subconscious which will play them naughty tricks.

But the organistic and mechanistic models, for all their lack of realism, indeed, because of all their lack of realism, also have cognitional value. This may, again in a subconscious sort of way, have been part of their attraction. They do not describe any society as it actually is, but between them they mark the limits within which societies can vary, and this is the reason why they can be built even into a completely realistic sociology. Organicism shows us the social maximum, as it were; mechanicism the social minimum. Organicism shows us what society would be like if the tendencies towards integration gained the upper hand, a complete victory, over the tendencies towards individual independence. The ant hill is a picture of this nightmare come true. Mechanicism on the other hand shows us what society would be like if the tendencies towards individual independence gained the upper hand, a complete victory, over the tendencies towards integration. Unlike the rigidly integrated community, it has no archetypal exemplification in nature, and it is doubtful whether it could ever be fully realised. Mutual throat-cutting would soon take the place of mutual equilibration. In this respect, as in some others noted in this book, sociological mechanicism, if it puts itself forward as a positive and not as a normative doctrine, is, if possible, even more unrealistic than sociological organicism. Yet sociological organicism, too, is unrealistic, where man is concerned. Dr. Imms, after describing the co-operative communism of the ant hill, ends his book by saying that 'a social system of this kind is unattainable [on the human level] by any coercive or repressive manifestations on the part of [even] the most ruthless . . . dictatorship'. He is right. Man, however much he can be cowed by social forces, would never be able to breathe, and consequently to live, without some private sphere of his own.

Every society will, for this reason, be situated somewhere along a line of which the organistic and the mechanistic models are the end points—end points lying, as it were, in infinity. Some will be nearer the collectivistic end of the scale, others nearer the individualistic; some will, at a given time, be moving towards the social maximum, others towards the social minimum. But at any and every moment, there will be some compromise, some mixture between social ordering and individual freedom. Sociologists must remember this, and if they can't, then they should give up sociology. A social theory which is not human, is, by definition and of necessity, no social theory at all. But to be human is to be torn between sociality and selfishness. No specious philosophising is needed to prove this fact. We are all walking demonstrations of it. The last answer to the question, what is the essence of society, must lie in our deepest self-experience as human beings—the awareness of our dividedness, and of the constant compromise between the strivings which divide us. Sumner's folkway concept (a typical example of dualism, of Dilthey's 'idealism of freedom') fully reflects this reality, and for this reason it is superior, both to organicism which would make us nothing but social, and to mechanism which would make us nothing but selfish. It rests securely on the knowledge that we are creatures of contradictions, precariously poised between freedom and determination, and that we are for ever condemned and privileged to tread the middle way.

INDEX